Lonely planet

LONELY PLANET'S

WHERE TO GO WHEN

2ND EDITION

THE ULTIMATE TRIP PLANNER FOR EVERY MONTH OF THE YEAR

CONTENTS

January

P8-31

February

P32-55

March

P56-79

April

P80-103

May

P104-127

June

P128-151

CONTENTS

October

P224-247

November

P248-271

December

P272-295

INTRODUCTION

➔ We ran out of space on the cover of this book. In our ideal world, the name wouldn't be just *Where to Go When*. It would be *Where to Go When, Why and How*.

The final title captures the basic concept, of course: it's a carefully curated menu of places, and the best time to be in them all. With 300 destinations split across 12 chapters – one for each month of the year – every entry outlines what makes that country, region, island or city so wonderful to visit at that moment. Carved out two weeks for a relaxing break? We'll advise where to go then: Bali or Belize, the Caribbean or the Cyclades. Dream of seeing the sun rise over the ancient temples of Angkor? We reveal when to plan that adventure (February, since you ask). Simple.

Except it isn't, not always; don't assume you should aim for the hottest weather or the most famous events. A rainforest may be best explored after rain, after all; prices soar during festivals; surf's often up in winter. And with some spots thronged to bursting in summer months, it pays to think outside the box – or, at least, outside high season. That's why we've highlighted alternative ways and times to enjoy famous experiences. Why not roam Amsterdam in quieter January, say, warming up with nips of local *jenever* in brown cafes between admiring Rembrandts and Van Goghs in peace? And sure, countless wildebeest thunder across Kenya's Masai Mara on the Great Migration in the middle of the year – but you'll discover a different facet to that spectacle in the southern Serengeti in February, when those herds calve en masse.

True, sometimes there is a perfect moment: you really do want clear skies to enjoy that idyllic beach or mountain view, and you don't want to miss that brief window for sailing to Antarctica during the austral

© DutchScenery / Shutterstock

summer. We've covered those here, too.

But this book is also about the why and the how. Because travel isn't just about the destination, nor even the journey – though sometimes that's the most unforgettable part, particularly if you eschew a quick flight for a lower-carbon option, maybe an iconic railway journey or even an on-foot pilgrimage.

At its heart, every great trip begins with a spark of curiosity – a discovery waiting to be made. So, to choose the locations in this book, we asked ourselves the why. That's where the flowcharts at the start of each chapter come in, helping you identify the themes, activities and travel styles that appeal to you. We also tackle the how: how can I experience that wildlife encounter, challenging hike or local cuisine within my budget, abilities and timeframe. So whether you're escaping for a month or a weekend, with family in tow or on a blow-out bucket-list epic, you'll find a host of suggestions, from well-known wonders to offbeat adventures – not only the where and when, but also the why and how.

By Sarah Baxter and Paul Bloomfield

(L) Wander around Amsterdam in winter; (R) Unwind in Ubud; (B) Find quiet patches of paradise in the Cyclades

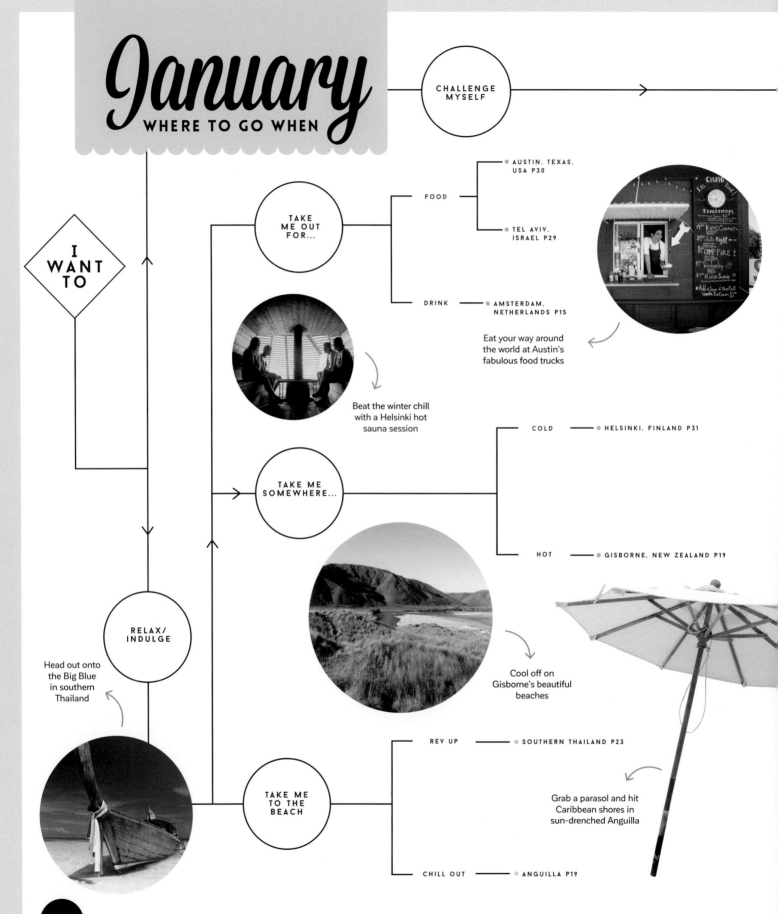

January
WHERE TO GO WHEN

CHALLENGE MYSELF

I WANT TO

TAKE ME OUT FOR...

FOOD
- AUSTIN, TEXAS, USA P30
- TEL AVIV, ISRAEL P29

DRINK
- AMSTERDAM, NETHERLANDS P15

Eat your way around the world at Austin's fabulous food trucks

Beat the winter chill with a Helsinki hot sauna session

TAKE ME SOMEWHERE...

COLD — HELSINKI, FINLAND P31

HOT — GISBORNE, NEW ZEALAND P19

Cool off on Gisborne's beautiful beaches

RELAX/ INDULGE

Head out onto the Big Blue in southern Thailand

TAKE ME TO THE BEACH

REV UP — SOUTHERN THAILAND P23

CHILL OUT — ANGUILLA P19

Grab a parasol and hit Caribbean shores in sun-drenched Anguilla

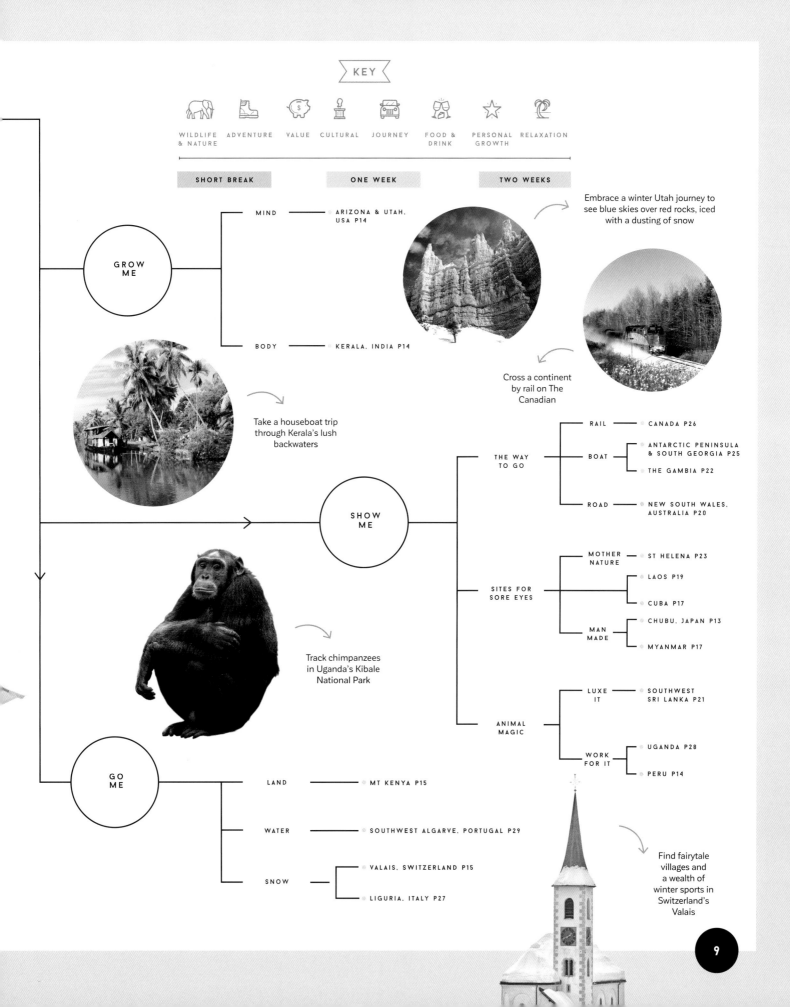

KEY

WILDLIFE & NATURE | ADVENTURE | VALUE | CULTURAL | JOURNEY | FOOD & DRINK | PERSONAL GROWTH | RELAXATION

SHORT BREAK | ONE WEEK | TWO WEEKS

GROW ME

MIND — ARIZONA & UTAH, USA P14

Embrace a winter Utah journey to see blue skies over red rocks, iced with a dusting of snow

BODY — KERALA, INDIA P14

Cross a continent by rail on The Canadian

Take a houseboat trip through Kerala's lush backwaters

SHOW ME

THE WAY TO GO
- RAIL — CANADA P26
- BOAT — ANTARCTIC PENINSULA & SOUTH GEORGIA P25 / THE GAMBIA P22
- ROAD — NEW SOUTH WALES, AUSTRALIA P20

SITES FOR SORE EYES
- MOTHER NATURE — ST HELENA P23 / LAOS P19 / CUBA P17
- MAN MADE — CHUBU, JAPAN P13 / MYANMAR P17

ANIMAL MAGIC
- LUXE IT — SOUTHWEST SRI LANKA P21
- WORK FOR IT — UGANDA P28 / PERU P14

Track chimpanzees in Uganda's Kibale National Park

GO ME

LAND — MT KENYA P15

WATER — SOUTHWEST ALGARVE, PORTUGAL P29

SNOW — VALAIS, SWITZERLAND P15 / LIGURIA, ITALY P27

Find fairytale villages and a wealth of winter sports in Switzerland's Valais

9

EVENTS
IN JANUARY

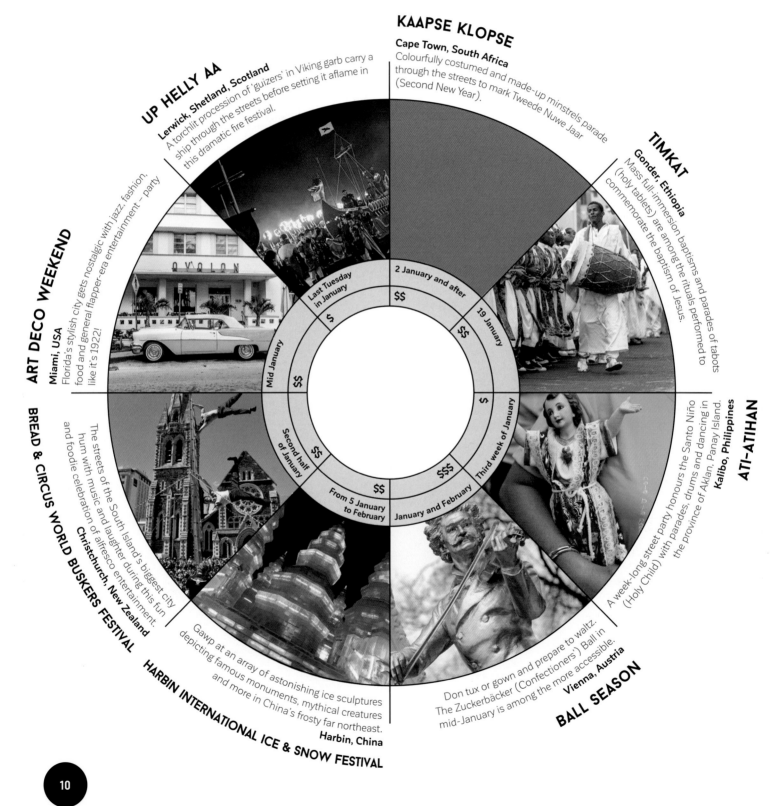

KAAPSE KLOPSE

Cape Town, South Africa
Colourfully costumed and made-up minstrels parade through the streets to mark Tweede Nuwe Jaar (Second New Year).

UP HELLY AA

Lerwick, Shetland, Scotland
A torchlit procession of 'guizers' in Viking garb carry a ship through the streets before setting it aflame in this dramatic fire festival.

TIMKAT

Gonder, Ethiopia
Mass full-immersion baptisms and parades of tabots (holy tablets) are among the rituals performed to commemorate the baptism of Jesus.

ART DECO WEEKEND

Miami, USA
Florida's stylish city gets nostalgic with jazz, fashion, food and general flapper-era entertainment – party like it's 1922!

ATI-ATIHAN

Kalibo, Philippines
A week-long street party honours the Santo Niño (Holy Child) with parades, drums and dancing in the province of Aklan, Panay Island.

BREAD & CIRCUS WORLD BUSKERS FESTIVAL

Christchurch, New Zealand
The streets of the South Island's biggest city hum with music and laughter during this fun and foodie celebration of alfresco entertainment.

HARBIN INTERNATIONAL ICE & SNOW FESTIVAL

Harbin, China
Gawp at an array of astonishing ice sculptures depicting famous monuments, mythical creatures and more in China's frosty far northeast.

BALL SEASON

Vienna, Austria
Don tux or gown and prepare to waltz. The Zuckerbäcker (Confectioners') Ball in mid-January is among the more accessible.

Last Tuesday in January — $

2 January and after — $$

19 January — $$

Mid January — $$

Third week of January — $

Second half of January — $$

From 5 January to February — $$

January and February — $$$

VALAIS, SWITZERLAND

Build a snowman or
hit the slopes
in Valais

Soak up the laid-
back surf scene in
Portugal's Algarve

SOUTHERN THAILAND

ALGARVE, PORTUGAL

Enjoy quiet beaches,
vivid reefs and mellow
nightlife in Southern
Thailand

Take a Snowy
Mountains road trip
along Kosciuszko
Alpine Way,
New South Wales

LIGURIA, ITALY

Embark on a wintry
wander to admire
Helsinki's grand
designs

LAOS

AUSTIN, TEXAS, USA

SOUTHWEST SRI LANKA

HELSINKI,
FINLAND

Find wildlife-
watching nirvana
in Sri Lanka

NEW SOUTH WALES,
AUSTRALIA

ANGUILLA

ARIZONA & UTAH, USA

CHUBU, JAPAN

AMSTERDAM,
NETHERLANDS

GISBORNE, NEW ZEALAND

Book a yoga retreat
or a backwaters boat
trip in quiet Kerala

Discover the less-visited
Caribbean in picture-
perfect Anguilla

Savour
'Veganuary' in
Tel Aviv, Israel's
plant-based
foodie hotspot

CUBA

THE GAMBIA

KERALA, INDIA

UGANDA

Sip a rum
cocktail and
soak up the
son in Santiago
de Cuba

MT KENYA

MYANMAR

TEL AVIV, ISRAEL

Mingle with chimps in
Uganda's Kibale, or seek
out silverbacks in Bwindi

CANADA

Become a citizen
scientist as a
conservation
volunteer in Peru

ANTARCTIC PENINSULA
& SOUTH GEORGIA

ST HELENA

PERU

CHUBU JAPAN

→ **Why now?** Discover a winter wonderland of steaming hot springs, traditional villages and snow sports.

Winter's a magical time to explore the historic settlements of central Honshu, when snow dusts temples, castles and traditional wooden houses. Outside of the ski resorts, crowds thin after the late-December holidays and before cherry-blossom season, so you can roam sites in peace (prices can be lower, too). In the Japanese Alps, 'snow monkeys' (Japanese macaques) soak in hot springs near Yudanaka, and there's glorious hiking, snowshoeing and downhill skiing. Visit Kanazawa on the north coast, dubbed 'Little Kyoto' for its castle, Kenroku-en garden, and geisha and samurai districts; *zuwai-gani* (snow crab) is in season here now, too. To the south, the fairytale thatched hamlets of Shirakawa-go and Gokayama lie on the wooded eastern flanks of Hakusan National Park; the lively town of Takayama, with its compact old centre, makes a fine stop en route to the magnificent castle of Matsumoto. Chilly? There's always a steaming *onsen* (hot spring) and warm sake nearby.

Trip plan: From Tokyo, cross the Japanese Alps – stopping for snowy fun near Nagano – to explore Kanazawa, then meander south through Shirakawa-go and Gokayama, Takayama and Matsumoto, ending in Kyoto.

Need to know: *Kaga-ryori* (Kanazawa cuisine) is delicious but expensive – look for lunch deals or noodle restaurants serving *soba* (hot, filling buckwheat noodles).

Other months: Dec & Feb – cold, crisp, snow in mountains; Mar-May – spring, cherry blossom, busy; Jun-Sep – hot, humid; Oct-Nov – mild, autumn colours.

(L) A 'snow monkey' enjoys a hot-spring soak; (R) Shirakawa-go blanketed in snow

ARIZONA & UTAH
USA

PERU

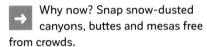

KERALA
INDIA

Why now? Contribute to conservation and citizen science in cloud and rain forests.

If your new year resolution is to give back, volunteering might be just the ticket – and few destinations have such a wealth of opportunities as Peru, where you could help with community engagement, education and poverty alleviation, or nature conservation and citizen science. The country's generous tranche of the Amazon region covers a range of habitats, many in need of study and conservation. So you might find yourself surveying biodiversity, tracking animals or analysing camera-trap footage to identify and count species in the cloud forest of Parque Nacional Yanachaga-Chemillén. Or you could join the long-running Tambopata Macaw Project, studying the ecology of these colourful but vulnerable parrots at the bustling clay licks which they throng to in January, at the height of the rainy season.

Trip plan: Parque Nacional Yanachaga-Chemillén is usually accessed from Lima via Oxapampa; Reserva Nacional Tambopata, in the far southeast, is typically reached from Cusco or by plane from Lima.

Need to know: When choosing your project, check that the organisation provides relevant training and support, and that the work has meaningful benefits to science, the environment and/or local people. Ask questions and, ideally, speak to someone who's previously volunteered.

Other months: Dec & Feb-Mar – wet in highlands and interior, sunnier on coast; Apr-May & Sep-Nov – less rain; Jun-Aug – drier in highlands and rainforest, busy.

Why now? Snap snow-dusted canyons, buttes and mesas free from crowds.

The red-rock ravines and outcrops of the region straddling the Utah and Arizona borders look even more delectable with a topping of snow – and in January you'll share these wonders with far fewer people. Make no mistake, you'll need to wrap up warm: surrounded by peaks and plateaus topping 3000m (9843ft), temperatures dip well below freezing. But don the right clothes and boots (better still, snowshoes), and you'll discover dramatic landscapes made even more magical in the absence of crowds: Zion, Canyonlands and Capitol Reef national parks, Antelope and Bryce canyons, Monument Valley, Canyon de Chelly. To better understand the natural and cultural heritage of the Navajo people who've long called this land home, join a tour with a local operator affiliated with Navajo Nation Parks & Recreation (navajonationparks.org) – some special spots, such as Antelope Canyon, are accessible only with an expert guide – or bed down in a traditional *hogan* dwelling.

Trip plan: Plot a loop from Las Vegas, Salt Lake City or Flagstaff, allowing at least a week with time for hikes and snowshoe excursions off the beaten path.

Need to know: Heavy snowfalls can close roads and trails – be flexible with plans and allow a few days' buffer in case of delays.

Other months: Dec & Feb – very cold, widespread snow; Mar-May & Sep-Nov – cool, popular; Jun-Aug – very hot.

Why now? Find your inner glow on a winter sun and yoga break in 'God's own country'.

Over the past couple of decades, the beaches of Varkala and Kovalam have morphed from the peaceful preserves of fishermen and Hindu devotees into backpacker hangouts and on into fullblown resorts studded with exclusive hotels. But with serene stretches of sand still to be found here and there, you can take your pick of the trance parties, hot hotels and restful homestays. After the overindulgence of Christmas, Kerala offers opportunities for taking stock and detoxing on a yoga retreat, and exploring the backwaters on a rice barge or heading into the Western Ghats for cool air and wildlife-watching among the forested slopes and tea plantations.

Trip plan: Fly to Kochi via Delhi or Mumbai for the short transfer to Varkala, Kovalam or a homestay or retreat in the inland foothills. Alleppey (Alappuzha) is the starting point for most backwater cruises, while Munnar is a great hill-station centre for hiking and wildlife-watching in Chinnar Wildlife Sanctuary.

Need to know: Most visitors to India require a visa. Apply for an e-visa at least a week before travel.

Other months: Dec & Feb-Mar – dry, not too hot; Apr-May – very hot; Jun-Jul – very wet; Aug-Nov – slightly less rainy, heating up.

AMSTERDAM
NETHERLANDS

→ **Why now? Warm the cockles with a tot of *jenever* between crowd-free visits to cultural highlights.**

Winters in northern Europe can be cold and grey – but also quiet and cheap. Amsterdam, its canals and cobbled streets jammed with museums, bars and the traditional pubs known as 'brown cafes', is ideally set up for a January visit. In many ways this is a wonderful time to be in this most popular Dutch city, after the crowds thronging Christmas markets and New Year celebrations have subsided and with great deals on accommodation to boot. Its world-class cultural attractions – including the art treasure-trove Rijksmuseum, Van Gogh Museum and Stedelijk Museum, the Anne Frank Huis and more – remain open. And if frostbite threatens, ward off the chill with a shot of *jenever* (Dutch gin) in a venerable bar such as Wynand Fockink or De Drie Fleschjes, both dating from the 17th century.

Trip plan: Spend a day or two touring the museums and historic sights of Amsterdam, allowing plenty of time to refresh yourself in brown cafes, and add on trips to nearby cities such as Utrecht and Den Haag.

Need to know: Depending on your bent, an I amsterdam card (covering public transport, many museums, a canal cruise and bike hire) or Netherlands Museum Pass is a sound buy.

Other months: Dec & Feb-Mar – chilly; Apr – tulip festivals, busy; May-Jun – pleasant; Jul-Aug - warm, busy; Sep-Nov – autumn colours, seasonal beers.

VALAIS
SWITZERLAND

→ **Why now? Crunch and swoosh through a snowsports playground.**

January means snow means skiing in Switzerland. But though the glitzy resorts – St Moritz and Zermatt, Davos and Verbier – attract the wealthy with perfect powder and aprés-ski, elsewhere you'll find peaceful valleys where winter walking, snowshoeing and cross-country skiing take you deep into the mountains, among fairytale chalet villages and pine forests clad in white frosting. Try Goms and neighbouring villages in the Valais, strung along a valley topping 1200m (3937ft) high; with around 80km (50 miles) of marked winter hiking trails, eight tested and signed snowshoe treks and over 100km (62 miles) of cross-country skiing routes, plus zippy connections along the valley on the Matterhorn Gotthard Railway, it's a district custom-made for slower travel. Add options for fatbiking, sledging and ice-skating, with equipment and expert guides on hand, and you've the recipe for an exhilarating off-piste winter adventure.

Trip plan: Trains to Goms run from Brig, linked to Zürich and Geneva airports as well as cities including Lausanne and Basel by direct services.

Need to know: German is the language of the Goms region, though locals speak a Highest Alemannic dialect that can be tricky for outsiders to understand at first.

Other months: Dec & Feb-Mar – winter, snow; Apr-May & Oct-Nov – shoulder seasons, some facilities closed; Jun-Sep – summer, great hiking and cycling.

MT KENYA
KENYA

→ **Why now? Summit Africa's second-highest peak in the dry season.**

Kilimanjaro, 'Africa's roof', may be loftier but Kenya's namesake peak offers a more achievable, beautiful and wildlife-rich trekking experience, best attempted during this driest period. Conquering Point Lenana (4895m/16,060ft) is no picnic, demanding a good level of fitness and careful acclimatisation, but it is a walk in the park – Mt Kenya National Park, protecting bountiful wildlife as well as those rusty, jagged spires. Spy elephants, elands, baboons and turacos on the verdant lower flanks; higher up, cheeky rock hyrax and bold sunbirds scamper and flit among giant lobelias. Camping at over 4000m (13,123ft) on summit night, prepare for subzero temperatures and a pre-dawn start, navigating by star- and moonlight for the final push. But icy fingers and a throbbing head can't dent the thrill of watching the sun rise across the African plains from your mountaintop eyrie.

Trip plan: Drive north from Nairobi to trek from the Sirimon, Burguret, Naro Moru or Chogoria gate, descending along a different route for variety; spend at least three nights on the mountain. Combine with a safari in Meru National Park, the Aberdares or the Laikipia Plateau.

Need to know: Mt Kenya's two highest peaks, Batian (5199m/17,057ft) and Nelion (5188m/17,021ft), are technical climbs.

Other months: Feb-Mar – driest, warmest; Apr-Jun & Oct-Nov – long rains; Jul-Sep & Dec – some rain.

Classic-car cruising
in downtown
Havana, Cuba

CUBA

→ Why now? Delve into southeastern Cuba's colourful heritage and culture in comfort.

Cuba in January is warm enough to enjoy days in the hills yet cool enough to roam southeastern cities, stifling in summer months. Having absorbed the regenerating pastel grandeur of Habana Vieja (Old Havana), time-travel east to discover more historic big-hitters of the Spanish colonial era: the cobbled streets and colourful houses of Trinidad – perhaps sneaking off to La Boca or Playa Ancón for some low-key beach time – and the Neoclassical architecture of Camagüey. Move to the sounds of *son* in music capital Santiago de Cuba, lubricated with a drop or two of rum (Bacardi was founded here), and hike the highlands of the Sierra Maestra to Castro's revolutionary headquarters at Comandancia de la Plata. Bookend your trip in Baracoa, discovering indigenous Taíno culture and spotting manatees and the world's smallest avian species, the bee hummingbird, in nearby Alejandro de Humboldt National Park. Throughout, a burgeoning roster of *casas particulares* (family-owned guesthouses) provide characterful, good-value accommodation, and a new wave of restaurants offer relief from basic rice-and-beans fare.

Trip plan: Fly to Havana, then head east to Trinidad, Camagüey, the Sierra Maestra, Santiago de Cuba and Baracoa.

Need to know: Local currency is the Cuban peso (CUP); convertible pesos (CUC) are no longer legal currency – don't accept CUC as change. Bring euros, Canadian dollars or UK pounds.

Other months: Dec-Apr – cooler, dry; May-Jun – wetter; Jul-Nov – hot, rainy.

Fishing Myanmar-
style on Inle Lake

© Matt Munro / Lonely Planet

MYANMAR (BURMA)

→ Why now? Cruise the Ayeyarwady River and explore the temples of Bagan under a warm sun.

Myanmar is, it could fairly be claimed, Asia's warmest country. Not measured in celsius or fahrenheit, but in the smiles of its unfailingly welcoming people. Its roster of sights, sounds and smells is enticing, too: the 'winking wonder' of golden Shwedagon Paya in former capital Yangon; the pony-drawn carriages and strawberries of hill station Pyin Oo Lwin; the temples and leg-rowing fishermen of serene Inle Lake. The ideal 'road to Mandalay' is a ribbon not of tarmac but water: the Ayeyarwady (Irrawaddy) River, snaking between Yangon and that former royal capital, and in full flow in January. Board an old-style riverboat for a cruise past rural landscapes, villages and ancient sites – none more jaw-dropping than the vast plain of Bagan, studded with thousands of millennium-old stupas, pagodas and temples.

Trip plan: Yangon and Mandalay receive international flights. A two-week counterclockwise circuit from Yangon takes in the golden-boulder-balanced stupa at Kyaiktiyo, Inle Lake and hilltribes around Kalaw, Pyin Oo Lwin and Mandalay's temples and palace before cruising downstream via Bagan and the Ayeyarwady Delta.

Need to know: The entrance fee for Bagan Archaeological Zone, currently 25,000 kyat (about US$22), is valid for five days.

Other months: Oct-Dec & Feb-Apr – dry (Dec-Feb: peak season, cooler); May-Sep – rainy, hot, prices lower.

(A) Gisborne's Waikanae Beach, New Zealand; (L) The Mekong's 'Four Thousand Islands', Laos; (R) Wreck at Sandy Ground Beach, Anguilla

© Justin Foulkes / Lonely Planet

18

GISBORNE
NEW ZEALAND

→ **Why now?** Be the first to greet the midsummer sun in New Zealand's mild east.

Early bird? Gisborne claims to be the first city in the world to see the sunrise. Whether or not you're up with the dawn, this chirpy burg is a dream destination for a short break in summer, when long, sunny, dry days are ideal for exploring the city and surrounding Tairāwhiti region. Captain James Cook was less impressed on his first landing in what's now New Zealand, naming this patch of coast Poverty Bay. But today it's rich in Māori culture: find out more on the Tupapa Heritage Trail, visiting the Tairāwhiti Museum and admiring the magnificent carvings on Maunga (Mt) Hikurangi. Make time for more recently introduced innovations, too: specifically, grapes – tour the boutique wineries of New Zealand's unofficial 'Chardonnay capital', where you'll also taste excellent Sauvignon Blanc, Pinot Gris and Gewürztraminer. Moderate surf makes this a good place to learn boardriding; beginners try Waikanae Beach, more experienced surfers hit Wainui Beach. For a very different marine experience, head a little east of town to meet friendly stingrays with Dive Tatapouri.

Trip plan: Spend two or three days discovering Gisborne's rich Indigenous heritage, learning to surf and visiting the area's wineries.

Need to know: Public transport in and around Gisborne is limited – explore by car or, better still, bike.

Other months: Dec & Feb – summer, warm; Mar-May & Sep-Nov – cooler; Jun-Aug – winter, biggest swells.

LAOS

→ **Why now?** Explore temples, islands and mountains while temperatures and rainfall are low.

Southeast Asia's sleeper hit was long the Cinderella of the region, a landlocked nation lacking the world-wonder monuments and soft-sand beaches luring tourist throngs to its neighbours. Yet the subtle allure of Laos is more varied and absorbing still, particularly during dry, relatively cool January – the perfect time to discover its cultural and natural wonders. Luang Prabang, with its gilt-roofed temples, provides an obvious jumping-off point for exploring the north, where clouded leopard, elephant and gaur roam protected areas and hilltribes preserve traditional lifestyles in remote villages. To the east, huge stone vessels lie scattered across the Plain of Jars near Phonsavan, while in the far south you'll find elaborately carved temples around Champasak and the laidback charms and Irrawaddy dolphins of Si Phan Don – the 'Four Thousand Islands' scattered across the Mekong River.

Trip plan: Starting in Luang Prabang, loop through the north – visiting caves and hilltribe villages around Phongsali, Muang Khua and Nong Khiaw, and spotting wildlife in Nam Ha or Nam Et-Phou Louey national protected areas. Then turn south to admire the karst scenery of Vang Vieng, the pre-Angkor Wat temple at Champasak and the waterfalls of the Bolaven Plateau.

Need to know: Temperatures at higher altitudes can get chilly on January nights – bring warm layers if you're heading into the mountains.

Other months: Nov-Dec & Feb-Apr – cooler, dry; May-Oct – wet, hot, humid.

ANGUILLA

→ **Why now?** Chill in a quieter corner of the Caribbean.

In January, hordes of heat-seeking European and North American travellers looking to flee winter head for the Caribbean. Yet few of them find their way to long, skinny little Anguilla (the name means 'eel' in Spanish), which remains determinedly low-key and relatively undeveloped. More fool them – this British Overseas Territory boasts all the ingredients of the Caribbean dream: friendly folk, an uplifting reggae soundtrack and some of the region's most beautiful palm-fringed beaches, notably lively Shoal Bay on the north coast and sleepier Rendezvous Bay in the south. You'll find top-end resorts and the high quality of cuisine their guests expect, headlined by fresh lobster and crayfish. But smaller, characterful guesthouses give mere mortals the chance to sample some dozen white-powder-sand strands – all free to access, mind – plus ample opportunities to enjoy the other attractions. There's fine snorkelling, particularly around offshore islands such as Prickly Pear, while divers can explore bustling coral reefs and the extraordinary wreck of an 18th-century Spanish galleon, *El Buen Consejo*.

Trip plan: Few direct flights serve Anguilla; fly via Puerto Rico, Antigua, St Maarten or St Kitts.

Need to know: January is peak season, when less-expensive accommodation is at a premium – book well ahead.

Other months: Jun-Oct – rainy, hurricanes possible; Dec & Feb-Apr – drier, milder; Nov & May – some rain, lower prices.

NEW SOUTH WALES AUSTRALIA

Snowy Mountains scenery at lovely Lake Jindabyne

© Taras Vyshnya / Shutterstock

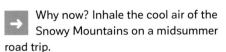

➡ **Why now?** Inhale the cool air of the Snowy Mountains on a midsummer road trip.

While Canberra, Melbourne and Sydney sizzle, the Snowy Mountains rising between them offer an escape from summer heat, plus a host of outdoor adventures. Plot a short break with a difference on a road trip along the Kosciuszko Alpine Way, following a historic route tramped first by Aboriginal people then used as a drovers' stock road, into the verdant highlands immortalised in the poetry of Banjo Paterson. Cooma marks the gateway to the region and the official start of the route; pause here to learn about the Snowy Mountains Hydro-electric Scheme that transformed local landscapes – notably in Jindabyne, your next stop, relocated when the old town was flooded to create Lake Jindabyne. Then it's into Kosciuszko National Park, to climb the namesake 2228m (7310ft) peak – Australia's highest – or to hike or bike the trails. Drink in the vistas from Scammells Ridge Lookout before exiting the park at Khancoban Pondage, a great venue for fishing and kayaking.

Trip plan: Drive south from Canberra on the B23 to Cooma, west on the Kosciuszko Road to overnight around Jindabyne, continuing on the Alpine Way to Thredbo and finishing at Khancoban. Add extra days for hiking or cycling.

Need to know: Buy a national park pass from NPWS visitor centres or entry stations.

Other months: Dec & Feb – summer, warm days; Mar–May – autumn; Jun–Sep – winter, skiing; Oct-Nov – spring, wildflowers.

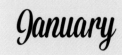

Elephants rehydrate
in Udawalawe
National Park

SOUTHWEST SRI LANKA

→ **Why now?** Marvel at marine behemoths, hike the hills and relax on beaches during dry days.

Timing is everything in Sri Lanka, where monsoons hit the southwest and northeast over different months. January is a sweet spot for sunning yourself on the south coast and hiking in the central highlands, among the tea plantations around Hatton and the cooler grasslands and cloud forest of Horton Plains. It's also a magical spell for wildlife-watchers: between December and April blue, sperm and Bryde's whales cruise coastal waters, and you can also encounter big herds of elephants and profuse birdlife in Udawalawe National Park. A string of lovely beaches studs the shore: Bentota and Unawatuna are popular resorts famed for nightlife and watersports, Hiriketiya is a quieter retreat to the southeast, while Mirissa is the main departure point for whale-watching tours. Don't miss the 17th-century Dutch fort that forms the heart of Galle, an alluring city with ancient mosques, churches and temples.

Trip plan: From Colombo, head into the central highlands before turning south to Udawalawe, hitting the beach at Hiriketiya, spotting whales from Mirissa and exploring Galle's historic sites.

Need to know: The Galle Literary Festival hosts major international authors in late January, when it can get very busy – book accommodation well in advance.

Other months: Nov & Feb – driest; Mar–Oct – heavy rains in southwest, dry in north and east.

Green and serene: a bird's-eye view of the Gambia River's mangrove forests

THE GAMBIA

→ **Why now?** Venture upriver into the heart of West Africa on cool, sunny days.

The Gambia *is* the river: nowhere in continental Africa's smallest country is more than a few kilometres from its namesake waterway. Few international visitors venture far from the gleaming Atlantic beaches, but voyage east along the Gambia River during this coolest, driest month and you'll not only discover relics of troubling colonial history – Fort James on Kunta Kinteh Island, and other sites from which enslaved African people were shipped to the New World – but also a wealth of wildlife. Birds are the biggest draw, with more than 500 species spotted here, but you might also spy dolphins, hippos and crocs in the river, and primates including baboons, red colobus monkeys and even rehabilitated chimps on islands in the River Gambia National Park.

Trip plan: Board your vessel at Senegal's capital, Dakar, to sail south to the mouth of the Gambia River, pausing at the Saloum Delta for some spectacular birding. Spend a few days navigating upstream to Kuntaur, calling at nature reserves, villages and historic sites.

Need to know: Most passenger vessels are too large to continue upriver past Kuntaur – take a local ferry or *pirogue* (local fishing boat) to visit the River Gambia National Park and Janjanbureh (Georgetown).

Other months: Nov-Dec & Feb – dry, cooler, best time for wildlife; Mar-May & Oct – hotter, mostly dry; Jun-Sep – wet, very hot, humid.

© Curioso.Photography / Shutterstock

(R) Longwood House, Jamestown; (B) Jonathan, the giant tortoise

© Umomos / Shutterstock

ST HELENA

→ **Why now? Encounter gentle giants on land and at sea.**

Adrift in the South Atlantic, St Helena remains little-visited, even since its long-awaited airport opened in 2017. Little-visited by humans, that is; this tropical, volcanic speck, a remote British Overseas Territory nearly 2000km (1243 miles) from the African coast, is a popular destination for whale sharks. Between December and March, the world's largest fish – growing over 10m (33ft) long and weighing 20 tonnes – congregate in large numbers here; January, in the warmer 'summer' (though St Helena doesn't really have seasons per se), is the ideal time to swim alongside them. Back on land, meet another big character: Jonathan the giant tortoise, believed to be nearly two centuries old, who lumbers around the grounds of Plantation House. To get the lie of the land, climb the 699 steps of

Jacob's Ladder to Half Tree Hollow or tackle Diana's Peak, the island's highest point at 823m (2700ft). Also explore the Georgian architecture of the capital, Jamestown, and visit Longwood House where Napoleon spent his final years in exile.

Trip plan: Flights from South Africa serve St Helena weekly from Johannesburg, with an extra midweek flight in high season (typically Nov-Feb).

Need to know: The St Helena pound is equivalent to the UK pound sterling, which is also accepted; there are no ATM machines, and credit/debit cards are not yet widely used.

Other months: Dec & Feb-Mar – warmer, whale sharks; Apr-May – wetter; Jun-Nov – slightly cooler.

© Oliver Berry / Lonely Planet

SOUTHERN THAILAND

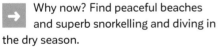

→ **Why now? Find peaceful beaches and superb snorkelling and diving in the dry season.**

The islands and beaches of Thailand's southwest are hardly terra incognita – Phuket, Krabi and Ko Phi Phi have long been popular sun-sea-sand destinations, particularly during the European winter when the Andaman Coast is reliably sunny and dry. Head further south, though, to find lesser-known corners that would make even Leo DiCaprio salivate. The Trang Islands – Ko Kradan and craggy Ko Muk – have escaped

large-scale development, despite their gleaming beaches, pellucid waters and the latter's beautiful Tham Morakot (Emerald Cave). Keep going to Tarutao National Marine Park, an archipelago of 51 islands just north of the Malay border; Ko Lipe has the beaches and, in Pattaya, the tourists and nightlife (seek out Hat Sunset for a mellower vibe). Ko Adang has waterfalls, wildlife and black sands; and larger Ko Tarutao has cliffs, caves, rainforest hikes and dramatic karst scenery. Coral reefs in the surrounding waters teem with marine life, offering

memorable snorkelling and diving.

Trip plan: Take an overnight train from Bangkok to Trang, then a ferry from Hat Yao Pier to Ko Muk or a longtail boat to Ko Kradan. Speedboats from Pak Bara serve Ko Lipe; longtails connect to Ko Adang and Ko Tarutao.

Need to know: Avoid Thailand's southernmost border region, widely considered unsafe – check your government's travel advice.

Other months: Dec & Feb-Mar – dry, warm; May–Oct – heavy rain; Apr & Nov – shoulder, some rain.

ANTARCTIC PENINSULA & SOUTH GEORGIA

→ **Why now? Bask in near permanent daylight in this enormous white wilderness at the end of the world.**

High summer on the Antarctic Peninsula brings endless, warm days – well, it's all relative, isn't it? Temperatures 'soar' to freezing point or even a little higher in the middle of the austral summer. Certainly the locals appreciate it. In January you'll see – and hear – vast penguin colonies at their most raucous, with chicks (hatched at new year) demanding to be fed, and seal pups on South Georgia, while whale sightings rise towards the end of the month. Weather can't be guaranteed, of course, not least on the Drake Passage between Tierra del Fuego and the peninsula – you might get the 'Drake Shake' (a rough crossing) or just as easily the 'Drake Lake' (water as calm as a lake) – but at least in January you have a good chance of sailing among gargantuan icebergs and soaring cliffs while sunshine glints off water and ice.

Trip plan: Most cruises heading for the Antarctic Peninsula sail from Ushuaia on Tierra del Fuego, southern Argentina, and last around 11 to 14 days. Adding South Georgia increases duration by a few days.

Need to know: The Drake Passage crossing takes at least two days in each direction. It's possible to fly from Punta Arenas (Chile) to King George Island on one or both legs, avoiding the crossing.

Other months: Nov-Dec & Feb-Mar – summer, Antarctica accessible to tourist ships; Apr- Oct – winter, dark, cold, difficult to visit.

South Georgia promises king penguins, seal pups and dramatic coastline

CANADA

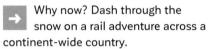 **Why now? Dash through the snow on a rail adventure across a continent-wide country.**

When does Canada look at its most spectacular? We'd argue that winter's the, er, hot ticket, when snow blankets mountains, forests and plains. True, in January the mercury plummets well below freezing – but if you're admiring that epic scenery from the comfort of a well-heated railway carriage, preferably a dome car with glass all around, why worry? VIA Rail's The Canadian service does all that, taking four days and four nights to trundle 4466km (2775 miles) from Toronto to Vancouver via Winnipeg, Saskatoon, Edmonton, Jasper and Kamloops, making the journey twice-weekly year-round. Of course, chances are you'll want to hop off – to gawp at Niagara Falls choked with ice, perhaps, or to detour along the Icefield Parkway through the heart of the Rockies from Jasper to Banff. And for a true cross-continental odyssey, start further east still in Halifax, breaking your journey in Montréal to experience the world's second-largest Francophone city.

Trip plan: From Halifax, take the overnight Ocean service to Montréal; connect to one of the four-times-daily direct trains to Toronto, then board The Canadian for the four-day journey to Vancouver.

Need to know: The Canadian runs between Toronto and Vancouver twice a week; check all times online (viarail.ca).

Other months: Dec & Feb-Mar – very cold, often snowy; Apr & May – spring, wildflowers, animals emerge from hibernation; Jun-Sep – warmest, driest; Oct-Nov – autumn colours.

© VIA Rail Canada

See the sights from the comfort of your carriage aboard The Canadian

© Susan Wright / Lonely Planet

Don't leave Liguria without sampling some classic pesto

LIGURIA ITALY

Why now: Tramp snowy paths and munch fabulous food in the quietest season.

Italy has more than one set of Alps. As well as its share of the headline peaks tracing its northern border, there's a range arcing around the Med: the Ligurian Alps. In summer, hikers tackle the Alta Via dei Monti Liguri, a long-distance trek of around 440km (273 miles). In winter, though, wonderfully crisp air and snowy forest trails lure showshoers to Aveto and Antola natural regional parks and yet-more-rugged Beigua Geopark, where snowshoe hire is available and marked circular trails offer sea views. All are within touching distance of regional capital Genoa, deliciously quiet in January yet as tasty as ever, the narrow *caruggi* (alleys) of its labyrinthine old town

studded with *palazzi* (mansions), *piazze* (squares), cafes and restaurants serving typical cuisine: pesto, salt cod, focaccia and *farinata* – moreish chickpea pancakes. To work off those calories, head just along the coast to the picture-perfect cliff-wedged villages of the Cinque Terre, connected by 120km (74.5 miles) of walking trails that are generally emptiest this month.

Trip plan: Genoa is well served by flights, but also linked by rail to Milan, Nice and Pisa, and the Cinque Terre.

Need to know: Many hotels, particularly in the Cinque Terre, close over winter – book ahead.

Other months: Nov-Dec & Feb-Mar – cool, snow at higher altitudes; Apr-May & Oct – warmer but crowds still sparse; Jun-Sep – hot, busy.

Seek out silverbacks
in Uganda's Bwindi
Impenetrable
National Park

UGANDA

→ **Why now? Track the world's biggest primates in the dry(ish) season.**
Gazing into the deep brown eyes of an endangered mountain gorilla is a precious experience: perhaps a thousand or so individuals survive worldwide, of which nearly half roam the dense forests of Uganda's Bwindi Impenetrable National Park. It's an experience you'll need to earn, tackling steep, muddy trails at altitudes up to 3000m (9483ft), possibly for several hours. But if you snag one of only eight permits available for each of the park's 19 habituated families, the rewards are luminous: an hour in the company of these gentle giants (a silverback male can reach 180kg/397lbs) is unforgettable. The rest of the country holds its own, too. Nearby Queen Elizabeth National Park is renowned for tree-climbing lions, while you can track chimpanzees in Kibale National Park. Beyond the far tip of Lake Albert, the Nile thunders over Murchison Falls; and there's also fine trekking to be had in the Rwenzori Mountains.

Trip plan: From Entebbe, Uganda's international airport, fly to an airstrip near Bwindi. Add time in Queen Elizabeth, Kibale and Murchison Falls national parks.

Need to know: Gorilla-tracking permits valid for one day must be purchased in advance, currently US$700 for foreign non-residents. Under-15s aren't permitted on gorilla-tracking excursions.

Other months: Dec & Feb & Jun-Sep – driest months, best for trekking; Mar-May – wet, good birding; Oct-Nov – wet, gorilla permits may be easier to obtain.

TEL AVIV
ISRAEL

→ **Why now:** New year, new diet – discover plant-based eating in the global 'vegan capital'.

As one year ticks over into the next, many of us ponder positive changes in our lives. Now's the time to try going vegan – and Tel Aviv, with more than 400 vegetarian restaurants, some 50 or so of them completely vegan, is the place to kick-start your new diet. It helps that classic dishes such as falafel and hummus are meat-free, of course, but there's more to this 'vegan capital of the world' than these simple but delicious snacks, with sophisticated plant-based restaurants booming across the Israeli capital. With its pleasantly mild days, January makes good browsing weather; join restaurateurs delving into the *shuks* (markets) for the freshest produce, perhaps picking up a bottle of fine local wine or haggling for antiques in Jaffa's Flea Market while you're in the mood for shopping. Then head for hip neighbourhoods such as Florentin to taste vegan cuisine from rising-star chefs. And if the mercury rises, you've 16 Mediterranean beaches to choose from for a post-prandial loll.

Trip plan: Frequent Israel Railways (rail.co.il) trains shuttle passengers from Ben Gurion Airport to central Tel Aviv in around 10min.

Need to know: Check schedules of religious festivals, when accommodation can be full.

Other months: Dec & Feb – mild, wetter; Mar-May & Sep-Nov – pleasantly warm, drier; Jun-Aug – very hot and dry.

Sizing up the swell in the southern Algarve

© Westend61 / Getty Images

SOUTHWEST ALGARVE PORTUGAL

→ **Why now?** Ride wide waves on mild seas.

Portugal's southwestern tip is swell in winter. The coastline at the corner of the Iberian Peninsula has a wide swell window, and can pick up wave surges from almost any direction; in winter, that's often big nor'westers, which slap Cabo de São Vicente and Sagres, and wrap right into the coves beyond. This means impressively gnarly waves for experienced riders – fun to watch even if you don't want to get into the water. And there's always a protected bay somewhere that will be suitable for beginners; local surf schools operate year-round. While it's hardly bikini weather, it's pleasant for winter: the air averages 13°C (55°F), the water no less than 14°C (57°F), so you won't need more than a 4/3mm wetsuit. It's also relatively tourist-free – this bit of the Algarve has more of a friendly, laid-back local vibe, especially in the off-season. Head for a chilled-out surfer town like Sagres, where you'll find cheap cafes and an outdoorsy vibe.

Trip plan: Sagres is around 120km (75 miles) west of Faro airport. It's easiest to get there by car; or you can take the train from Faro to Lagos, then a bus to Sagres.

Need to know: Beware of ocean currents. Check beaches' flags: chequered means it's unsupervised; red means it's unsafe; yellow means paddle but don't swim; and green means swimming is safe. Blue means the beach is safe and clean.

Other months: Oct-Dec & Feb-Mar – mild climes, big waves; Apr-Sep – warm to hot (heat and crowds peaking Jul-Aug).

AUSTIN, TEXAS
USA

→ Why now? Forage and feast from food trucks in the mild Texas January.

Over the past decade or so, food-truck culture has boomed across the US, and you'll find the epitome of mobile munching in the Texan capital. Long famed for its barbecue and Tex-Mex, today there's a world of cuisines to discover here, from American regional classics – Philly cheesesteaks, Cajun jambalaya, fried chicken – to dishes from all corners of the globe: pick up West African jollof rice, Syrian shawarma, Venezuelan arepas, Thai Tom Kha soup, plus plenty of vegetarian and vegan options. Mild January, when temperatures hover at around 15°C (59°F), brings fine weather for alfresco eating and enjoying the outdoor lifestyle that Austin does so well along the trails of the Barton Creek Greenbelt and Lady Bird Lake. And you're never far from a cool tequila cocktail and a hot gig – particularly during the Red River Cultural District Free Week at the start of the month, with dozens of live performances.

Trip plan: Hop between the dozen-plus food-truck parks scattered around the city, or just follow your nose – working off those calories in Austin's many green spaces.

Need to know: The SXSW film, media and music festival in March sees crowds boom and prices soar. Book festival-time accommodation well in advance if you're planning on an extended Austin stay.

Other months: Dec & Feb – mild, quiet; Mar-May – pleasantly warm, busy; Jun-Aug – very hot; Sep-Nov – comfortable, popular.

Alfresco eating and drinking at Banger's

WHOLE HOG

BBQ

© Jussi Hellstén / MyHelsinki

Enjoy the great outdoors in
Helsinki, from city-centre
skating to skiing the suburbs

HELSINKI FINLAND

Why now: Ski, sledge, swim and soak in a city made for winter.

Despite – or perhaps because of – the subzero temperatures, the Finnish capital is very much an outdoor destination in midwinter. Sure, you wouldn't want to miss Helsinki's grand Art Nouveau, Neoclassical and Modernist architecture, nor the hulking 18th-century Suomenlinna sea fortress. But this is the time when locals don cross-country skis to swoosh along almost 200km (124 miles) of well-kept trails around the city. They lace up skates to glide across the frozen Baltic or one of the rinks that pop up around the centre. They grab a *pulkka* (sledge) and clamber up the slopes of Sinebrychoff Park and waterfront Kaivopuisto to toboggan down with a wild whoop. And they plunge into the icy waters for an, um, invigorating swim – before, of course, reheating in a sauna, of which Finland reputedly has more than two million; the modern Löyly public sauna and restaurant complex in Hernesaari is a hot ticket for cold days. You'll want to grab a glug of *glogg* (mulled wine), too, or bar-hop through the hip Kallio district.

Trip plan: Helsinki is connected to many international airports.

Need to know: Regular ferries make the 2hr crossing between Helsinki and Tallinn, Estonia, making a two-country break easy.

Other months: Dec & Feb-Mar – very cold, short days; Apr-May – spring, pleasant; Jun-Aug – warm, long days; Sep-Nov – getting chillier, autumn colours.

31

February

WHERE TO GO WHEN

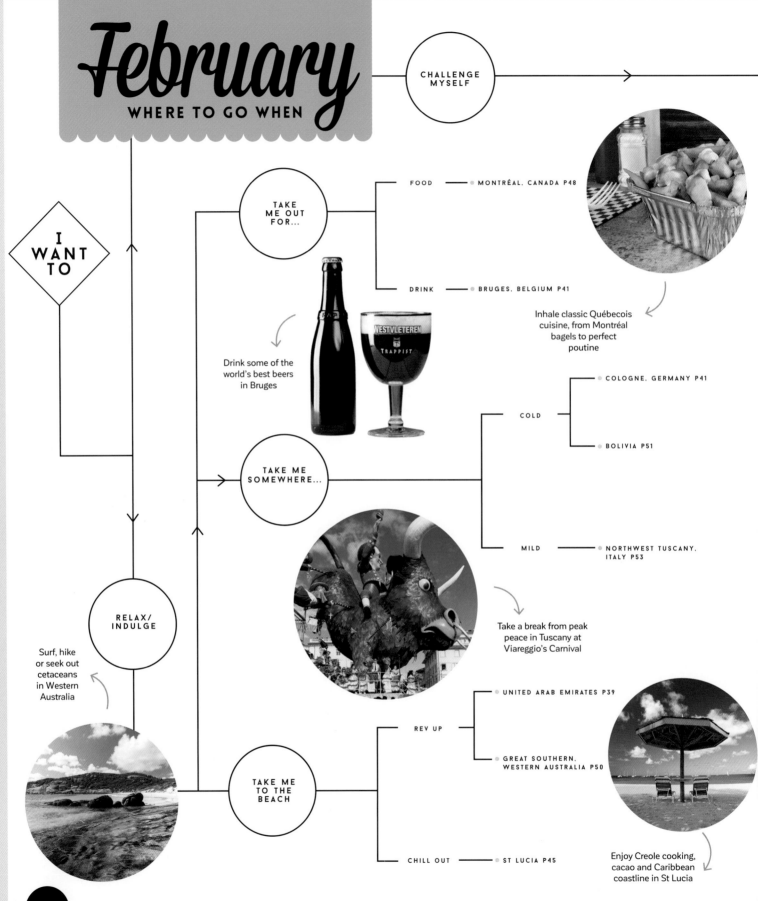

CHALLENGE MYSELF

I WANT TO

TAKE ME OUT FOR...

FOOD ━━ MONTRÉAL, CANADA P48

DRINK ━━ BRUGES, BELGIUM P41

Inhale classic Québecois cuisine, from Montréal bagels to perfect poutine

Drink some of the world's best beers in Bruges

TAKE ME SOMEWHERE...

COLD
- COLOGNE, GERMANY P41
- BOLIVIA P51

MILD ━━ NORTHWEST TUSCANY, ITALY P53

Take a break from peak peace in Tuscany at Viareggio's Carnival

RELAX/ INDULGE

Surf, hike or seek out cetaceans in Western Australia

TAKE ME TO THE BEACH

REV UP
- UNITED ARAB EMIRATES P39
- GREAT SOUTHERN, WESTERN AUSTRALIA P50

CHILL OUT ━━ ST LUCIA P45

Enjoy Creole cooking, cacao and Caribbean coastline in St Lucia

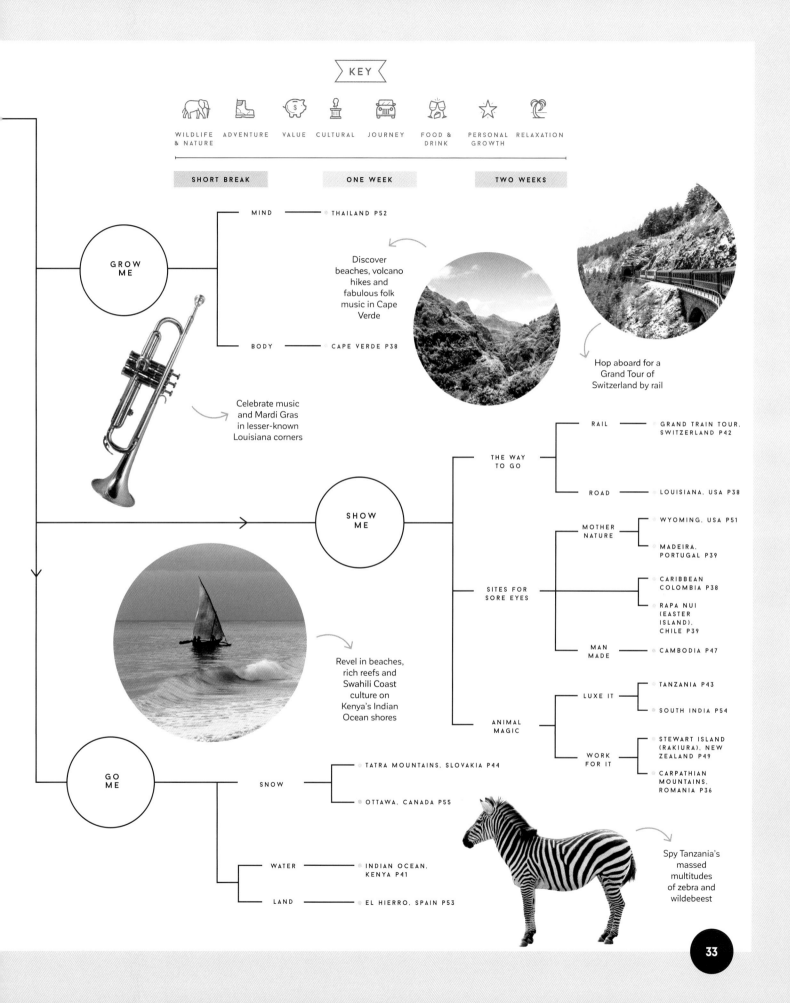

WILDLIFE & NATURE   ADVENTURE   VALUE   CULTURAL   JOURNEY   FOOD & DRINK   PERSONAL GROWTH   RELAXATION

SHORT BREAK   ONE WEEK   TWO WEEKS

GROW ME

MIND ——— THAILAND P52

Discover beaches, volcano hikes and fabulous folk music in Cape Verde

BODY ——— CAPE VERDE P38

Hop aboard for a Grand Tour of Switzerland by rail

Celebrate music and Mardi Gras in lesser-known Louisiana corners

SHOW ME

THE WAY TO GO

RAIL ——— GRAND TRAIN TOUR, SWITZERLAND P42

ROAD ——— LOUISIANA, USA P38

SITES FOR SORE EYES

MOTHER NATURE ——— WYOMING, USA P51

MADEIRA, PORTUGAL P39

CARIBBEAN COLOMBIA P38

RAPA NUI (EASTER ISLAND), CHILE P39

MAN MADE ——— CAMBODIA P47

ANIMAL MAGIC

LUXE IT ——— TANZANIA P43

SOUTH INDIA P54

WORK FOR IT ——— STEWART ISLAND (RAKIURA), NEW ZEALAND P49

CARPATHIAN MOUNTAINS, ROMANIA P36

Revel in beaches, rich reefs and Swahili Coast culture on Kenya's Indian Ocean shores

GO ME

SNOW ——— TATRA MOUNTAINS, SLOVAKIA P44

OTTAWA, CANADA P55

WATER ——— INDIAN OCEAN, KENYA P41

LAND ——— EL HIERRO, SPAIN P53

Spy Tanzania's massed multitudes of zebra and wildebeest

EVENTS
IN FEBRUARY

ADELAIDE FRINGE
Adelaide, Australia
The southern hemisphere's biggest arts festival brings a month of cabaret, comedy, circus, music, theatre and more to South Australia's capital.

FIESTA DE LA VIRGEN DE LA CANDELARIA
Copacabana, Bolivia
Wild revelry (with a touch of reverence) marks celebrations honouring a 16th-century effigy of the Virgin Mary in the town on the shore of Lake Titicaca.

WHALE WATCHING
Mirissa, Sri Lanka
Blue whales, the world's largest creatures, cruise through the Indian Ocean off southern Sri Lanka – head out on a tour to spot them.

FLOWER FESTIVAL
Chiang Mai, Thailand
Be dazzled by displays of damask roses, chrysanthemums and other colourful blooms during this three-day celebration of the floral world.

ST VALENTINE'S DAY
Terni, Italy
Celebrate the most romantic saint with performances, poetry, painting, street art and more in his Umbrian birth- and resting place.

CARNAVAL DE QUÉBEC
Québec City, Canada
Reputedly the world's largest winter carnival is packed with activities and events including parades, ice-carving, music, ice-canoe racing and more.

ABU SIMBEL SUN FESTIVAL
Egypt
Shafts of light from the rising sun pierce the gloom of Abu Simbel Temple to illuminate three great statues within.

LEMON FESTIVAL
Menton, France
Some 140 tonnes of the versatile citrus adorn sculptures, floats and gardens during this two-week fruit-fest on the Côte d'Azur.

Mid-February to mid-March — $$
2 February — $$
November–March — $$
First weekend in February — $
14 February — $
First half of February — $$
22 February (also 22 October) — $$
From mid-February — $

VERY FAMILY FRIENDLY

Share Great Southern shores with orcas, surfers and even beach kangaroos

- GREAT SOUTHERN, WESTERN AUSTRALIA

Head to the UAE for biking, hiking, beaches and world-class galleries like Louvre Abu Dhabi

- UNITED ARAB EMIRATES

- MONTRÉAL, CANADA

Graze your way through foodie Montréal hotspots like pretty Plateau Mont-Royal

- CAPE VERDE

Lace up some skates and zoom along Ottawa's iced-over Rideau Canal

- OTTAWA, CANADA

- TATRA MOUNTAINS, SLOVAKIA

- INDIAN OCEAN, KENYA

- SOUTH INDIA

- CARPATHIAN MOUNTAINS, ROMANIA

Hike El Hierro's biodiverse trails then cool off in the turquoise waters of Charco Azul

Sharpen your tracker skills with a Carpathian expedition in search of wolves and lynx

- CAMBODIA

- EL HIERRO, SPAIN

- LOUISIANA, USA

EXPENSIVE BUT WORTH IT

GOOD VALUE

- GRAND TRAIN TOUR, SWITZERLAND

- TANZANIA

Spot Stewart Island species like the endangered kaka

- COLOGNE, GERMANY

- STEWART ISLAND (RAKIURA), NEW ZEALAND

- ST LUCIA

- RAPA NUI (EASTER ISLAND) CHILE

Take in monolithic *moai* and the Rapa Nui Tapati culture-fest on Easter Island

- BRUGES, BELGIUM

Climb the Belfort tower in Bruges without the crowds

- NORTHWEST TUSCANY, ITALY

- MADEIRA, PORTUGAL

- THAILAND

- WYOMING, USA

Train-trip through Thailand to see ancient treasures like Wat Phra Kaew's Emerald Buddha

- CARIBBEAN COLOMBIA

Trek high into Colombia's Sierra Nevada to the jungle-swathed 'Lost City'

- BOLIVIA

Dive right in to the wet, wild and wonderful Carnaval in Oruro, Bolivia

LEAVE THE KIDS AT HOME

CARPATHIAN MOUNTAINS
ROMANIA

→ Why now? Track wolves and lynx through snow-clad wilderness.

The children of the night, what music they make... and in Transylvania in February, that unearthly music – the nocturnal howls of wolves, the growls and yelps of courting lynx – is certainly the food of love. Late winter is the breeding season for both species in Romania's share of the Carpathian Mountains, which host perhaps 2500 wolves and about the same number of the magnificent cats. Now's the time to track them across the snowy wilderness of Piatra Craiului National Park, joining an expert local guide to learn to read spoor and follow the peregrinations of these elusive predators as they search for mates; early morning and evening expeditions into the mountains from the town of Zărnești might, if you're fortunate, also yield a rare sighting. Make the most of free time exploring nearby

14th-century Bran Castle (often whimsically linked with Dracula) and Brașov's medieval and Baroque monuments.

Trip plan: Closest international transport hubs to Zărnești, gateway to Piatra Craiului National Park, are Sibiu and Bucharest, both about 2hr 30min away by road. Allow at least two days' tracking to increase chances of a sighting of either species.

Need to know: Bring warm clothes – temperatures are likely to dip below freezing in the early mornings and evenings.

Other months: Dec-Jan – often subzero, snowy; Mar-Apr – warming, still chilly; May-Sep – warmest, bears active, wildflowers; Oct-Nov – temperatures fall, bears bed down for winter.

Follow wolves across the wilderness in a wintry Carpathian wonderland

LOUISIANA
USA

→ **Why now?** Take a deep dive into the vibrant, turbulent, tuneful heritage of the Bayou State.

February in New Orleans is all about Mardi Gras, that full-fat festival of music, dancing, parades and overindulgence of all kinds, bringing crowds (and higher prices) to the Big Easy. But Mardi Gras is celebrated across the state, and there are also opportunities to uncover more troubling and thought-provoking aspects of Louisiana's past in this relatively cool month, pleasant for exploring. Two specially curated trails now showcase the state's African American Heritage and Civil Rights Movement, highlighting key sites from Shreveport in the northwest to New Orleans' French Quarter in the southeast. Discover these spots and more historic mind-openers on a road trip, steering first south from New Orleans into the gator-infested swamps of the Barataria Preserve then along the River Road, visiting extravagant plantation houses en route to state capital Baton Rouge.

Trip plan: New Orleans' Louis Armstrong Airport (where you can rent a car) has connections to most US cities and several international destinations.

Need to know: Keep your ear to the ground for an old-time *boucherie* – a traditional communal hog-butchering event often held before Mardi Gras, yielding Cajun delicacies such as *boudin* sausages and *cracklins* (fried pork skin).

Other months: Dec-Jan – relatively cool and quiet; Mar-May – getting steamier; Jun-Sep – consistently hot, rain peaks in Jul, risk of hurricanes; Oct-Nov – slightly cooler and drier.

CAPE VERDE

→ **Why now?** Be blown away by this Atlantic archipelago.

Part of Africa, historically influenced by Portugal and Brazil, and dubbed the 'new Caribbean', the 10-island archipelago of Cape Verde is quite unlike anywhere else. That's largely due to its location, adrift in the Atlantic Ocean, 1000km (621 miles) west of Senegal. Such remoteness means a distinct fusion culture thrives here – perhaps best expressed through Cape Verde's intoxicating *morna* folk music. There are also sandy beaches, lively bars (especially on São Vicente and Sal) and excellent hiking – notably on Fogo island's volcanic Pico and amid the mountains of Santo Antão. The islands' year-round warmth – 26-30°C (79-86°F) – is especially appealing to northern-hemisphere-dwellers seeking sun. As one of the breezier months, February is also ideal for sailors, surfers, windsurfers and kitesurfers – regular tradewinds make it a world-class watersport destination.

Trip plan: Plan a twin-centre break to Sal and Boavista islands for the best combination of beaches, nightlife and watersports. Flights link the islands.

Need to know: Sal, Santiago, Boavista and São Vicente have international airports.

Other months: Dec-Jan – dry, windiest, warm; Mar-Jun –warm, dry; Jul-Nov – rainy.

CARIBBEAN
COLOMBIA

→ **Why now?** Discover a long-lost city amid coastal mountains.

For nearly four centuries, a set of ancient plazas and terraces lay shrouded in jungle high in Colombia's Sierra Nevada de Santa Marta: a settlement known to indigenous peoples as Teyuna (meaning 'Mother Nature') and now as Ciudad Perdida – the 'Lost City'. Rediscovered in the 1970s, today the only way to reach this extraordinary site is on a four- to six-day, 51km (32-mile) return trek through humid jungle, culminating in a climb up some 1200 stone steps from the Buritaca River – a challenging but hugely rewarding adventure on which you'll immerse yourself in the forest and meet the Wiwa people who call it home. February is a particularly pleasant month to visit Colombia's Caribbean region, typically with fewer visitors (and lower prices) than December or January, and when on-shore breezes provide welcome respite from the year-round heat – though it can rain at any time on the northern slopes of the Sierra Nevada. Relax post-trek on the rainforest-fringed beaches of Parque Nacional Natural Tayrona, and explore the cobbled streets, churches, well-preserved mansions and bougainvillea-strewn balconies of Cartagena's atmospheric old walled city.

Trip plan: Santa Marta, the gateway town for the trek, is served by flights from Bogotá and Medellín; buses to Cartagena take about 4hr.

Need to know: Parque Nacional Natural Tayrona often closes for some or all of February for ecological recovery.

Other months: Dec-Jan & Mar-Apr – dry, hot (busiest Dec-Jan); May-Nov – wet, hot.

MADEIRA
PORTUGAL

→ **Why now?** Have outdoor fun in the winter sun.

Madeira is an island without climatic extremes, but with plenty of topographical ones. Adrift in the Atlantic, closer to Morocco than to its Portuguese motherland, there's barely any flatland to be found – every inch seems dramatically ruptured – and the sun shines all year round. Suffice it to say, in February, when most of Europe shivers, Madeira can bask in temperatures of up to 20°C (68°F), and even if it rains, there are so many microclimates that you can travel to a different spot and find better weather. The mild winter is ideal for strolling the island's network of *levadas* (old irrigation channels) or simply for relaxing with a *poncha* (sugarcane-spirit cocktail) in an ocean-view bar. Capital Funchal has plenty to divert: the ornate Sé (cathedral); the Art Deco Mercado dos Lavradores; the cable car up to Monte, where the Monte Palace Tropical Gardens bloom year-round; or an elegant afternoon tea at Reid's Palace hotel. Or base yourself in the pretty fishing village of Câmara de Lobos, favoured bolthole of Winston Churchill. Madeira promises numerous activities, too, from trail running to mountain-biking and canyoning.

Trip plan: Madeira's airport is a 25min drive east of Funchal. Driving can be nerve-wracking – use buses and tours to make forays across the island.

Need to know: Carnival, one of the island's biggest events, falls in February/March (40 days before Easter). As well a grand parade through Funchal, events take place around the island during Carnival week.

Other months: Oct-Jan & Mar-Apr – mild, wetter; May-Sep – hotter, driest.

UNITED ARAB EMIRATES

→ **Why now?** Mix sun, sand, shopping and surprising cultural and active experiences.

The recent reinvention of Dubai as a tourism and trade hub grabbed the world's attention – but another six emirates await discovery in this relatively comfortable month, when daytime temperatures linger around the 24°C mark (75°F). Sure, there are beaches to lounge on, but don't limit yourself to the resort strands of Dubai: seek out sandy stretches such as Black Palace Beach, Khor Fakkan, Jebel Ali or Dibba in Fujairah, where you can enjoy some fine snorkelling against the backdrop of the Hajar Mountains. Those crags also host biking and hiking trails, including the region's first multi-day trail in Ras Al Khaimah. Cool off with some culture: explore the old centre and forts of oasis city Al Ain; 10 millennia of history at the expansive Mleiha Archaeological Centre; and the world-class museums and galleries of Sharjah and Abu Dhabi, including the Louvre and Guggenheim.

Trip plan: Dubai and Abu Dhabi receive most international flights. Bus services between cities are reasonable, but exploring further is easier by car or taxi. Allow a week to explore Dubai's souks and creek, the museums of Abu Dhabi and Sharjah, oasis city Al Ain and the beaches, forts and mountains of Fujairah and Ras Al Khaimah.

Need to know: Though most emirates are generally fairly relaxed, it's respectful to cover shoulders and knees in public. Drinking alcohol is illegal in Sharjah.

Other months: Nov-Jan & Mar-Apr – hot, occasional rain, busiest; May-Oct – extremely hot.

RAPA NUI (EASTER ISLAND)
CHILE

→ **Why now?** Experience the traditions, ancestral rituals and competitions of the annual Rapa Nui Tapati.

Calling Rapa Nui isolated doesn't come close – and neither does almost anywhere else: this volcanic speck lies adrift in the Pacific over 3600km (2237 miles) west of mainland Chile. No wonder its culture, seeded by Polynesian settlers in the first millennium CE, evolved a series of unique traditions and artefacts – most famously hundreds of colossal, mysterious *moai* (carved stone heads), looming up to 10m (33ft) tall. Centuries of clan strife, colonisation, assimilation and ecological collapse wreaked havoc on that heritage – but today it's celebrated once more during the two-week Rapa Nui Tapati at the start of February, a hot, dry month that's also prime time for exploring. Plot your route around key sites – Orongo Cultural Village, the Rano Raraku volcano from which part-quarried *moai* sprout, the monumental platform of Ahu Tongariki – making time to cheer on the horse-racing, running, swimming and boat-paddling competitions, the music and dance, and the final crowning of the Ariki (Queen) Tapati.

Trip plan: Rapa Nui is accessible by plane from Santiago, Chile and Lima, Peru – consider combining your visit with the highlights of either of those countries. Allow three or four nights on the island to explore fully.

Need to know: Mosquitoes sometimes carry dengue fever and Zika virus on Rapa Nui – cover up and bring insect repellent.

Other months: Nov-Jan & Feb-Mar – hot, driest, busiest; Apr-Oct – cooler, wetter (May is the rainiest month).

© quill23 / Getty Images

(L) Old meets new: Hohenzollern Bridge leading to Cologne Cathedral; (R) Sarongs for sale along Kenya's Indian Ocean coast; (B) Beautiful Bruges

COLOGNE
GERMANY

→ **Why now? Celebrate the 'fifth season'.**

The historic and high-spirited Rhineland city of Cologne doesn't just celebrate Carnival – it creates a whole new time period for it. The 'fifth season' officially starts on 11 November, but the party really kicks off the following February, on the Thursday before Lent. Then ensue the 'crazy days', between Fat Thursday and Ash Wednesday, when parading, masquerading, drinking, dancing and general revelry take over the streets. It's raucous good fun, and not at all out of character for Cologne, which is known for its liberalism, elan and generous number of traditional beer halls serving local-brewed Kölsch, hearty food and liberal dollops of *Gemütlichkeit* (aka hygge, German-style). There's plenty to see, too: the gargantuan twin-spired cathedral and the rambling lanes of the riverside Altstadt (Old Town), the modern art at Museum Ludwig and Cologne's Roman heritage at the Römisch-Germanisches Museum. A particularly moving way to move around the city is by following the Stolpersteins – brass plaques memorialising victims of the Nazis, part of a project by Cologne-based artist Gunter Demnig; they're especially dense in the Belgisches Viertel (Belgian Quarter), which is also one of the hippest hangouts, with lots of bars and boutiques.

Trip plan: Allow at least two days to explore, more if you plan to be nursing a Carnival hangover.

Need to know: Consider buying a MuseumsCard, which covers admission to many museums on two consecutive days.

Other months: Nov-Jan & Mar – cold (Christmas markets Dec); Apr-Jun & Sep-Oct – warm, less crowded; Jul-Aug – hottest, festivals.

INDIAN OCEAN
KENYA

→ **Why now? The air's hot, the water's gorgeous.**

In a country blessed with some of the world's greatest game parks, it can be easy to overlook the coast. But Kenya's Indian Ocean shore is far from second-rate. The fine, soft sand is blinding white, the sea is a swirl of crystal-clear blues, and picturesque fishing dhows, swaying palms and women sporting rainbow-bright kangas add photogenic touches. There is a distinct, spice-infused Swahili Coast culture too – evident in the Arabic houses of Mombasa and the region's signature curries, fragrant and full of seafood. Development has occurred, but most hotels are low-key and well-spaced and so don't interrupt the dreamy vibe. The snorkelling and diving are spectacular too, particularly in January and February, when the weather is hot and dry, and water visibility is at its best. Migrating whale sharks (February to April and September to October) also pass by.

Trip plan: Explore Mombasa's old town and Fort Jesus; if overlanding to Mombasa from Nairobi, break the journey with a safari in Tsavo. South of Mombasa, Diani offers traditional beach holidays; Watamu and Malindi, 120km (75 miles) north, are both protected by marine national parks.

Need to know: Check the security situation before travelling – the coast north of Malindi may be subject to travel advisories.

Other months: Jan – hot, dry, lush; Mar-May – long rains, very wet; Jun-Oct – dry, good game-viewing; Nov-Dec – short rains.

BRUGES
BELGIUM

→ **Why now? Imbibe ales and art during the city's delightfully sleepy winter season.**

With its glorious medieval architecture, cosy bars and romantic canal cruises, Bruges is a beautiful city indeed. Trouble is, that point hasn't gone unnoticed: more than eight million visitors cram its cobbled streets in the busiest years. The trick is in the timing. February is chilly, true, but also typically the driest month, and the quietest. Wrap up warm, amble those ancient alleys around the historic Markt and Burg squares, contemplate fine Flemish art at the Groeningemuseum, and climb the Belfort tower to drink in views without being jostled. Of course, that's unlikely to be the only drinking you'll contemplate: Belgium's celebrated beers are a lip-smacking delight at any time, and for a few days in early February you can sample more than 350 brews – international as well as local – during the Bruges Beer Festival. The chocolate's not half bad, either.

Trip plan: Allow at least two days – and nights, of course – to explore the medieval landmarks, admire the superb art collections and enjoy the nightlife. Bruges is 1hr by train from Brussels, with good connections Europe-wide.

Need to know: Carnival is celebrated in various towns across Belgium – notably Binche – in the days preceding Ash Wednesday, typically in February; make the short journey to experience the festivities.

Other months: Jan & Mar – cold, quieter; Apr-May – spring, warming; Jun-Aug – busiest; Sep-Nov – cooler, still popular; Dec – cold, busy during Christmas markets.

GRAND TRAIN TOUR SWITZERLAND

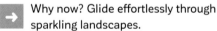

→ **Why now? Glide effortlessly through sparkling landscapes.**

The Swiss rail network doesn't give a jot about winter. Trains remain well-heated and punctual even after a dumping of snow. And my, what trains – the most scenic in the world, chugging between icy mountains, over gravity-defying viaducts and around frozen lakes. The biggest adventure is the Grand Train Tour, which covers around 1280km (795 miles), split into eight sections, using some premium trains and historic tracks. Ride the route in February and the panoramic carriages will be looking out onto a Narnian wonderland. Highlights include the city-to-summits Lucerne–Interlaken Express; the narrow-gauge Glacier Express between Zermatt and St Moritz, which glides past the mighty Matterhorn; and the St Moritz–Tirano

Bernina Express, which surges south towards Italian Switzerland on the Unesco-listed Rhaetian Railway.

Trip plan: A Swiss Travel Pass Flex covers train, bus and boat journeys on three, four, eight or 15 days in one month. Allow at least eight days to ride all sections of the Grand Train Tour; two weeks allows time to explore en route or add on some skiing.

Need to know: Seat reservations are recommended, and mandatory on some services (such as the Glacier Express) even if you have a pass. The Glacier Express doesn't run mid-October to mid-December; other services may have amended routings or timetables over winter.

Other months: Nov-Jan & Mar-Apr – winter timetable, snow scenes then spring wildflowers; May-Oct – summer rail timetable, warm to hot then cooling.

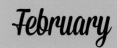

(L) Wildebeest and zebra on the move; (R) Tanzania's Ngorongoro Crater; (B) Bernina Express, Switzerland

TANZANIA

→ **Why now? Encounter hundreds of thousands of grazing wildebeest.**

If images of wildebeest plunging through croc-infested rivers or of lions stalking the herds across the vast Masai Mara have enticed you, think on this: each of those gnus came from somewhere. And that somewhere is their mother, who fattened up on the lush grasses of the southern Serengeti before calving in one of the world's great synchronised breeding events which produces up to half a million young each year. February is a great time to explore northern Tanzania, watching herds of these wildebeest, plus zebra munching their way across the short-grass plains of the southern Serengeti, stocking up on calories before giving birth, usually in early to mid February. Predator action can be thrilling now, before those 1.5 million gnus continue northwest on their cyclical migration. This short dry season also offers excellent birding, and some reserves such as Selous and Ruaha are relatively quiet, with lower rates at lodges. Make time, too, for Olduvai Gorge – the famed 'Cradle of Mankind' known for finds of early hominid remains – and the wildlife-dense Ngorongoro Crater.

Trip plan: For the southern Serengeti, fly into the Seronera airstrip. Small planes link to other sites countrywide.

Need to know: Many non-African nationals require a visa; apply for an electronic one online.

Other months: Mar – dry, wildebeest grazing; Apr-May – long rains; Jun-Oct – peak season, migration in north Serengeti and Masai Mara; Nov-Jan – short rains.

© chuvipro / Getty Images

© michelangeloop / Getty Images

TATRA MOUNTAINS
SLOVAKIA

➜ **Why now? Enjoy plenty of bang for few bucks in a snowy mountain playground.**

Embracing the thrills on the white stuff doesn't take too much of the green stuff in the Tatra Mountains. Downhill skiers and snowboarders find more moderate slopes and some uplifting off-piste rather than a host of testing black runs, but it's mainly the extensive menu of alternative snow sports that makes this region a hit with families and active types in February: winter hikes to frozen waterfalls, snowshoeing, cross-country skiing, husky sledding, tubing, skating, sledging and more. Feeling the chill? Soak in a steaming thermal pool or spa, or spark up your internal furnace with a tot or two of local firewater *slivovica* (plum brandy). There are cultural treats to discover, too, in the form of Goral villages inhabited by that ethnic group of the Carpathian highlands; and nearby Poprad's lovely Renaissance quarter, Spišská Sobota.

Trip plan: Poprad has the nearest airport, plus quick and frequent train and bus connections to mountain resorts such as Starý Smokovec and Tatranská Lomnica, where you'll find plenty of accommodation and activity providers. Košice, and Poland's Kraków, are also popular gateways.

Need to know: On days when weather is bleak, you'll find subterranean sanctuary among the extraordinary stalactites and underground lakes of otherworldly Belianska Cave (closed Mondays) in Tatranská Kotlina, about 10km (6 miles) north of Tatranská Lomnica.

Other months: Nov-Jan & Mar – cold, snowy in Tatra Mountains; Apr-Jun – mild, blossoms; Jul-Aug – hot, busiest across the country; Sep-Oct – balmy, settled weather, autumn colours.

Hike, ski, snowshoe or try husky-sledding in Slovakia's snowy Tatra Mountains

© Pawel Kazmierczak / Shutterstock

© Justin Foulkes / Lonely Planet

Enjoy gourmet eats and cacao treats in the shadow of St Lucia's Pitons

ST LUCIA

→ **Why now? Mix romance with relaxation – and perhaps a chocolate chaser – in this cooler, drier month.**

Among Caribbean destinations vying for the 'most romantic' crown, St Lucia has a couple of enviable attributes – and we're not talking about its voluptuous twin prominences, the Pitons, spectacularly photogenic as they are. Rather, we mean the roster of outstanding upmarket resorts overlooking gorgeous white-sand beaches lapped by the turquoise, bath-warm Caribbean, and a long heritage of cacao plantations – a legacy fuelling a passion for chocolate that's been reignited in recent years. February, when the air is coolest and clearest, is the time to fall in love with (or, indeed, in) St Lucia and its most sensuous pleasures. Plan a couples' retreat in the island's south for easy access to both those picturesque peaks and the cacao plantations, several of which offer chocolate tours, tastings and cookery classes.

Trip plan: Most long-haul flights arrive at Hewanorra Airport in the south of the island, closer to the majority of the cocoa plantations as well as several gorgeous resorts; regional services typically use George FL Charles Airport in the north, near a string of beach resorts further up the coast.

Need to know: Independence Day celebrations on 22 February include parades and local festivities – be prepared to party.

Other months: Dec-Jan – getting drier, very busy; Mar – coolest, driest, advance booking advised; Apr-May – rain building, better rates; Jun-Nov – heavy showers, hurricanes possible, prices lowest.

CAMBODIA

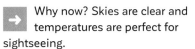

→ Why now? Skies are clear and temperatures are perfect for sightseeing.

The weather is dry and wonderful across Cambodia in February – right from the golden beaches of Sihanoukville to the temples of Angkor. Warmer than the early dry season (October to January) but not yet sweltering, this is a good month for exploring the vast, Unesco-listed complex. Long days of sightseeing are a more comfortable prospect in temperatures of around 27°C (81°F), and there's always shade to be found amid Angkor's stonework and jungly pockets. There's also just enough water left in Tonlé Sap Lake to take boat trips to floating villages that are still actually floating – as the dry season progresses, levels drop, leaving stilthouses

marooned in mud and Kampong Phluk (the 'flooded forest') inaccessible.

Trip plan: Start in Siem Reap, granting Angkor the time it deserves. Then cruise on Tonlé Sap Lake. Head south for the haunting museums of Phnom Penh before beach time in Kep or Sihanoukville; also consider hikes in the Cardamom Mountains.

Need to know: Angkor passes are available for durations of one (US$20), three (US$40) and seven (US$60) days.

Other months: Oct-Jan & Mar-Apr – dry; May-Sep – wet (Apr-Jun: hottest, most humid).

(L) Iconic Angkor Wat rises above the Cambodian jungle; (R) Still waters at sunset at Sihanoukville

MONTRÉAL
CANADA

➜ **Why now? Eat yourself heated in Québec's culinary epicentre.**

Let's not kid ourselves: February in Montréal is cold. Really, really cold – the mercury might sneak up towards zero, but then again it might plummet down below -20°C (-4°F), though it's typically dry and often clear. But Montréal is tailored to its climate (not least in its Underground City) and so is its eating scene. To inhale the extra calories you'll need to function in these icy climes, particularly after a stint skating, snowshoeing or cross-country skiing in the city's parks, you could chow down on classics: Montréal bagels and smoked meat sandwiches, and of course poutine, that gloopy, messy, delicious fries-curd-cheese-gravy combo. Yet Montréal is more ethnically diverse than ever – over a third of the population is of non-European origin – and its culinary offerings are similarly varied. So wrap up super-warm and plot a course between Korean fried chicken, Haitian *griot* (fried pork chunks), Syrian *kibbeh* and more.

Trip plan: From a base in Downtown or Old Montréal, graze your way north-northwest through Plateau Mont-Royal, Mile End, Little Italy, Mile-Ex, Villeray and Rosemont–La Petite-Patrie.

Need to know: February sees creative chefs showcase their craft during Montréal En Lumière, an annual gastronomy and music festival that promises a feast for the ears and stomach alike.

Other months: Dec-Jan & Mar – very cold, usually below freezing; Apr-May – warming; Jun-Sep – pleasantly warm; Oct-Nov – cooling, fall colours.

Work up an appetite with a snowy Park Ave run before diving in to Montréal's fabulous food scene

© martinedoucet / Getty Images

© R. Vickers / Shutterstock

Hit the
beach or take a
Rakiura wildlife hike

STEWART ISLAND (RAKIURA) NEW ZEALAND

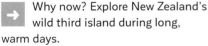

→ Why now? Explore New Zealand's wild third island during long, warm days.

The Māori of Stewart Island named their home Rakiura: the 'Land of Glowing Skies' – watch the flaming sun melt into the sea on a balmy February evening and you'll get an inkling why. Long, dry(ish), sunny days of the austral summer are perfect for roaming this little-visited wildlife haven, some 85% of which is protected within its namesake national park. The best way to explore is on foot: Stewart Island has only 25km (15.5 miles) of roads versus 245km (152 miles) of walking paths, and the rewards of tackling its trails – notably the headliner 32km (20 miles), three-day Rakiura Track – are largely feathered and floral. Cross the island through lush rimu and kamahi forest to Mason Bay for the best chances of spotting (or at least hearing) the elusive kiwi. And make the short boat crossing from Oban, the only real settlement, to Ulva Island – an astonishing natural aviary with a raucous cast of birds including endangered kaka, yellow- and red-fronted parakeets, bellbirds, fantails and tūī.

Trip plan: Stewart Island/Rakiura is a short (but often bumpy) flight from Invercargill or a 1hr (and also frequently rough) boat crossing from Bluff to Oban.

Need to know: Join a sea kayaking tour to access remote beaches and enjoy the best sunsets.

Other months: Dec-Jan – drier, temperatures nudging over 20°C (68°F); Mar-May & Oct-Nov – cooler, wetter; Jun-Sep – short, dark, colder days.

GREAT SOUTHERN
WESTERN AUSTRALIA

→ **Why now?** Chill on beautiful beaches, ride the waves and watch huge pods of killer whales.

It's been said that Australia's most beautiful beaches aren't around Sydney or on Queensland's tropical islands, but strung like a set of gleaming pearls along the south coast of Western Australia between Albany and Esperance. Yet this region, far from urban centres, is relatively quiet – and in February, after schools restart but while the mercury still hovers at a balmy 24°C (75°F) or so, it's the time to enjoy that soft sand by yourself. This isn't the place to simply lounge, mind: there's so much to do. Get a head for heights among the towering tingle trees in the Valley of the Giants; lace up your hiking shoes to explore Stirling Range and Fitzgerald River national parks; and grab your board to catch the waves at the various surf breaks. This is also the time of year to gawp at killer whales (orca) gathering in large numbers in Bremer Bay to snaffle squid and fish.

Trip plan: Fly (1hr) or drive (4hr 30min) from Perth to Albany, then steer east along the coast to Esperance – allow a week to explore Bremer Bay, Fitzgerald River National Park and the succession of golden-sand beaches en route.

Need to know: Public transport in this region is limited – you'll want a vehicle to get around.

Other months: Jan & Mar-Apr – warm, sunny, orca in Bremer Bay; May-Jun – cool, quiet; Jul-Nov – cooler, southern right whales calving; Dec – hot, busier.

© Matt Deakin / Shutterstock

Clear, clear water at Wharton Beach, Esperance

WYOMING USA

→ **Why now? Hot slopes, hot springs.**
When snow cloaks the cowboy state, special things happen. Skiers and boarders will love the Teton Mountains resort of Jackson Hole, nicknamed 'The Big One' on account of its steep terrain and great powder (driest and deepest January to February). There are some baby slopes, but this is best for intermediates and pros. Après-ski is lively too. Then, further north, quite different thrills await in Yellowstone National Park. Heaving in summer, Yellowstone empties in winter. Park roads close, and the only ways to explore are via snowcoach, snowmobile, cross-country skis or snowshoes. Geysers and hot springs steam in the icy air, and animals congregate at the thermal areas for warmth. Also, grey wolves stand out against the snowblanketed landscapes and their tracks are more easily followed – take a guided trip in the Lamar Valley for the chance of a sighting.

Trip plan: Jackson Hole keeps experienced powderhounds busy for weeks (nearby Snow King Resort is better for beginners). It's a scenic drive north to Yellowstone; free ranger-led tours still run in winter, or book a wildlife or snowsports package.

Need to know: Jackson Hole Airport is 12km (7 miles) north of Jackson, and 90km (56 miles) south of Yellowstone's south gate.

Other months: Nov, Jan & Mar – skiing, Yellowstone winter; Apr-May & Sep-Oct – mild, uncrowded; Jun-Aug – hot, busy.

Snow meets thermal water at Mammoth Hot Springs, Yellowstone National Park

© Terry W. Eggers / Getty Images

BOLIVIA

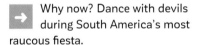

→ **Why now? Dance with devils during South America's most raucous fiesta.**
Visit Oruro in February and you're guaranteed to get wet. Not just because it's the rainy season – though you should expect downpours. Rather, the week before Lent, during Carnaval, heralds the most almighty water-fight (it puts all others in the shade) as well as huge parades headlined by the Diablada, the 'Dance of the Devils', joined by dozens of other colourfully costumed troupes. Other Bolivian towns including Tarija and Santa Cruz also celebrate Carnaval in kaleidoscopic style. As a bonus, crowds and prices typically shrink during the summer rains. Temperatures rise in the Altiplano, where the extra rain is less pronounced, and though delays in road and air transport are common, it's still a good time to explore cultural sites such as the Jesuit Missions of Chiquitos in peace. In the Amazon, trails become muddy – but more options for river transport open up, and birds such as macaws gather for the mating season.

Trip plan: From La Paz, head south to Oruro for the Carnaval chaos, then east to Santa Cruz and the Jesuit Missions. Add a visit to Madidi or Noel Kempff Mercado national parks for the full-on rainforest experience.

Need to know: In the Amazon, mosquitoes are even more annoying in the rainy season – use powerful repellent. Carnaval, almost always in February, falls occasionally in the first few days of March.

Other months: May-Oct – drier, clear skies, cold in the Andes; Nov-Jan & Mar-Apr – rainy, hotter.

Ayuthaya's Wat Mahathat complex and its bodhi-tree-entwined Buddha

THAILAND

→ **Why now? Trundle into the past on a train tour of ancient sites.**

In this cooler, dry season, Thailand's islands and shores ring with multifarious tongues – a true beach Babylon. Yet away from the coast, one of the few Asian nations never to be colonised reveals a diverse past stretching back many centuries. String together a daisy-chain of the most absorbing sites on a rail tour, tracing more or less in reverse the country's delicious history – and food, of course. Bustling Bangkok's Grand Palace, Wat Pho and Wat Phra Kaew – home of the Emerald Buddha – recall the founding of the modern capital in the late 18th century. To the west, contemporary Kanchanaburi echoes with reminders of more recent turmoil, particularly the so-called Death Railway built by forced labour during WWII. North of Bangkok, explore the evocative temple ruins of Ayuthaya, capital of Siam from the 14th century, itself usurping the Sukhothai Empire. After roaming Ayuthaya's fascinating remains, head to Chiang Mai, famed for its night markets and surrounded by gilded *wats* (temples) and the atmospherically tumbledown remains of Wiang Kum Kam, 13th-century heart of the Lanna Kingdom.

Trip plan: After exploring Bangkok, catch the train west to Kanchanaburi, stopping at Nakhon Pathom. Then veer north to Ayuthaya, continuing to Sukhothai and Chiang Mai.

Need to know: Sukhothai isn't on the train line; the connecting bus from Phitsanulok takes 1hr.

Other months: Nov-Jan & Mar-Apr – slightly cooler, dry (except Gulf of Thailand); May-Oct – rainy (drier on east-coast islands).

NORTHWEST TUSCANY ITALY

→ **Why now?** Admire medieval marvels in peace – aside from the clamour of Carnival celebrations.

Viareggio, on Tuscany's northwest coast, is a fairly regulation 20th-century beach resort, with a long stretch of sand and some eye-catching Art Nouveau-slash-Art Deco architecture. But on Sundays during February, its streets are invaded by huge *carri* (floats) adorned with elaborate, often hilariously satirical papier-mâché caricatures of celebs and politicians. Viareggio's Carnival is second only to Venice's in national prestige, but way more colourful and raucous, drawing thousands of participants and boisterous spectators. That event is, though, the exception that proves the rule: February brings peak peace to Tuscany. Sure, you're unlikely to bask in golden sun – temperatures hover at around 13°C (55°F), though this month is drier than autumn. But the relative absence of tourists makes this the perfect time for a triple-city break, admiring the marvels of Pisa – its beautiful squares, churches, palaces and that famed leaning *campanile* (bell tower) – and Lucca's exquisite duomo (cathedral) and Renaissance walls, so crammed from spring to autumn.

Trip plan: Viareggio, Lucca and Pisa (with its international airport) are connected by regular, fast train services. Any of the three would make a good base.

Need to know: Some hotels close over winter, and Viareggio is unsurprisingly popular during Carnival – book ahead.

Other months: Dec-Jan & Mar – chillier, quieter (outside Carnival); Apr-May & Oct-Nov – warm, relatively sparse crowds; Jun-Sep – hot, very busy.

El Golfo views from Mirador de Jinama, El Hierro

EL HIERRO SPAIN

→ **Why now?** Enjoy warm winter walking in the smallest Canary Island.

How far would you go for a hiking holiday now? To the ends of the Earth? El Hierro, the mildest, youngest and westernmost of the Canary Islands, was long thought to be just that: the edge of the known world. It still feels delightfully far-flung, with neither the beaches nor the tourist masses of larger Spanish islands. What it lacks in sand, El Hierro makes up for in spectacular landscapes and footpaths, irresistible in the warm, dry days of February, when the mercury reliably nudges 20°C (68°F). The spine of this appropriately boot-shaped volcanic speck is a steep volcanic scarp framing the vast sweep of El Golfo, clad in laurel forest and aromatic pinewoods and laced with trails. Pick of the bunch is the Camino de Jinama traverse – just 4km (2.5 miles) long but packed with rich biodiversity. You might encounter rock carvings of the pre-Spanish Bimbache culture, too, and cool off in natural pools including the pellucid turquoise waters of the Charco Azul.

Trip plan: There are no direct international flights to El Hierro. Fly from Tenerife North airport or make the 2hr 30min ferry crossing from Los Cristianos. The island has a reasonable bus system.

Need to know: La Restinga Marine Reserve, off the south coast, offers superb diving, with more than 40 sites and excellent visibility.

Other months: Nov-Jan & Mar – pleasantly mild, slightly more rain; Apr-Jun & Sep-Oct – warm, dry; Jul-Aug – hot.

SOUTH INDIA

➜ **Why now? Spot spectacular wildlife in lush uplands.**

Elephants, monkeys, dhole (Asian wild dog), boars, leopards and tigers and bears, oh my! These charismatic creatures and more prowl, snuffle and swing among the reserves of Karnataka, Kerala and Tamil Nadu – all far quieter than their northern counterparts in this cool-ish, dry month, so good for wildlife-watching. For example in Periyar, Kerala's original tiger reserve, some 2000 elephants lumber through wooded hills, along with perhaps 40 of those striped predators. In Nagarhole National Park, meanwhile, these biggest of cats are joined by a rare black panther; you'll also likely spot mongooses, macaques, langurs, gaur (hefty Indian bison) and dazzling birds. Anamalai Tiger Reserve is less touristed still, despite the mesmerising array of species endemic to the Nilgiri Hills. Mix up your South Indian odyssey with visits to beaches, tea plantations and cultural highlights – the mansions, synagogues and Chinese fishing nets of Kochi, the sleepy Kerala backwaters, the palaces and spice stalls of Mysuru (Mysore) and Hampi's magnificent 14th-century temples and bazaars.

Trip plan: From Bengaluru (Bangalore), head south via a selection of reserves – perhaps Nagarhole, Bandipur, Anamalai, Periyar and Wayanad – to Kochi.

Need to know: Rains fall hardest west of the Ghat Mountains; Tamil Nadu, to the east, tends to be drier. Winter nights can be cool in the mountains.

Other months: Dec-Jan & Mar – dry; Apr-May – very hot, rain building; Jun-Aug – very wet; Sep-Nov – rain gradually easing.

(T) Periyar boat trip;
(L) Bengal tiger, Nagarhole National Park;
(R) Boating through Kerala's backwaters

© ZisaPhoto / 500px

Oust the Ottawa winter with hot chocolate and pastries at BeaverTails

OTTAWA CANADA

 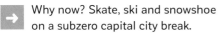

→ **Why now? Skate, ski and snowshoe on a subzero capital city break.**
The trickiest thing about ice-skating is manoeuvring the turns. That's not such a problem on the world's longest rink, created when the Rideau Canal in central Ottawa freezes over each winter. Typically it's skate-able from January to early March, so if you absolutely, positively have to zoom 7.8km (4.8 miles) along this icy speedway, get to Canada's perky capital in February. That's not the only reason to visit in this cold, driest month, when temperatures are consistently below freezing; the free Winterlude festival brings ice sculptures, music shows and other performances, plus food tastings, outdoor activities and a focus on Indigenous cultures. Groomed trails around the city draw cross-country skiers and snowshoers, while the array of world-class, state-of-the-art museums offer indoor retreats should the cold prove too intense. Warm up with a hot chocolate and a BeaverTail – a flat, fried, cinnamon-dipped pastry – at ByWard Market, also great for one-stop shopping.

Trip plan: Allow three days to zoom along the Rideau Canal, enjoy the fun of the Winterlude festival and imbibe art and culture at the galleries and museums.
Need to know: If you hear locals talking about Hull, they're referring to Ottawa's Francophone twin city across the river in Québec, renamed Gatineau in 2001.
Other months: Dec-Jan & Mar – very cold, often well below freezing; Apr-May – getting warmer; Jun-Sep – pleasant, sometimes hot; Oct-Nov – temperature dropping, autumn foliage.

March

WHERE TO GO WHEN

I WANT TO

CHALLENGE MYSELF →

TAKE ME OUT FOR...

- **FOOD**
  - NORTHWEST TASMANIA, AUSTRALIA P79
  - NEW BRUNSWICK, CANADA P62
- **DRINK**
  - URUGUAY P79

Food-trek through Tasmania during the bountiful harvest season

Discover the planet's best steaks in Uruguay's Montevideo

TAKE ME SOMEWHERE...

- **COLD**
  - COLORADO SPRINGS, USA P72
  - ISTANBUL, TURKEY P77
- **WARM**
  - CAIRO & ALEXANDRIA, EGYPT P74

Bargain amid medieval magnificence at Cairo's Khan el-Khalili bazaar

RELAX/ INDULGE

Seek sun, sand, sea and solitude at one of Antigua's 365 beaches

TAKE ME TO THE BEACH

- **REV UP**
  - ST KITTS & NEVIS P79
- **CHILL OUT**
  - ANTIGUA P63

Bask on uncrowded winter-sun shores in dinky St Kitts & Nevis

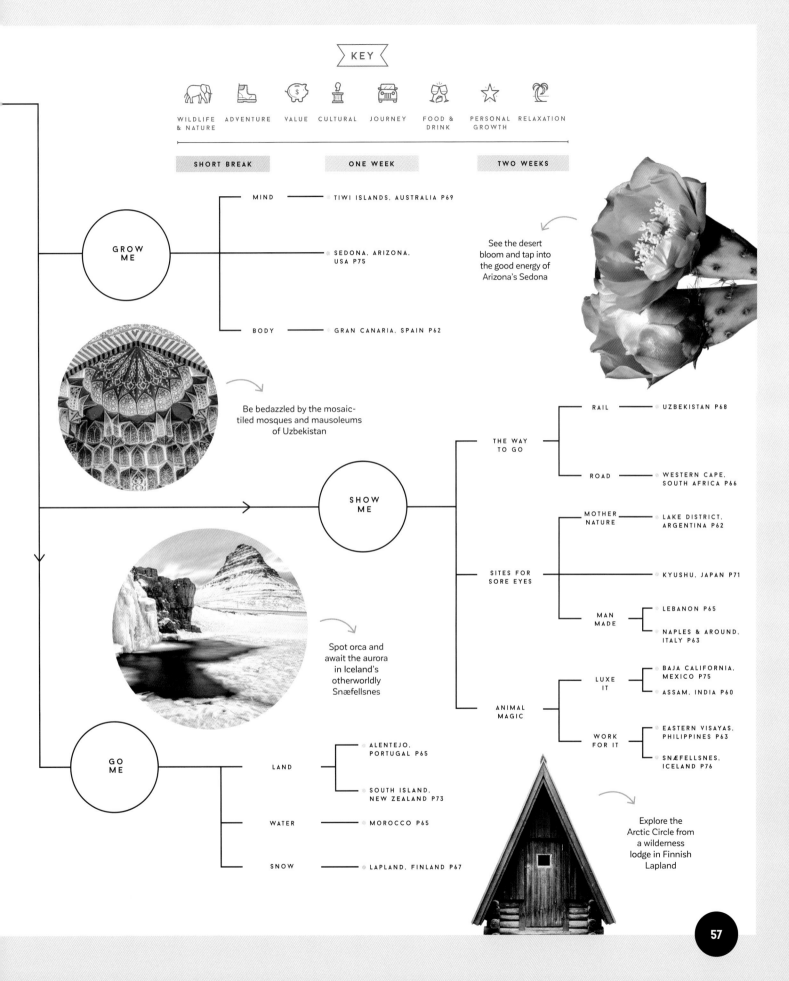

KEY

WILDLIFE & NATURE   ADVENTURE   VALUE   CULTURAL   JOURNEY   FOOD & DRINK   PERSONAL GROWTH   RELAXATION

SHORT BREAK   ONE WEEK   TWO WEEKS

GROW ME
- MIND — TIWI ISLANDS, AUSTRALIA P69
- SEDONA, ARIZONA, USA P75
- BODY — GRAN CANARIA, SPAIN P62

See the desert bloom and tap into the good energy of Arizona's Sedona

Be bedazzled by the mosaic-tiled mosques and mausoleums of Uzbekistan

SHOW ME

THE WAY TO GO
- RAIL — UZBEKISTAN P68
- ROAD — WESTERN CAPE, SOUTH AFRICA P66

SITES FOR SORE EYES
- MOTHER NATURE — LAKE DISTRICT, ARGENTINA P62
- KYUSHU, JAPAN P71
- MAN MADE — LEBANON P65
- NAPLES & AROUND, ITALY P63

ANIMAL MAGIC
- LUXE IT — BAJA CALIFORNIA, MEXICO P75
- ASSAM, INDIA P60
- WORK FOR IT — EASTERN VISAYAS, PHILIPPINES P63
- SNÆFELLSNES, ICELAND P76

Spot orca and await the aurora in Iceland's otherworldly Snæfellsnes

GO ME
- LAND — ALENTEJO, PORTUGAL P65
- SOUTH ISLAND, NEW ZEALAND P73
- WATER — MOROCCO P65
- SNOW — LAPLAND, FINLAND P67

Explore the Arctic Circle from a wilderness lodge in Finnish Lapland

EVENTS
IN MARCH

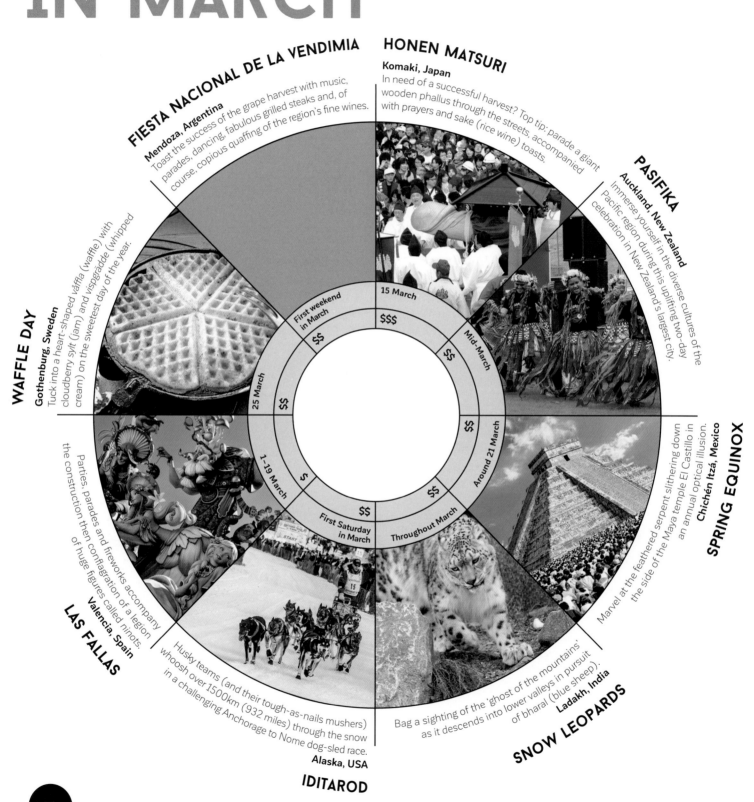

FIESTA NACIONAL DE LA VENDIMIA
Mendoza, Argentina
Toast the success of the grape harvest with music, parades, dancing, fabulous grilled steaks and, of course, copious quaffing of the region's fine wines.

HONEN MATSURI
Komaki, Japan
In need of a successful harvest? Top tip: parade a giant wooden phallus through the streets, accompanied with prayers and sake (rice wine) toasts.

PASIFIKA
Auckland, New Zealand
Immerse yourself in the diverse cultures of the Pacific region during this uplifting two-day celebration in New Zealand's largest city.

WAFFLE DAY
Gothenburg, Sweden
Tuck into a heart-shaped *våffla* (waffle) with cloudberry *sylt* (jam) and *vispgrädde* (whipped cream) on the sweetest day of the year.

SPRING EQUINOX
Chichén Itzá, Mexico
Marvel at the feathered serpent slithering down the side of the Maya temple El Castillo in an annual optical illusion.

LAS FALLAS
Valencia, Spain
Parties, parades and fireworks accompany the construction then conflagration of a legion of huge figures called ninots.

IDITAROD
Alaska, USA
Husky teams (and their tough-as-nails mushers) whoosh over 1500km (932 miles) through the snow in a challenging Anchorage to Nome dog-sled race.

SNOW LEOPARDS
Ladakh, India
Bag a sighting of the 'ghost of the mountains' as it descends into lower valleys in pursuit of bharal (blue sheep).

First weekend in March — $$
15 March — $$$
Mid-March — $$
Around 21 March — $$
Throughout March — $$
First Saturday in March — $$
1–19 March — $
25 March — $$

58

- LAPLAND, FINLAND

Wrap up warm for Arctic Circle snowsports in Finnish Lapland

Unfurl your yoga mat or walk the red-rock trails around picture-perfect Sedona

- ANTIGUA

Go beyond the beach to hike the hinterland of St Kitts & Nevis

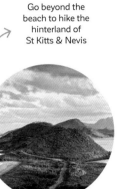

- SEDONA, ARIZONA, USA

- ST KITTS & NEVIS

- SNÆFELLSNES, ICELAND

- GRAN CANARIA, SPAIN

- NEW BRUNSWICK, CANADA

- COLORADO SPRINGS, USA

Combine culture and catching big waves in Morocco

- MOROCCO

- WESTERN CAPE, SOUTH AFRICA

- CAIRO & ALEXANDRIA, EGYPT

Find a slice of heaven in Colorado Springs' Garden of the Gods

- NORTHWEST TASMANIA, AUSTRALIA

- NAPLES & AROUND, ITALY

Island-hop the Philippines to climb Chocolate Hills and swim with turtles

- EASTERN VISAYAS, PHILIPPINES

- KYUSHU, JAPAN

Break from the blossom-watching with an Aso-San volcano hike in Kyushu

- BAJA CALIFORNIA, MEXICO

- TIWI ISLANDS, AUSTRALIA

Follow grey, blue, Bryde's and humpback whales to Mexico's Baja California

- ASSAM, INDIA

Wildlife-spot during dry season in Kaziranga National Park, Assam

Admire ancient architecture and buzzing bazaars in İstanbul

- ISTANBUL, TURKEY

- ALENTEJO, PORTUGAL

- SOUTH ISLAND, NEW ZEALAND

- LAKE DISTRICT, ARGENTINA

- URUGUAY

Drink it all in at Uruguay's Vendimia (grape-harvest) festivals

- LEBANON

- UZBEKISTAN

Discover little-visted Lebanese treasures like Baalbek's Temple of Bacchus

ASSAM INDIA

→ **Why now?** Track tigers and rhinos in the best season for wildlife-watching.

Back in 1905, just 12 'armoured unicorns' remained in the area that was then designated Kaziranga National Park. Thanks to ongoing conservation efforts, today an estimated 3700 greater one-horned rhinoceros survive in northern Indian and Nepal – and perhaps two-thirds of those graze the grasslands of this 430-sq-km (166-sq-mile) reserve flanking the mighty Brahmaputra River. You've a good chance of spotting them in March, towards the end of the cooler dry season, when orchids bloom and elephant grass has withered or been burned. And with the eagle eyes and experience of an expert guide, you might also spy tiger (Kaziranga has one of the densest populations), leopard, gaur, elephant, sloth bear, hoolock gibbon and a host of birds including black kite and Pallas's fish eagle. Boost your chances of a wildlife encounter by adding a visit to Manas National Park, in the foothills of the Himalaya on the Bhutanese border, which hosts many of the same big-ticket species.

Trip plan: Fly to Guwahati and either drive to a comfortable lodge in Kaziranga (5hr) or board a riverboat to cruise upstream along the Brahmaputra River to the park.

Need to know: Holi, the Festival of Colours, is celebrated in March with perfumed paint-powder – if you visit during this boisterous event, wear old clothes!

Other months: Oct-Feb – cooler, dry, busier; Apr-Jun – increasingly warm, lower prices; Jul-Sep – monsoon, hot, very wet.

March is a great time to spot one-horned rhino in Kaziranga National Park

LAKE DISTRICT
ARGENTINA

→ **Why now?** Roam watery mountain wilds among flaming fall hues.

The lake-studded stretch of the Andes sweeping through Argentina's share of northern Patagonia has been dubbed 'Little Switzerland', but though its peaks, tarns, woods and chalets bear a passing resemblance to the Alps, its charms are wilder and more dramatic. Early autumn – when forests spark into fiery foliage and trails start to empty, but before snow carpets those trekking routes – is a dream time to explore. Centrepieces of the region are Parque Nacional Nahuel Huapi – the country's oldest and among the largest, spanning over 7500 sq km (2896 sq miles) around its namesake 100km-long (62-mile) lake – and adjacent Parque Nacional Lanín, both laced with hiking trails and offering opportunities for kayaking, cycling, whitewater rafting, swimming and spotting wildlife including cougar, deer and river otter.

Trip plan: From Bariloche – whose airport is served by flights from Buenos Aires – traverse the Nahuel Huapi and Lanín national parks on an epic Ruta de los Siete Lagos (Route of the Seven Lakes) drive via Villa la Angostura to San Martín de los Andes. If time permits, add the stretch south to El Bolsón and the temperate rainforests of Parque Nacional Los Alerces.

Need to know: This part of Patagonia is renowned for its beers – make time to taste the wares of Bariloche's many breweries.

Other months: Dec-Feb – warm, dry, popular; Apr-May – cooling, rainy days increasing, autumn colours; Jun-Aug – cool, rainiest; Sep-Nov – warming, wildflowers.

NEW BRUNSWICK
CANADA

→ **Why now?** Succumb to your sweet tooth amid snowy landscapes.

March is maple syrup month in New Brunswick, a province as peaceful and little-touristed as it is packed with natural beauty and history. In this 'fifth season', temperatures start to peek above freezing and the sap rises in maple trees, which are tapped by producers to yield an ambrosial syrup with a distinctively sweet flavour. Sugar camps (or shacks) welcome hungry visitors to sugarbush events with cooked breakfasts of eggs, bacon, sausage, beans and pancakes – all smothered with that sticky syrup, of course. With snow lingering on the ground, work up an appetite cross-country skiing, snowshoeing or winter hiking in spectacular settings such as Fundy National Park, then savour maple taffy on ice (very sticky lollipops, basically) and hop between the bars and eateries of Victorian-era Fredericton and the historic heart of St John's.

Trip plan: VIA Rail Canada links towns in eastern New Brunswick with Québec and Nova Scotia; buses serve the rest of the province. Allow several days to tour sugar camps and ski backcountry trails across the province.

Need to know: Some accommodation options, attractions and tourist facilities close outside the summer season – check and book in advance.

Other months: Nov-Feb – very cold, snowy, quiet, many tourist facilities closed; Apr-May – warming, snow melting, spring flowers; Jun-Aug – warm, busy, whales feeding and breeding in Bay of Fundy; Sep-Oct – rich autumn colours, lower accommodation prices.

GRAN CANARIA
SPAIN

→ **Why now?** Spring clean mind and body with a tai chi and chill-out break.

Perhaps it's the captivating Spain-meets-Africa vibe that makes Gran Canaria a suitably exotic-feeling destination for a wellness escape amid sand dunes and blissfully balmy weather, with temperatures reliably above 20°C (68°F) and over seven hours of sunshine daily in March. The beautiful belly-button of the Canary Islands is a hotbed of yoga, meditation, tai chi and qigong retreats, with several clustered around Las Palmas, Gran Canaria's culturally diverse capital. Pick a location according to your interests – after your early-morning tai chi session, you'll have plenty of time to relax or get active. You'll find beaches galore on which to get horizontal, but consider striking out onto the trails, too. Wildflowers bloom on the flanks of the *cumbres* (summits) in the central highlands, where you can hike among forests, *barrancos* (ravines) and delightful villages such as Artenara, the island's highest, with its troglodyte dwellings.

Trip plan: Base yourself in Las Palmas for sand and city life, Maspalomas for lively beach action and vast sand dunes, Puerto de Mogán for a picturesque harbour, or the central north for hiking.

Need to know: Take a boat trip from Puerto Rico in the island's south to spot dolphins and, if you're lucky, pilot, sperm, humpback and possibly even blue whales.

Other months: Nov-Feb – cool, some rain, vibrant Carnival celebrations in Feb; Apr-May & Sep-Oct – pleasantly warm; Jun-Aug – very hot.

EASTERN VISAYAS
PHILIPPINES

→ **Why now?** Meet big-eyed tarsiers, climb Chocolate Hills and lounge on pristine beaches in warm, dry conditions.

The Philippines is dauntingly vast – more than 7000 islands spread over some 300,000 sq km (115,830 sq miles) – so focus on the central cluster known as the Visayas to max your adventure and animal tally. Tourist numbers drop off in March, but this is a wonderfully dry and warm time to explore the islands of Cebu, Bohol, Leyte, Siquijor and surrounding specks. Between sun-worshipping sessions on the white-sand beaches of Malapascua, Biliran, Sumilon and Panglao islands, roam Bohol's curiously domed Chocolate Hills before gazing into the oversized eyes of an impossibly cute Philippine tarsier at the nearby sanctuary. There's more mesmerising wildlife to encounter beneath the waves, too: swim with whale sharks at Sogod Bay off southern Leyte, shimmering shoals of sardines at Moalboal on western Cebu, and *pawikans* (sea turtles) around Apo Island – one of the planet's top dive sites. In this culturally diverse region, you'll also discover historic Spanish churches and older animist traditions, including the famed natural healers of Siquijor. Overheating? You're never far from a waterfall beneath which you can take a cooling dip.

Trip plan: Cebu City is well served by international flights, and regular ferries link the islands.

Need to know: In some locations, whale-shark swims are poorly regulated and the fish are fed, altering behaviour – check ethical credentials before booking.

Other months: Jan-Feb & Apr – driest, getting hotter; May-Dec – hot and wet, rainfall peaking Jul-Aug.

ANTIGUA

→ **Why now?** Bright Caribbean sunshine and cool breezes in the perfect season.

Antigua has a beach for every day of the year – or so the legend goes. Whether or not there are 365 separate stretches of sand on the island, it's true that you won't want for a patch of soft, golden-tinted shoreline on which to lounge. March sees a lull in tourist arrivals after the midwinter peak and before Easter, but the weather is still dry and hurricane-free. Antigua is a family-friendly paradise, too, with activities galore and a piratical air – venture to Nelson's Dockyard or the atmospheric, 18th-century Fort James for a bit of maritime history, snorkel the colourful reefs or try a bit of bodysurfing.

Trip plan: International flights serve VC Bird Airport in Antigua's north, near the capital, St John's; the other significant centre is around the dual coves and historic sites of Falmouth Harbour and English Harbour in the south. But with its compact 21km (13 miles) length and beaches all around the island, it's easy to access all parts of Antigua.

Need to know: March is towards the end of the mating season for frigate birds – look for the throat sacs of courting males at Codrington on neighbouring sister island Barbuda, one of the world's largest breeding colonies.

Other months: Dec-Feb & Apr – driest; May & Jun – hot; Jul-Nov – showers; Jul – Carnival.

NAPLES & AROUND
ITALY

→ **Why now?** Quieter sites and a gritty city in early spring.

Naples is unapologetic. This southern Italian sprawl is a bit grimy in parts, scruffy around the edges, but has an indefatigable spirit, a dramatic location (on the Bay of Naples, in the shadow of Vesuvius) and, of course, the best pizzas in the country. Off-season March is neither too hot nor too cold, and well before most visitors descend. That means unmissable sights such as the Museo Archeologico Nazionale (packed with Pompeiian artefacts) are crowd-free, as is Pompeii itself, just a 45-minute train ride south. Join a walking tour around the untouristy Naples neighbourhoods made famous by Elena Ferrante's *Neapolitan Novels*. And, if the weather is a bit inclement, sign up for Napoli Sotterranea, a dip into the city's ancient underground aqueducts, burial chambers and air-raid shelters.

Trip plan: Allow two or three days in Naples, plus a day for Pompeii. Also consider out-of-season visits to Capri, blissfully quiet compared with summer, and Sorrento, where the famed lemons will already be on the trees (the best ones are harvested March-July).

Need to know: Circumvesuviana and Campania Express trains connect Naples and Pompeii; avoid crowds at the archeological site by starting with the areas furthest from the entrance and working back.

Other months: Nov-Feb – cool, low season (except Christmas); Apr-May – warm, quiet; Jun-Aug – hot, busiest, many shops close in Aug; Sep & Oct – mild, warm, potentially rainier.

(A) See the 13th century-built sea castle at Saida, Lebanon; (L) Hiking the trails along Portugal's Costa Vicentina; (R) Catching a break at Taghazout, Morocco

LEBANON

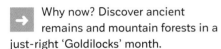

Why now? Discover ancient remains and mountain forests in a just-right 'Goldilocks' month.

A historic crossroads in the eastern Mediterranean, Lebanon has long been a focus for trade, cultural exchange and, sadly, conflict. The legacy is a melange of Phoenician and Roman remains, European and Middle Eastern influences, delectable cuisine and a society in which Christianity and Islam rub shoulders. Spring brings pleasantly warm temperatures to the coast and wildflowers in the mountains, without the crowds (and prices) of summer – an ideal time to explore the ancient sites, hike among the monasteries and 1000-year-old cedars lining slopes above the Qadisha Valley, and stroll the palm-lined esplanades of cosmopolitan capital Beirut. A quartet of historical big-hitters demand your attention: the vast, beautifully decorated Roman Temple of Bacchus at Baalbek; the Phoenician cities and souqs at Saida (Sidon) and Byblos, both boasting Crusader sea castles; and the remains of nearly 5000 years of occupation at Tyre. But make time, too, to taste the wines of the Bekaa Valley and chill on golden beaches.

Trip plan: Spend a week making a clockwise circuit from Beirut through Byblos, the Qadisha Valley, Baalbek and Saida, branching south to Tyre.

Need to know: Repairs are ongoing following the major explosion that devastated Beirut's port area in 2020.

Other months: Dec-Feb – winter, rainier, skiing in mountains; Apr-May – warm, drier, wildflowers; Jun-Sep – hot on coast, busy; Oct-Nov – pleasant temperatures, more rain, lower prices, grape harvest.

ALENTEJO
PORTUGAL

Why now? Stroll or cycle the trails as springtime sweeps the southwest.

Along Portugal's Atlantic seaboard, change is afoot – or at your feet. In spring, storks return to nest on clifftops and wildflowers spangle the coastal path leading north from mainland Europe's southwesternmost point, Cabo de São Vicente, along the shore of Alentejo province. Brainchild of a local association dedicated to developing nature-based tourism, the Fishermen's Trail is one strand of an ambitious project nurturing community renewal and a fresh understanding of the region's natural heritage. This 226km (140 miles) route along the Costa Vicentina, Europe's largest coastal natural park, passes slumberous fishing villages (seafood is a delight here), cork-oak woods and immaculate beaches where egrets forage. The alternative 263km (163 miles) Historical Way veers inland, tackling ridges, farms and valleys, while a network of mountain-bike trails offers adrenalin rushes, and a 500km (310 miles) cycle-touring route links Faro and Lisbon airports. Whichever you choose, you'll enjoy unique insights into a less-visited corner of southern Portugal.

Trip plan: Fly into Faro and out of Lisbon; cyclists can pedal directly between the two, while hikers transfer to Lagos or Cabo de São Vicente to start walking, finishing at Santiago do Cacém or São Torpes.

Need to know: The association that created the routes (rotavicentina.com) provides excellent planning information, and plenty of tour operators offer supported trips.

Other months: Nov-Feb – cooler, wetter, quieter; Apr-May – pleasantly warm, lots of festivals; Jun-Aug – hot, coast busy; Sep-Oct – mellow, grape harvest.

MOROCCO

Why now? Ride reliable waves in a surf and yoga hotspot.

It's over half a century since board-riders first discovered the awesome swells that surge onto Morocco's Atlantic coast throughout the winter. Those early surf pioneers established the reputations of the breaks between Agadir and Essaouira – Sidi Kaouki, Banana Beach, Devil's Rock, Panorama Point, Hash Point, Tamri and La Source for all levels, and fierce Anchor Point, Killer Point, Boilers, Dracula's and Desert Point for pros. Today, a string of surf camps stud the coast, most clustered around Taghazout and the quieter fishing village of Tamraght. The surf is reliably good between October and March, when the weather starts to warm up but waves are still big, long and consistent. Most camps offer a simple recipe: limber up with a sunrise yoga session, then grab a board and find the best breaks, sparing time to explore the galleries and souqs of Essaouira's fortified medina.

Trip plan: There are plenty of places to stay around Essaouira, Taghazout and Tamraght, so it's easy to book your own trip, but surf camps typically offer good-value packages including accommodation, surf lessons, board hire, yoga classes, food and transfers from Agadir airport.

Need to know: The Atlantic is at its coolest during March – you'll want at least a 3/2mm wetsuit.

Other months: Oct-Feb – big swells, pleasant temperatures, more rain; Sep – reliable surf, warm; Apr-Aug – increasingly hot, stronger winds, flatter seas.

© Gary Latham / Lonely Planet

WESTERN CAPE
SOUTH AFRICA

Strolling crowd-free
sands at Cape Town's
Table View Beach

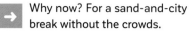

→ **Why now? For a sand-and-city
break without the crowds.**

The quirks of the African climate mean that
during the austral summer, while much of
the rest of the country soaks, South Africa's
Cape region basks in warm sunshine. The
peak of summer – from mid-December
through January and into February – sees
tourists flock here, which is why March
is the ideal time to arrive, with blue skies
but without the crowds. Cape Town
celebrates now, too: in March, the city and
surrounding region sings and dances with
festivals and events including its annual
Carnival. Drive east from Cape Town on the
N2, then duck off the highway and down to

the coast to explore the gems of the forest-
lined Garden Route. Discover glorious
beaches and charming villages, surf with
the dolphins of Plettenberg Bay, kayak the
waterways of Wilderness National Park,
wander pretty seaside towns, and roam the
ancient forests of Knysna and Tsitsikamma
National Park.

Trip plan: By flying into Cape Town and
out of Port Elizabeth, or vice versa, you can
plan a one-way route and avoid doubling
back on yourself.

Need to know: For high-flyers, March is the
end of the primo paragliding season.

Other months: Nov-Feb – summer, dry,
warm; Apr-Oct – cooler, rainy.

LAPLAND
FINLAND

→ **Why now? For dog-sleds and dancing lights.**

The Arctic Circle sparkles at this time of year. The landscape is buried in snow and lakes are frozen. Polar night (the period of 24-hour darkness) is over, and the sun puts in ever-longer appearances. And the magical Northern Lights are quite likely to dance: according to the Finnish Meteorological Institute, the best time to look for aurora is February to March and September to October. This is also a great time for everyone – young, old, families, couples – to get into the great outdoors. Though still chilly, temperatures start to rise this month, and wilderness lodges offer full programmes of activities: husky-sledding, snowmobiling, sleigh rides, snowshoeing, cross-country skiing – all guaranteed to warm you up. If all else fails, a visit to a traditional Finnish sauna should do the trick.

Trip plan: Rovaniemi and Ivalo airports offer access to Finland's north. Spend four or more nights at a wilderness lodge to maximise chances of seeing the aurora, and to pack in plenty of snowy fun.

Need to know: Many lodges offer 'aurora alerts' – a wake-up call if the lights emerge.

Other months: Dec-Feb & Apr – snow activities (Sep-Apr: aurora); May-Aug – long days, warmest; Sep-Nov – brief autumn, cooling.

The dancing waves of the Aurora Borealis light up the Lapland sky

Wander through – and
wonder at – Samarkand's
mosaic-tiled marvels

© Marina Sorokina / 500px

UZBEKISTAN

→ Why now? Ride the rails among ancient Silk Road monuments in spring.

Though the moniker 'Silk Road' was first coined in the 19th century, that sleek textile was first carried along various routes between China and the Middle East at least two millennia earlier. Probably the most splendid reminders of those disparate trails' glory days lie in Uzbekistan's ancient cities: the majestic Registan of Samarkand, the holy city of Bukhara and Khiva's Ichon-Qala (walled city), graced still with beautiful mosaic-tiled mosques, mausoleums and *medressas* (Islamic schools). The train's the way to travel today, offering comfortable, sustainable and economical transport between the main centres, particularly since the recent introduction of fast Afrosiyob trains and a station at Khiva. Visit Uzbekistan now, as it enters a long-welcomed spring, both literally – March sees the celebration of colourful spring festival Novruz, with feasting and dancing – and figuratively, as the country eases border restrictions to offer visa-free visits for more nationalities.

Trip plan: From Tashkent, trace a route south and west through Samarkand, Shakhrisabz and Bukhara to Khiva, detouring into the Kyzylkum Desert to discover crumbling fortresses, continuing up to the Aral Sea if time permits.

Need to know: For dramatic mountain views, take a seat on the left (southern) side of the train heading west.

Other months: Nov-Feb – very cold, air clear, sites quiet; Apr – warming up, still uncrowded, some rain; May-Jun & Sep-Oct – pleasantly warm, sites busy; Jul-Aug – very hot and dry.

Soak up the arts scene
on the Tiwis' Bathurst
and Melville islands

TIWI ISLANDS AUSTRALIA

→ **Why now? Revel in the excitement of the annual Football Grand Final and Art Sale.**

If you thought the rest of the country was footie mad, wait till you experience the extraordinary levels of fandom among the Indigenous people of this two-island archipelago, 80km (50 miles) north of Darwin: more than one-third of the population of under 3000 play the Aussie-rules game, many at the highest level. As March ebbs and the rains start to ease off, the annual Tiwi Islands Football Grand Final

and Art Sale draws lovers of both sport and culture, who hop across from mainland Northern Territory to watch the match and pick up unique pieces from the 'Islands of Smiles'. This is a fascinating place to visit at any time, though, its Polynesian-influenced culture subtly different from that of mainland Aboriginal peoples after centuries of relative isolation. Learn about painted ironwood *pukumani* (taboo) burial poles, and discover distinctive screen-printing, painting, pottery and carving. Stop off to enjoy white-sand beaches and cool off

under Taracumbi Falls en route between the arts centres at Milikapiti, Pirlangimpi and main settlement Wurrumiyanga.

Trip plan: Visitors to the Tiwi Islands (outside Wurrumiyanga) require a permit – book a guided tour, including the flight or boat from Darwin.

Need to know: Melville Island is a hotspot for catch-and-release fishing – keen anglers hook barramundi, mangrove jacks and dozens of other species.

Other months: Nov-Feb – hot, wet; Apr-Oct – cooler, drier.

69

KYUSHU
JAPAN

→ **Why now? Be dazzled by cherry blossoms during early *sakura* season.**

A cherry tree in bloom is a delightful sight, sure. But two thousand cherry trees blossoming in the clear spring air – now, that's a mind-boggling spectacle. No wonder the Japanese celebrate *sakura* season with *hanami* (flower-viewing) outings, thronging parks to picnic beneath pink canopies. The warmer southwestern island of Kyushu blushes before the better-known spots on Honshu, its Somei Yoshino and Yamazakura trees blooming from mid-March in parks around Fukuoka and magnificent Kumamoto castles, and in Yoshino Park in Kagoshima, set against the dramatic backdrop of aptly named Mt Sakurajima. Kyushu makes an ideal destination for a spring break, combining *hanami* with visits to the moving memorials of Nagasaki, hikes on volcanic slopes, soaks in Oita's hot springs, and steaming bowls of Tonkotsu ramen.

Trip plan: From Fukuoka, linked by Shinkansen to Tokyo (5hr), Kyoto (2hr 45min) and Hiroshima (1hr), visit Nagasaki, Kumamoto and Kagoshima, making time for diversions to volcanoes – perhaps mighty Aso-san, the largest active volcano in Japan – hikes in Unzen-Amakusa National Park, a soak in an *onsen* and offbeat sights such as the deserted industrial ghost-island of Hashima.

Need to know: JR Kyushu rail passes, valid for three, five or seven days, offer good value but aren't valid for private railways serving some destinations on the island.

Other months: Dec-Feb – cold; Apr-May – spring, blossoms, busy; Jun-Aug – hot, rainy; Sep-Nov – cooling off, autumn colours.

A feast for both belly and eyes: Tonkotsu ramen and sakura

COLORADO SPRINGS USA

→ **Why now? Enjoy mild days hiking urban wilds.**

The Centennial State's second-biggest city, Colorado Springs, has a split personality. Partly that's down to geography – Great Plains to the east, Rockies to the west – and partly inhabitants, a unique mix of military staff, conservative evangelicals and typically laid-back Colorado types. Which makes this a delightfully diverse short-break destination, particularly in the comfortable climate of early spring, perfect for exploring the outdoor marvels on its doorstep. Hike or ride the red sandstone crags in downtown Garden of the Gods Park; delve into rubicund Red Rock Canyon; and haul up 4302m (14,115ft) Pikes Peak, just to the west, for far-reaching views (there's a cog railway for those short on time or puff). You'll find pockets of history, too, in the relocated Puebloan cliff dwellings and old-town vibes of nearby Manitou Springs, and echoes of the Wild West in the saloons and casinos of Cripple Creek, an hour's drive away.

Trip plan: Colorado Springs is a 1hr 30min bus ride from central Denver; direct buses (2hr) run from Denver airport. Allow at least two or three days to explore the city, ascend Pikes Peak and roam the surrounding area.

Need to know: For a taste of Wild West gambling saloon action, head 80km (50 miles) west to the cluster of casinos in Cripple Creek.

Other months: Nov-Feb – cold, dry; Apr-May & Sep-Oct – comfortable temperatures, uncrowded, lower prices (fiery fall foliage in autumn); Jun-Aug – hot, several festivals, busiest.

Lace up your boots and hike scenic trails through aptly named Garden of the Gods Park

© Sean Pavone / iStock | Getty Images Plus

© Jason Friend / Alamy Stock Photo

Lush, stream-laced
rainforest lining the
Hump Ridge Track

SOUTH ISLAND NEW ZEALAND

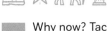

→ **Why now? Tackle the newest Great Walk in beautiful autumn.**
New Zealand's roster of Great Walks is no secret. In fact, huts on the most popular treks – Milford, Routeburn, Kepler – get booked out many months in advance. So the addition of a new option, the recently upgraded (but already highly respected) Tuatapere Hump Ridge Track in Fiordland's remote far south, is one to welcome, albeit in a whisper: this is a true wilderness tramp on which to escape the crowds, at least for now. Early autumn's a fine time to take

to the trail, a 62km/38 miles, three-day loop leading walkers along empty beaches from where rare Hector's dolphins can be spotted; over historic viaducts running through lush native forest; and up to the subalpine landscapes and rocky tors of the eponymous Hump Ridge for sweeping views over Fiordland, along the south coast and across to Stewart Island (Rakiura).
Trip plan: The Humpridge Shuttle bus links Tuatapere, closest town to the trailhead, with Queenstown (2hr 30min), Invercargill (1hr) and Te Anau (1hr 15min).

Various levels of service, including guided and 'luxury' options, are offered by the community-led charitable organisation that manages the track and huts (humpridgetrack.co.nz).
Need to know: The hike can be extended by combining Hump Ridge with the 62km/38 miles, four-day South Coast Track to Big River.
Other months: Nov-Feb – summer, peak trekking season; Apr – early autumn, quieter; May-Aug – colder, wetter; Sep-Oct – spring, often pleasant hiking.

© krechet / Shutterstock

Freshly restored Fort
Qaitbey, Alexandria's Med-
side guardian since 1480

CAIRO & ALEXANDRIA EGYPT

→ **Why now? Delve into the ancient past without the crowds of winter or stifling heat of summer.**

Egypt's capital has far more to offer than just pyramids. True, those three Brobdingnagian monuments and their guardian Sphinx at Giza are unmissable – less busy in mild March than in the preceding months, too, and not yet sizzling in the Saharan summer. This is also the time to haggle in the medieval Khan el-Khalili bazaar, get lost in the labyrinthine alleys of Islamic Cairo, and marvel at the mummies in the recently inaugurated National Museum of Egyptian Civilization. Good transport links with Egypt's second city, Alexandria, make stitching together a two-centre break a cinch and, though blazing sunshine isn't guaranteed in March, you can expect dry, warm days perfect for exploring the Mediterranean city's world-class museums – particularly the cluster housed in the spectacular Bibliotheca Alexandrina, channelling the spirit of its legendary library of antiquity – and curios such as the catacombs of Kom Ash Shuqqafa.

Trip plan: Split your week according to interests – for superb modern museums, beaches and dive sites, weight your trip towards Alexandria; for medieval mosques, bustling bazaars and ancient monuments, spend more time in Cairo.

Need to know: Frequent buses run between Cairo and Alexandria in about 3hr; the train takes almost 1hr longer and is slightly cheaper.

Other months: Dec-Feb – cool, high season; Apr – pleasantly warm, quieter; May-Jun – getting hotter; Jul-Sep – very hot; Oct-Nov – balmy, less crowded.

BAJA CALIFORNIA
MEXICO

→ **Why now? To meet a whale.**
The grey whales that congregate off this spindly, untamed Mexican peninsula are a friendly bunch. Around 10,000 of them migrate from the Arctic down the west coast of North America to over-winter in the Baja's Pacific lagoons, where they mate and calve; numbers peak February to April. In San Ignacio Lagoon in particular the whales are extremely curious, often bopping boats and courting cuddles. Eyeballing one of these barnacled leviathans is one of the planet's most emotional wildlife encounters. Even better, Baja's waters are chock-full of other species. The Pacific Coast attracts still more whales, including humpbacks, plus dolphins and fur seals. On Baja's east coast, La Paz Bay is a whale-shark hangout, while the Sea of Cortez is one of the world's best places to spot Bryde's and blue whales.

Trip plan: Expedition cruises heading south from San Diego offer the most comprehensive marine experience. Alternatively, take day-boat excursions from shore camps at San Ignacio, Cabo San Lucas (for the Sea of Cortez) and La Paz.

Need to know: Loreto is the closest international airport to the lagoons; Cabo San Lucas (a 10hr drive from San Ignacio) receives more flights.

Other months: Jan-Feb & Apr – main whalewatching season; Jul-Sep – rainiest; Sep-Dec – whale shark numbers peak.

© Nikolas_jkd / Shutterstock

Hike ravishing red-rock Sedona trails like the Devil's Bridge

SEDONA, ARIZONA USA

→ **Why now? Recharge spiritual and physical batteries among energy vortexes and desert blooms.**
The flaming-red sandstone formations of central Arizona, backdrop for countless movies, might be the most recognisable emblems of Sedona. But it's a less visible attraction that draws many of today's visitors. A cluster of four major 'energy vortexes' identified in the 1980s lures crowds of New Age adherents, who enjoy various mystical and spiritual healing practices and workshops (as well as some top-notch restaurants to nourish body as well as mind and soul). March brings delightfully warm weather, wildflowers and the annual yoga and mountain bike festivals. Pack loose clothes and a mat for yoga sessions at one of the many studios, but also cycling gear and hiking boots – more than 200 trails traverse the surrounding countryside, notably among the striking outcrops of Red Rock Crossing – and an empty memory card for this most photogenic city.

Trip plan: Shuttle buses make the 2hr 30min journey between Phoenix and Sedona several times daily. You'll easily fill two days with yoga, hikes, rides and restaurants – allow longer to discover the ancient pictographs of the Palatki Heritage Site or explore Red Rock State Park's trails.

Need to know: Several companies offer vortex tours; save money by picking up a free map from shops around the city.

Other months: Dec-Feb – cool, quieter, prices lower; Apr-May – balmy, desert flowers bloom, popular; Jun-Aug – very hot, some rain; Sep-Nov – pleasant temperatures, crowds and prices diminishing.

SNÆFELLSNES
ICELAND

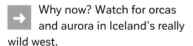

→ **Why now? Watch for orcas and aurora in Iceland's really wild west.**

Iceland's not short on killer attractions in any season, its otherworldly volcanic landscapes as dramatic in snow as they are in sunshine. But in late winter, nights are long enough to maximise chances of marvelling at the Aurora Borealis' celestial dance, but lengthening days give ample light to head out on a whale-watching tour. March is one of the most reliable months for an encounter with the orca that feast on herring in Breiðafjörður, off the Snæfellsnes Peninsula. This gnarled finger stretching into the North Atlantic has plenty more adventure to enjoy among the lava flows, stegosaur-sail ridges – Kirkjufell above Grundarfjörður must surely be Iceland's most-photographed peak – and monstrous icecap Snæfellsjökull, which inspired Jules Verne's epic *Journey to the Centre of the Earth*.

Trip plan: Base yourself in Grundarfjörður, a 3hr drive from Keflavík Airport. Allow at least two days for whale-watching to maximise your chances of an orca encounter. Add two or three more days to explore Reykjavík and the sights of the Golden Circle – the spouting hot springs at Geysir, Gulfoss waterfall and the scenic marvels of Þingvellir National Park.

Need to know: Humpback and male sperm whales are most commonly seen in late spring and summer, along with puffins, which usually arrive in April.

Other months: Oct-Feb – cold, dark, aurora possible; Apr-May & Sep– warmer; Jun-Aug – long days, inland routes accessible.

© ariet / Shutterstock

(A) The Northern Lights blaze over Snæfellsnes; (B) An orca cruises Breiðafjörður

© Arctic-Images / Getty Images

A tempting array of food stalls cluster in İstanbul's Eminönü Square

ISTANBUL TURKEY

→ Why now? Discover bazaars, ancient wonders and culinary secrets in peace.

You might debate which is the greatest treasure of the former Constantinople: the incredible 6th-century basilica-mosque of Aya Sofya? Sprawling, opulent Topkapı Palace? The domes, minarets and ornate azure tilework of the Blue Mosque? Wander among them all to decide for yourself, by all means – and in March, as things begin to warm up towards the end of the low season, you can enjoy discounts, smaller crowds and more forgiving weather. But save some time for the greatest legacy the Ottomans left the world: food. Why else would the Spice Bazaar be so huge and bustling? From simple kebabs to *meze* feasts and the luscious aubergine masterpiece, *İmam bayıldı*, there are few cuisines as indulgent as Turkish. Over the past couple of decades a roster of excellent food-themed walking tours and cookery schools has sprung up in İstanbul, providing the opportunity to combine a spring city break with a culinary reboot.

Trip plan: Base yourself in the Sultanahmet district, on the west (European) side of the Bosphorus, for easy access to the Grand Bazaar, Spice Bazaar and most historic sites.

Need to know: Turkish etiquette decrees that you shouldn't point your finger or the sole of your foot towards anyone.

Other months: Nov-Feb – cold, damp; Apr-May & Sept-Oct – mild, quiet; Jun-Aug – hot, busy.

Colonia del Sacramento's Barrio Histórico, Uruguay

Emerald hills and turquoise Caribbean seas in St Kitts

NORTHWEST TASMANIA
AUSTRALIA

→ **Why now?** Get a taste for Tassie food and drink on an epicurean road trip in this fruitful season.

Australia's island ark is, unsurprisingly, most famed for its wild nature. Some 40% of the state is protected as national parks and reserves, their mountain slopes, forests, rivers and grasslands bustling with wallabies, wombats, Tasmanian devils, little penguins, platypuses, pademelons and more, while trails and whitewaters draw trekkers and rafters from across the world. Quietly, though, the artisan growers and producers of the northwest have been building a reputation for the finest flavours – and early autumn, season of harvests and hearty feasts, is an ideal time to navigate the Cradle to Coast Tasting Trail, a curated itinerary snaking between Launceston and Smithton. Steer between dozens of wineries, breweries and distilleries, chocolatiers and cheesemakers, seafood fisheries and fruit farms, gelato geniuses and even truffle hunters, plus a selection of cafes and restaurants creating culinary delights with local produce. Work up an appetite on a detour to hike the trails around Cradle Mountain, that magnificently scalloped peak in its namesake national park.

Trip plan: Take the overnight ferry from Melbourne to Devonport or fly to Launceston, Devonport or Burnie, then drive – or even cycle, if you're feeling energetic – between artisan producers.

Need to know: Much Tasmanian wildlife is nocturnal and not traffic-savvy – if driving after dusk, go extremely slowly to avoid collisions.

Other months: Nov-Feb – driest, warmest, sunniest; Apr-Oct - cooler, wetter.

URUGUAY

→ **Why now?** Toast the grape harvest in balmy early autumn.

This compact country might be overshadowed by neighbours Argentina and Brazil, but it's not ignored by them – certainly not in summer (December to February), when holidaymakers hop across borders to enjoy stylish beach resorts such as Punta del Este that stud its 660km (410 miles) of sandy shoreline. In March, when crowds have thinned but sun and sea are still warm, you can explore Uruguay's coast and cultural heritage in relative peace – with the added bonus of Vendimia (grape-harvest) festivals heralding new vintages. Between roaming the Barrio Histórico of Colonia del Sacramento, its Unesco-listed architecture dating from the Portuguese era, and taking to the saddle in a traditional *estancia* (cattle ranch), fuel up with some of the planet's finest steaks at a *parrilla* (grill) in capital Montevideo's Mercado del Puerto.

Trip plan: Head west from Montevideo through the wineries of Canelones and Carmelo to Colonia and up the Río Uruguay to Fray Bentos, then back east via an *estancia* to the Atlantic beaches and restaurants in and around José Ignacio, detouring to the bird-bustling lagoons of Rocha province.

Need to know: Montevideo receives few long-haul flights. For international travellers it can be cheaper and more convenient to fly to Buenos Aires and catch the ferry across the River Plate to Colonia (1hr 15min) or Montevideo (2hr 15min).

Other months: Nov-Feb – warm, dry, busy; Apr-May – autumn, quieter, sea warmest; Jun-Oct – cooler, wetter, southern right whales breed off the coast.

ST KITTS & NEVIS

→ **Why now?** Soak up Caribbean sun and make a splash on offbeat islands.

As much of the northern hemisphere tentatively prepares to shed winter coats, the Caribbean basks in warm, dry days. But while similarly paradisiacal destinations nearby are thronged, most of the lush volcanic speck of St Kitts and little sister Nevis remain far less touristed. Both serve up a feast of beautiful beaches with a side order of fascinating (and often troubling) history: Old Road Town, Bloody Point and hulking hilltop Brimstone Hill Fortress speak of 17th-century clashes between French and English colonisers and indigenous Kalinago, while estates such as Wingfield recall sugar plantations worked by enslaved African people. Things are more peaceful today – though the air is rent with yells and splashes each March during the Nevis to St Kitts cross-channel event, when swimmers traverse the 4km (2.5 miles) Narrows between the islands.

Trip plan: International flights touch down at Robert L Bradshaw Airport near Basseterre in the far south of St Kitts. Ferries and water taxis run between St Kitts and Nevis. Spend at least a couple of days exploring the historic sites, snorkelling and hiking the islands' forested interiors.

Need to know: The 'green' (vervet) monkeys scampering around St Kitts are non-native and damage crops. If you're offered 'tree mutton', you'll be eating monkey.

Other months: Dec-Jan – mostly dry, popular; Feb & Apr – warm, driest, busy; May-Jun – rain and heat increasing, prices falling; Jul-Nov – heavy showers, quietest, risk of tropical storms.

April

WHERE TO GO WHEN

CHALLENGE MYSELF

I WANT TO

TAKE ME OUT FOR...
- FOOD — PELOPONNESE, GREECE P97
- DRINK
  - RICHMOND, VIRGINIA, USA P87
  - WAIRARAPA, NEW ZEALAND P96

Take a Wairarapa wine-and-food wander during grape-harvest season

Sample terrific *tagines* or snap up some spices in Marrakesh

TAKE ME SOMEWHERE IN...
- SPRING
  - MARRAKESH & THE ATLAS, MOROCCO P93
  - PHILADELPHIA, USA P91
- AUTUMN — MELBOURNE, AUSTRALIA P86

Combine Maya ruins with beachtime and *cenote* swims in the Yucatán

Grab a board and ride the waves in Brazil's surf-savvy Florianópolis

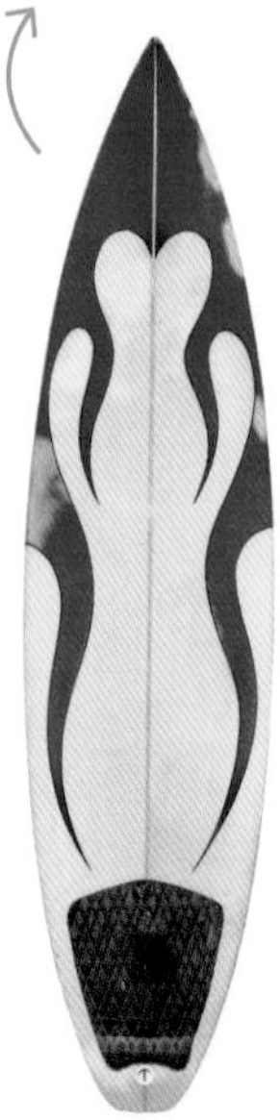

RELAX/ INDULGE

Discover the true unhurried Caribbean in boat-mad Bequia

TAKE ME TO THE BEACH
- REV UP
  - YUCATÁN, MEXICO P103
  - BEQUIA, ST VINCENT & THE GRENADINES P89
- CHILL OUT — FLORIANÓPOLIS, BRAZIL P86

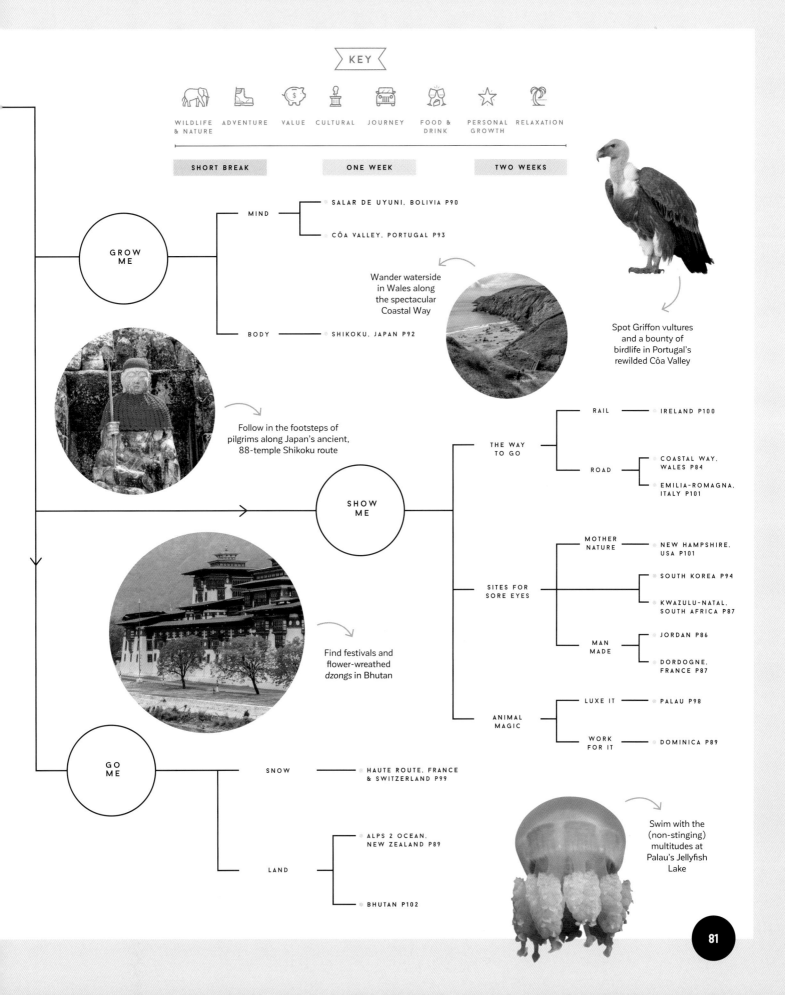

KEY

WILDLIFE & NATURE ADVENTURE VALUE CULTURAL JOURNEY FOOD & DRINK PERSONAL GROWTH RELAXATION

SHORT BREAK | ONE WEEK | TWO WEEKS

GROW ME

MIND
- SALAR DE UYUNI, BOLIVIA P90
- CÔA VALLEY, PORTUGAL P93

BODY
- SHIKOKU, JAPAN P92

Wander waterside in Wales along the spectacular Coastal Way

Spot Griffon vultures and a bounty of birdlife in Portugal's rewilded Côa Valley

Follow in the footsteps of pilgrims along Japan's ancient, 88-temple Shikoku route

SHOW ME

THE WAY TO GO
- RAIL — IRELAND P100
- ROAD
  - COASTAL WAY, WALES P84
  - EMILIA-ROMAGNA, ITALY P101

SITES FOR SORE EYES
- MOTHER NATURE
  - NEW HAMPSHIRE, USA P101
  - SOUTH KOREA P94
  - KWAZULU-NATAL, SOUTH AFRICA P87
- MAN MADE
  - JORDAN P86
  - DORDOGNE, FRANCE P87

ANIMAL MAGIC
- LUXE IT — PALAU P98
- WORK FOR IT — DOMINICA P89

Find festivals and flower-wreathed *dzongs* in Bhutan

GO ME

SNOW — HAUTE ROUTE, FRANCE & SWITZERLAND P99

LAND
- ALPS 2 OCEAN, NEW ZEALAND P89
- BHUTAN P102

Swim with the (non-stinging) multitudes at Palau's Jellyfish Lake

EVENTS
IN APRIL

FERIA NACIONAL DE SAN MARCOS
Aguascalientes, Mexico
Join thousands of revellers celebrating St Mark's feast with parades, feasting and plenty of tequila at the country's oldest fair.

WALPURGISNACHT
Thale, Germany
On the night when witches gather in the Harz Mountains, join the throngs on the Hexentanzplatz (Witches' Dance Square) for music and merriment.

INTERNATIONAL CHOCOLATE FESTIVAL
Óbidos, Portugal
Admire and inhale the delectable confectionery, used to create monumental sculptures during Óbidos' annual extravaganza.

PANIGIRAKI
Arachova, Greece
The most renowned of the Greek festivities on the Feast of St George involves parades, sports and other celebrations.

TOONIK TYME
Iqalit, Nunavut, Canada
Celebrate the return of spring and admire displays of traditional Inuit skills, games, throat-singing and dancing in the Arctic.

SONGKRAN FESTIVAL
Thailand
Expect to get soaked by water balloons and pistols during the world's biggest water fight.

NAGHOL (LAND DIVING)
Pentecost Island, Vanuatu
Witness young men hurl themselves off lofty, ramshackle-looking towers, their fall broken only by liana vines, in a stomach-lurching rite of passage.

BVI SPRING REGATTA & SAILING FESTIVAL
British Virgin Islands
Cheer on dozens of fleet vessels navigating the balmy waters during a series of races through the alluring Caribbean archipelago.

Inner wheel labels:
- 30 April — $$
- 23 April — $
- Late April — $$$
- First week in April — $$$
- Saturdays April to June — $$$
- 12-15 April — $
- Late April — $
- 25 April and around — $

VERY FAMILY FRIENDLY

NEW HAMPSHIRE, USA

Devour syrup-drenched feasts on a New Hampshire road trip in maple sugaring season

Delve into history and take a springtime park walk in blossoming Philadelphia

PHILADELPHIA, USA

FLORIANÓPOLIS, BRAZIL

Swim with sperm whales or hike the hills in green, serene Dominica

DOMINICA

PALAU

YUCATÁN, MEXICO

Cycle through dazzling South Island scenery on New Zealand's Alps 2 Ocean trail

ALPS 2 OCEAN, NEW ZEALAND

Take a craic-filled Ireland train trip to all corners of the Emerald Isle

MARRAKESH & THE ATLAS, MOROCCO

IRELAND

COASTAL WAY, WALES

MELBOURNE, AUSTRALIA

JORDAN

Plot a Peloponnese produce pilgrimage to find vanilla fir honey or classic Kalamata olives

KWAZULU-NATAL, SOUTH AFRICA

PELOPONNESE, GREECE

EXPENSIVE BUT WORTH IT

GOOD VALUE

SOUTH KOREA

See Seoul and Silla on a cherry-blossom circuit of South Korea

BHUTAN

Find your inner happiness in ever-blissful Bhutan

Combine Wairarapa's wine trail with a side-trip to Putangirua Pinnacles

WAIRARAPA, NEW ZEALAND

HAUTE ROUTE, FRANCE & SWITZERLAND

BEQUIA, ST VINCENT & THE GRENADINES

EMILIA-ROMAGNA, ITALY

Tick off Emilia-Romagna's top tourist sights in cool, crowd-free climes

CÔA VALLEY, PORTUGAL

DORDOGNE, FRANCE

Go underground to find rock art and cave-bear claw marks in the Dordogne

SALAR DE UYUNI, BOLIVIA

Snap the perfect saltflat shot and stargaze by night on the Salar de Uyuni

SHIKOKU, JAPAN

RICHMOND, VIRGINIA, USA

LEAVE THE KIDS AT HOME

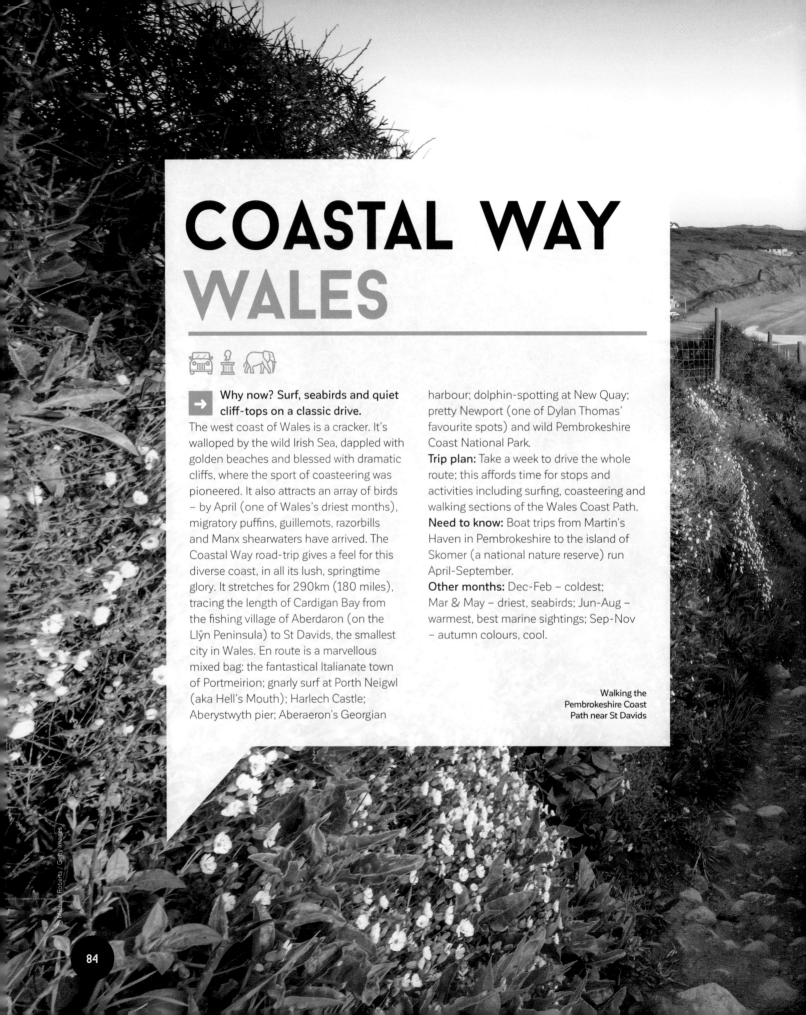

COASTAL WAY
WALES

Why now? Surf, seabirds and quiet cliff-tops on a classic drive.

The west coast of Wales is a cracker. It's walloped by the wild Irish Sea, dappled with golden beaches and blessed with dramatic cliffs, where the sport of coasteering was pioneered. It also attracts an array of birds – by April (one of Wales's driest months), migratory puffins, guillemots, razorbills and Manx shearwaters have arrived. The Coastal Way road-trip gives a feel for this diverse coast, in all its lush, springtime glory. It stretches for 290km (180 miles), tracing the length of Cardigan Bay from the fishing village of Aberdaron (on the Llŷn Peninsula) to St Davids, the smallest city in Wales. En route is a marvellous mixed bag: the fantastical Italianate town of Portmeirion; gnarly surf at Porth Neigwl (aka Hell's Mouth); Harlech Castle; Aberystwyth pier; Aberaeron's Georgian harbour; dolphin-spotting at New Quay; pretty Newport (one of Dylan Thomas' favourite spots) and wild Pembrokeshire Coast National Park.

Trip plan: Take a week to drive the whole route; this affords time for stops and activities including surfing, coasteering and walking sections of the Wales Coast Path.

Need to know: Boat trips from Martin's Haven in Pembrokeshire to the island of Skomer (a national nature reserve) run April-September.

Other months: Dec-Feb – coldest; Mar & May – driest, seabirds; Jun-Aug – warmest, best marine sightings; Sep-Nov – autumn colours, cool.

Walking the Pembrokeshire Coast Path near St Davids

© Michael Roberts / Getty Images

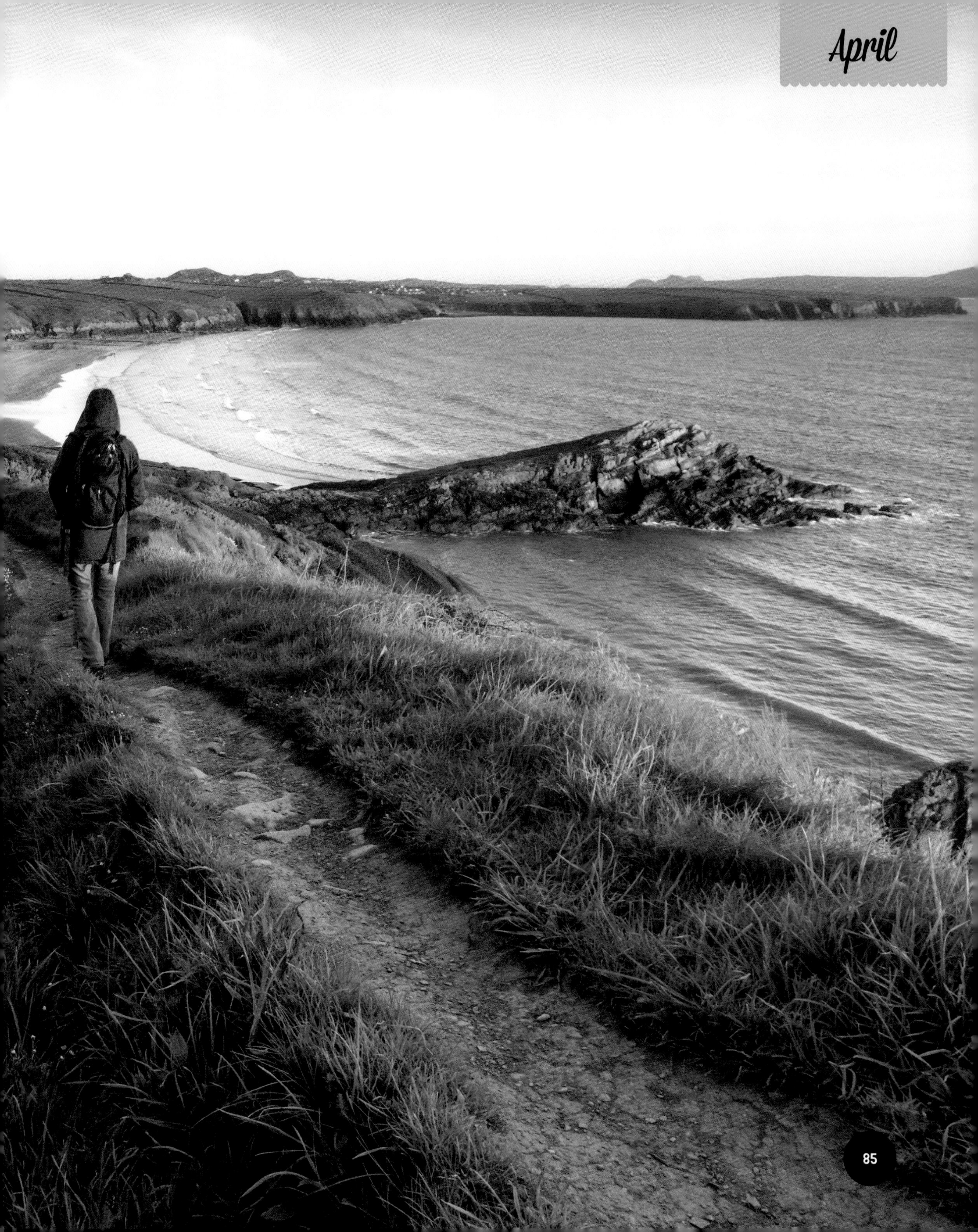

JORDAN

 Why now? For desert adventures in the kindest temperatures.

Compact Jordan is the complete package. Ancient wonders? Visit the 2000-year-old rock-hewn city of Petra or Kerak's Crusader castle. City sights? Try Roman Jerash or the souks of Amman. Jaw-dropping landscapes? Camp in the other-worldly deserts of Wadi Rum. Wildlife? Explore Dana Nature Reserve. Beach? Pick between the salty Dead Sea or snorkel-friendly Red Sea. More surprisingly, Jordan can also be very green – especially at this time. In April, humidity and rainfall are low, temperatures loiter delightfully at a mild 20-23°C (68-73°F), the central valleys are lush from winter rains and there are wildflowers everywhere. In particular, Ajloun Forest is abloom with strawberry trees and rock roses, while Dana's oases are bright with oleander and birds. Also, the vastness of Petra can be explored without breaking a sweat. In short, a beautiful time to travel across the country.

Trip plan: From Amman, nip north to Jerash and Ajloun before veering south towards Aqaba, stopping at the Dead Sea, Dana, Petra and Wadi Rum en route.

Need to know: The *khamseen* (hot, sandy wind) can hit Jordan in spring; it usually only lasts a few days.

Other months: Mar & May – springlike, ideal; Jun-Sep – very hot; Oct – fleeting autumn, pleasant; Nov-Feb – cold in many areas, Aqaba warm.

FLORIANÓPOLIS
BRAZIL

 Why now? Autumn magic in Ilha da Magia (the 'Magic Island').

Sitting pretty on Brazil's Atlantic coast, 800km (497 miles) south of Rio, the city of Florianópolis encompasses the idyllic isle of Santa Catarina – and it's not hard to see why it got its magical moniker. The island has 60 golden beaches, with one to suit all sorts – some are party-pounding, some wave-crashed, some peacefully tucked away. April marks the start of autumn, but the weather is still divine (average highs of 25°C/77°F; 195 hours of sunshine) while the summer crowds have ebbed away. It's a culturally mixed place, home to Azorean fisherfolk, Germanic villages and Italian-run vineyards making the most of the fertile soil. You could put in a bit of effort: Praia do Campeche and Praia do Santinho are top spots for surfing, while on the mainland, the lush Serra Geral mountains will tempt hikers. Or you could simply seek out a shack selling *caldo de cana* (sugarcane juice) and the island's famed oysters and sink your toes into the sand.

Trip plan: Florianópolis has an airport. Spend a weekend or a week exploring. The south of the island is quieter than the centre and north.

Need to know: Buses connect Florianópolis to other cities, including Rio (19hr), São Paulo (10hr 30min) and Montevideo, Uruguay (18hr).

Other months: Dec-Mar – hot, busy, rainier; May – warm, quieter; Jun-Sep – clear, cool; Oct-Nov – mild, drier, Blumenau Oktoberfest (Oct).

MELBOURNE
AUSTRALIA

 Why now? For laughs, mellow weather and fewer people.

It's all happening in Melbourne in March. The city explodes with events: Fashion Festival, Food & Wine Festival, Formula 1 Grand Prix. Which is great – if you want to fight your way to the bar and pay a premium for your bed. Alternatively, wait until April and visit Australia's culture capital when there's more room to breathe. The Comedy Festival (the world's third-largest laugh-fest) runs to the middle of the month; the pleasant autumnal weather continues (highs around 20°C/68°F), but the city isn't so overrun. That means you'll have more space while browsing the creative laneways, walking in the Botanic Gardens (aflame with autumn colour), cycling the buzzy neighbourhoods of Fitzroy, Collingwood and Carlton, and strolling seaside St Kilda. If you do get some autumn rain, shelter in one of Melbourne's 100-plus art galleries or aboard the free City Circle Tram.

Trip plan: Allow at least three days. Make time to explore the inner-city suburbs, where the best bars and cafes are found. The vineyard-streaked Yarra Valley makes a lovely, easy escape, especially during autumn's grape harvest.

Need to know: Free wi-fi is available in public spaces across the city, including in Federation Sq.

Other months: Dec-Feb – very hot; Mar & May – milder, festivals; Jun-Aug – cold, wet; Sep-Nov – mild, quieter.

DORDOGNE
FRANCE

→ **Why now?** To revel in rock art without the masses.

The Dordogne is all that's fabulous about France, in miniature: perfect pastoral scenes; chateaux-flecked riverbanks; a deep, rich history; markets overflowing with local produce; slopes streaked with vines. It's also home to some of the earliest and finest examples of prehistoric rock art anywhere – highlights include Lascaux, where the caves are festooned with hundreds of paintings and engravings; the vast subterranean system of Rouffignac (aka the Cave of the Hundred Mammoths); Font de Gaume, home to fine, multicoloured paintings; and Cougnac, where you'll find stalactites and stalagmites and the claw-marks of cave bears. Come summer, the Dordogne is heaving. But in mild, wildflower-y April the crowds are yet to descend. And, if it does rain a little, simply ride it out inside another of those jaw-dropping caves.

Trip plan: The Dordogne's capital is Périgueux. Rock art sites are clustered southwest of the city. Les Eyzies, in the Vézère Valley, makes a good base. The best way to explore is by car.

Need to know: Most villages in the Dordogne host a farmers' market at least once a week; check locally as market day varies village to village.

Other months: Nov-Mar – cold, truffle season; May-Jun – warm, quieter; Jul-Aug – hot, busiest, best for canoeing; Sep-Oct – mild, harvest.

RICHMOND, VIRGINIA USA

→ **Why now?** To raise a glass to better climes.

There's a buzz about the Virginian capital – and it's not just the coming of spring (though April is nice, bringing longer days and warmer weather). A burst of creative energy has given the handsome but old-fashioned-feeling 'River City' a new vitality. The booze scene is certainly booming, garnering Richmond the nickname 'America's Beer City'. Indeed, it has more than 20 craft breweries, which can be visited on the Richmond Beer Trail. Drop in to the huge taproom at Hardywood, one of Virginia's craft-revival pioneers; brave an 11.5% honey ginger beer at Ardent; try beers and barrel-aged barleywines at Triple Crossing; and catch live music while you drink at Three Notch'd. The ale-averse may be happy to discover that Richmond has a growing cocktail scene, too – order something fabulous at The Jasper, which oozes speakeasy style, or settle in at classic dive bar, the Fuzzy Cactus.

Trip plan: Spend two or three days bar-hopping. Also worth visiting are the Museum of Fine Arts, the Edgar Allen Poe Museum and leafy Hollywood Cemetery (where two presidents are buried).

Need to know: Richmond has an international airport, a Greyhound bus station and three Amtrak train stations.

Other months: Jan-Mar – quiet, cold; May-Jun – warm, uncrowded; Jul-Aug – muggy, busiest; Sep-Dec – cooling, Oktoberfest, Christmas festivities.

KWAZULU-NATAL
SOUTH AFRICA

→ **Why now?** For stable weather, mighty mountains, moving history and massive mammals.

For an excellent South African all-rounder, look no further than KwaZulu-Natal. The province has golden Indian Ocean frontage, the country's highest peaks and brilliant big-game parks (including some of Africa's best rhino-spotting). Its earth is soaked with history too, most notably the bloody skirmishes of the 1879 Anglo-Zulu War, best appreciated on guided trips to the battlefield sites of Isandlwana and Rorke's Drift. Soak it all up in austral autumn, when the weather is still warm (24°C/75°F) and the skies dry. Conditions are generally stable in the spear-like Drakensberg Mountains too, opening a world of wonderful walking of all levels via geological amphitheatres, pools and waterfalls, imposing spires and San rock art.

Trip plan: Head inland from coastal Durban to the Drakensberg (Lesotho is an easy detour, country-tickers). Continue to the battlefields for guided tours. Finish with a safari in Hluhluwe-Imfolozi Game Reserve.

Need to know: In Durban, try local speciality *bunny chow*, a hollowed-out loaf of bread filled with curry.

Other months: Sep-Nov & Mar & May – stable weather; Dec-Feb – hot, thunderstorms; Jun-Aug – cold, snowy.

(A) Scotts Head, Dominica; (L) Admiralty Bay, Bequia; (R) Cycling Waitaki Valley, NZ

DOMINICA

→ **Why now? For warm, wild times on the Nature Isle.**

Dominica isn't like other Caribbean countries. Black sand, rampant jungle, a relative dearth of slick-and-swanky resorts – this is tropical paradise as nature intended, rustic and authentic. It's a great place for hikes (unusual for the region). It's arguably even better for spotting huge marine creatures: around 200 sperm whales plus porpoises and dolphins live here year-round, while migrating humpbacks pass by (January-April) and four species of sea turtle – leatherbacks, loggerheads, greens and hawksbills – come to nest (March-October). Short-finned pilot, false killer and melon-headed whales are also known to visit. Boats venture out to try to spot the cetaceans, with warm, dry April providing good weather for this. It's also possible, if conditions allow, to scuba dive or swim with the 20m-long (65ft) sperm whales.

Trip planner: Allow at least a week. Head to Soufriere Scotts Head Marine Reserve, in the southwest; boat trips and dive excursions can be arranged. For turtles, join guided nighttime tours with the Dominica's Sea Turtle Conservation Organization; hotspots include Rosalie Bay and Calibishie Beach.

Need to know: Douglas–Charles Airport is in Dominica's northeast; journeys from outside the region usually require a plane change on another island.

Other months: Jan-Mar – warm, driest, wildlife; Dec & May – rainier, hot, cheaper; Jun-Nov – hurricane season.

BEQUIA
ST VINCENT & THE GRENADINES

→ **Why now? Go bananas for boats under cloud-free skies.**

St Vincent & the Grenadines somehow manages to fly under the radar. This low-key archipelago – comprising 32 islands, only nine of which are inhabited – has all the lushness and beach-beauty you'd expect from the Caribbean, but only a fraction of the tourists you'll find elsewhere in the region. And if that's true of main isle St Vincent, it's even truer of laidback Bequia. The largest of the Grenadines, Bequia (pronounced 'beh-kwee') is a charming speck of blinding-white sands, coconut groves and historic boat-building villages. Indeed, sailing has long been important here, and is celebrated with gusto during the Bequia Regatta, which features both fancy yachts and local-style dinghies, plus plenty of Bequia culture. Helpfully, it's held over Easter (often April), when the weather averages 29°C (84°F) but peak-season crowds have gone away.

Trip planner: Explore St Vincent (Botanic Gardens, rainforest walks, La Soufrière volcano) before catching the ferry from Kingstown to Bequia (1hr). Explore tiny capital Port Elizabeth, stroll the Princess Point Trail, snorkel at Lower Bay and learn about the island's seafaring heritage at the Bequia Maritime Museum.

Need to know: Dollar vans (open-backed taxis) gather near Bequia's ferry jetty.

Other months: Dec-Mar – driest, warm, busiest, most expensive; May – warm, cheaper; Jun-Nov – hurricane season, Vincy Mas Carnival (Jul).

ALPS 2 OCEAN
NEW ZEALAND

→ **Why now? Cycle the South Island in cooler weather.**

It's possible to cycle the length of New Zealand. The Nga Haerenga New Zealand Cycle Trail is a network of 22 Great Rides, totalling 2500km (1553 miles), top-to-tailing the country. Quite an undertaking. If you've less time, concentrate on a super section, like the 312km (194 miles) Alps 2 Ocean. Graded easy-moderate, the trail runs from the snow-capped peaks of Aoraki/Mt Cook National Park to Oamaru, on the Pacific coast, via dazzling lakes, braided rivers, dramatic Mackenzie Basin and the geological wonders and Māori rock art of the Waitaki Valley. Southern hemisphere autumn is a lovely time to ride: cooler than summer, with some flaming fall colours and a chance to pass vineyards heavy with fruit (and pop in for tastings).

Trip planner: Allow five-seven days to cover the nine sections. A classic six-day itinerary from Aoraki/Mt Cook to Oamaru, with stops at Twizel, Lake Ohau, Omarama, Kurow and Duntroon, means moderate daily distances (40-50km/25-31 miles), with time for sightseeing.

Need to know: Trail surfaces vary; a mountain bike is the best option but the route is also doable on a touring or hybrid bike.

Other months: Dec-Feb – summer, hot, busier; Ma & May – cooler, fall colours; Jun-Sep – cold, snow possible; Oct-Nov – wildflowers, potentially more rain/wind.

© Benedikt Juerges / Shutterstock

SALAR DE UYUNI BOLIVIA

Big skies and
blinding whites in
the Salar de Uyuni

➜ **Why now? Few places are as wonderfully weird as Bolivia's Salar de Uyuni, the world's largest salt flat.**
The leftovers of long-since-evaporated prehistoric lakes, Salar de Uyuni is a near-eternity of blinding-white crystals that crusts the altiplano and plays fast and loose with the rules of perspective. In short, it's a photographer's dream. Indeed, it's hard to take a bad picture here. But April, at the end of the wet season, offers a particular treat. As the weather increasingly dries out – better for touring elsewhere in the country – it's the last chance to capture the Salar underwater: when the rain pools on the surface, it creates a glassy sheen, reflecting the sky above in mind-bending fashion. Nights are more likely to be clear in April, too, so you may get to capture a gazillion galaxies mirrored in the pan below.

Trip plan: The Salar de Uyuni is in southern Bolivia, accessible from Chile and Argentina; take a tour out of San Pedro de Atacama (Chile) to combine the salt flats with the wider altiplano, exploring the region's high-altitude lakes, volcanoes, deserts and geysers.

Need to know: The Salar can flood during rainy season, causing some areas, such as Isla Incahuasi, to become inaccessible.

Other months: Dec-Mar – rainy season, warmer; May-Nov – dry, cool.

Cherry blossom adds a pop of April colour to Philly's financial centre

PHILADELPHIA
USA

Why now? To see history abloom.
The USA's original capital, Philly is not short on history. It's here that you can visit Independence Hall (where the Declaration of Independence was adopted), the Benjamin Franklin Museum and the Liberty Bell. But it's also a city of excellent outside spaces, which are arguably at their finest in spring when its many cherry trees are in full bloom. Huge Fairmount Park, 2000 landscaped acres hugging the banks of the Schuylkill River, is pick of the spots – as well as the Shofuso Japanese Cultural Center, which holds an annual *sakura* festival, and Kelly Drive, which is lined with blossoming boughs, the park is home to biking and hiking trails, a venerable zoo, the interactive Please Touch Museum and the Museum of Art (of Rocky-running-up-the-steps fame). April's mild temperatures (average highs of 19°C/66°F) and lack of crowds make exploring a pleasure too.

Trip plan: Allow at least three days to tour the main sites and outside spaces. Combine Philly with Washington DC (1hr 45min by train), which also holds a springtime cherry blossom festival.

Need to know: If you're here in late April, look out for the Penn Relays, the USA's oldest, biggest track and field competition held on the University of Pennsylvania campus.

Other months: Mar & May – quieter, warm, blossom; Jun-Aug – hottest, busy; Sep-Oct – cooler; Nov-Feb – quiet, cold.

91

SHIKOKU
JAPAN

→ Why now? Prime pilgrimage weather.

Walking around an entire island, ticking off visits to 88 temples on a journey of around 1200km (750 miles) is hard enough without worrying about the weather. Which is why cool, clement April (highs of 17°C/63°F; pre-cyclone season) is one of the best times to embark on the ancient Shikoku Pilgrimage, a sacred stroll between temples associated with Kobo Daishi, founder of Shingon Buddhism. You don't have to do the whole route at once, of course – you could walk *kugiri-uchi*, which means completing the trail in segments; try the section between Temple 11 (valley-tucked Fujii-dera) and 21 (mountain-top Tairyu-ji). Other key spots to visit include gorge-perched Iwaya-ji (Temple 45) and Zentsu-ji (Temple 75), where Kobo Daishi was born in CE 774.

Trip plan: A full pilgrimage takes six to eight weeks. Many start at Temple 1 (Ryozen-ji in Tokushima) and walk clockwise; it's easier to follow waymarks in this direction. It is also possible to complete the route by bike, bus tour or taxi.

Need to know: Traditional attire for *ohenro-san* (pilgrims) is a white *hakui* (jacket), *sugegasa* (conical hat) and *kongozue* (wooden walking stick); pilgrims carry a book, which is stamped at each temple.

Other months: Dec-Mar – very cold; May – warmer, cherry blossoms; Jun-Aug – hot, wet, cyclones possible; Sep-Nov – mild, dry.

Temple 1 (Ryozen-ji), where the Shikoku pilgrimage begins

© Amehime / Shutterstock

CÔA VALLEY
PORTUGAL

→ **Why now? See prehistoric art in a reviving wilderness.**

The Côa Valley is a special slice of northeast Portugal. Running from the Serra da Malcata mountains to the banks of the Douro, it's a region that's been occupied for millennia – the oldest rock art here dates back 25,000 years. But, more recently, it's also become a pioneering place for wildlife. Part of the Endangered Landscapes Programme, the over-grazed Côa Valley is being rewilded in an attempt to increase biodiversity and help species such as griffon vultures, Bonelli's eagles, wild boar and Iberian wolf reestablish and thrive. In the privately owned Faia Brava Reserve you can join a safari, sleep in fly-camps and track wolves on foot – spring is an especially lovely time, when the weather's not too hot and the landscape green. It offers good temperatures, too, for walking, biking or horse-riding the Côa Valley Grande Route, a 200km (124 miles) trail linking the Douro's headwaters to its mouth via remote, rugged hills.

Trip plan: Porto is the closest airport. The easiest way to explore is to hire a car – it's a 200km (124 miles) drive from Porto to the Foz Côa Archaeological Park; the Faia Brava Reserve is a little further south.

Need to know: The scenic Linha do Douro railway connects Porto and Pochino, near Vila Nova de Foz Côa.

Other months: Nov-Mar – cool, wet; May-Jun – warm, green; Jul-Aug – hottest; Sep-Oct – warm, less lush.

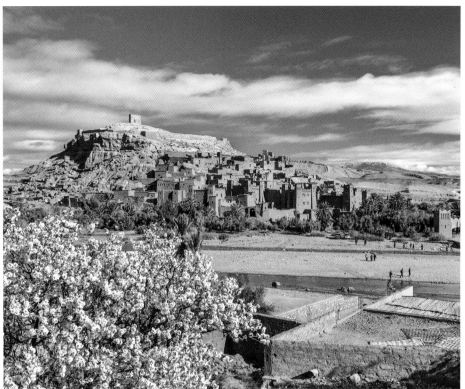

© Leonid Andronov / Shutterstock

MARRAKESH & THE ATLAS
MOROCCO

Head into the Atlas from Marrakesh to explore fortified Aït Ben Haddou

→ **Why now? Mild medinas and mountains.**

Ah, Morocco in spring: almond blossom blooming and hillsides green. Temperatures in the lowland are sitting happily at around 25°C (77°F) – just right for city wandering – and in the highlands it's a little cooler making it pleasant for hikes. First, head for marvellous Marrakesh. Get swept up with the snake-charmers, orange juicers and acrobats thronging the sprawling Djemaa El Fna square (where every night feels like a festival); barter for spices, scarves and *babouches* (slippers) in the medina's souks; and admire the heady mix, from exquisite Islamic architecture to the Jewish district to leafy Ville Nouvelle. Marrakesh is a good place for the peckish, too: eat traditional *tagines* and modern Moroccan-with-a-twist, or take a food tour. Then make a break for the Atlas mountains. Morocco's mightiest peaks (including 4167m/13,671ft Jebel Toubkal, highest of all) are within easy reach, and flush with wildflowers at this time. Take a hike and immerse yourself in Amazigh (Berber) culture.

Trip plan: Spend at least three days in Marrakesh before heading into the Atlas. Imlil (90km/56 miles from the city) is a good hiking hub. Toubkal is conquerable by anyone of average fitness.

Need to know: Consider starting your visit with a tour, to help orientate yourself within the confusing medina and to pick up some shopping/restaurant tips.

Other months: May & Sep-Oct – warm, pleasant; Jun-Aug – hot in the city; Nov-Mar – cool, winter hiking possible.

SOUTH KOREA

Why now? Perfect petals, with a generous side of culture too.

Think cherry blossom means Japan? Think again. South Korea puts on equally dazzling displays come springtime. Several flower-related festivals are held in capital Seoul in April (when temperatures average a pleasant 17°C/63°F); wander beneath dreamy blooms at Seokchon Lake, on Yeouido Island and around 15th-century Changgyeonggung Palace. Further south, around Busan, the port city of Jinhae is pretty as a picture – stroll over 'Romance Bridge' to see petals reflected in the stream below. Gyeongju hosts an annual Cherry Blossom Marathon in early April. The city, former capital of the ancient Silla dynasty, is also home to more temples, tombs, pagodas and palaces than anywhere else in the country – explore Gyeongju National Park's scenic and historic gems, and walk out to sacred Namsan to follow trails used by Buddhist monks amid temples and 180 peaks.

Trip plan: With ten days, start in Seoul, take a tour up to the DMZ and ride the bullet train to Busan to explore Gyeongju and Gamcheon Culture Village. With extra time, head over to Jeju Island.

Need to know: April can see dust from the Gobi Desert blown over to South Korea, which may irritate those with allergies.

Other months: Dec-Feb – very cold, skiing; Ma & May – warm, cherry and azalea blossoms; Jun-Aug – hot, wet; Sep-Nov – warm, dry.

Cherries in bloom around Gyeongju's Lake Bomunjeong

© Pete Monk / Luna Estate

Thriving vines
in Wairarapa's
vineyards

WAIRARAPA NEW ZEALAND

Why now? Raise a glass outside the capital.

Come grape harvest season, when the vines are ready to be plucked and blaze autumnal-orange across the hillsides, raise a glass like a true Wellingtonian. The Wairarapa Wine Region, only an hour's drive northeast of the New Zealand capital, has a climate similar to Burgundy and a wild, rural, undiscovered feel. Make for Martinborough, the charming old town at the heart of the local wine industry. Top quality Pinot Noir hails from the family-owned vineyards hereabouts – Luna has a

restaurant on site; smaller, more intimate options include Nga Waka and Schubert. Gourmet tours and food-and-wine pairing experiences are possible, which combine visits to some of the 20-odd local vineyards; wines are sipped alongside beers from the region's craft breweries and platters of world-class cheeses. Or take a self-guided cycle amid the vines – the cellar doors here are conveniently close and easy to link by bike.

Trip plan: Wairarapa makes a tasty weekender from Wellington. Hire a car, drive over the Remutaka Range or out to

Aorangi Forest Park (home of the needle-sharp Putangirua Pinnacles), and base yourself in Martinborough or nearby Greytown, a village of wooden Victorian-era buildings and good restaurants.

Need to know: For cellar door tastings at smaller vineyards, advance bookings may be required, especially for groups of six or more.

Other months: Dec-Feb – hottest; Mar & May – grape harvest, autumn colours; Jun-Sep – winter, chilly; Oct-Nov – warmer, wildflowers.

© Pit Stock / Shutterstock

PELOPONNESE GREECE

Seaside drinks at
sunset in Kalamata

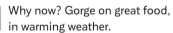

**→ Why now? Gorge on great food,
in warming weather.**

Hanging south of mainland Greece, the
mountainous Peloponnese peninsula,
one-time heartland of the Spartans, is both
historically rich and fantastically fertile. So
come in mild, sunny spring, to walk the
ruins – Olympia, Mycenae, Epidaurus – in
pleasant temperatures (average maximum
21°C/70°F) and to eat yourself silly.
Speciality produce ranges from Kalamata
olives to *tsakoniki* aubergines and roast
suckling pig, from Mani *lalaggia* (bread

fritters) to the Menalon mountains' vanilla
fir honey, which has protected origin
status. Even better, tourism here is more
community-focused than mass-market,
with family-run food tours, guesthouses
and tavernas enabling you to sample
authentic flavours. The wine is good too:
try super reds from Nemea and sweet white
Malvasia from Monemvasia.

Trip plan: Buses, trains and ferries run from
near Athens to the Peloponnese (Athens-
Corinth is 85km/53 miles). Allow a week
or more, especially if heading south. Visit

Kalamata, then graze around the Messinia,
Mani and Monemvasia peninsulas; wild
Mani is an especially good choice for
wildflower hikes and taverna eating.

Need to know: Be mindful of Easter: on the
plus side it brings fireworks, festivities and
oh-so-tender *kleftiko* (slow-cooked lamb);
on the minus, places can get busy and
prices hiked.

Other months: Nov-Feb – cool, olive
harvest; Mar & May – warming, wildflowers;
Jun-Aug – hot, busiest; Sep-Oct – warm,
quieter.

97

PALAU

 Why now? For underwater adventures in paradise.

The Micronesian nation of Palau looks pretty amazing above water: it's a sprinkle of 200-odd lush-green limestone outcrops, sheltered lagoons, white sands and blindingly turquoise seas. But it's under water where things become truly spectacular. This is the sub-aqua Serengeti, with 1500 fish species, soft corals and sea fans, sheer drop-offs and WWII wrecks. Palau is balmy year-round, and there's no really bad time to dive here. However, dry-season April, when seas are calmer and clearer, is a good choice. Also, whale sharks and manta rays are more likely January to April, while green and hawksbill turtles are most often seen April to July. The icing on the cake? Jellyfish Lake, a lagoon pulsating with a million translucent, stingless jellies – it's like snorkelling through the chorus line of an immense submarine ballet.

Trip plan: Keen divers should consider a liveaboard trip, to maximise dive opportunities and ease access to the best sites (including Blue Corner and German Channel).

Need to know: Roman Tmetuchl International Airport is on Babeldaob island; it's a 1hr 30min flight from Guam (which has US connections), 4hr from Tokyo.

Other months: May-Oct – wetter, typhoons a little more likely; Nov-Mar – drier, best diving.

© BlueOrange Studio / Shutterstock

Snorkel a surreal sub-surface dreamworld at Jellyfish Lake

HAUTE ROUTE
FRANCE & SWITZERLAND

👢 ☆

➡️ **Why now? Tackle a tough Alpine classic when conditions are best.**
The 120km (74 miles) Haute Route links Chamonix/Mont Blanc and Zermatt/the Matterhorn via some of the Alps' finest terrain. It ticks off two countries, skirts beneath most of the range's highest summits, crosses cols, traverses lakes and descends glaciers. Simply put, it is the crème de la crème of ski-touring, and only for those with experience. Long days at high altitude (it tops out at 3790m/12,434ft Pigne d'Arolla) make it a challenging prospect. The main Haute Route ski-touring season runs from mid-March to late April. This is when the glaciers are safely covered in powder, the weather is generally milder, and the mountain huts are open, heated and cooking up hearty hot meals. Don't ski? Come back in summer to do it on foot.

Trip plan: Skiing the Haute Route takes around six days, but allow time to enjoy lively Chamonix and Zermatt at either end. Both towns are accessible by public transport from Geneva and Zürich (the most convenient airports), as well as scenic train routes: the narrow-gauge Mont Blanc Express runs up to Chamonix from Martigny, while Zermatt is the end of the line for the Glacier Express from St Moritz.

Need to know: You will need both euros (France) and Swiss francs (Switzerland).

Other months: Mar – best snow conditions; Jun-Sep – route hikeable; Oct-Feb & May – conditions not ideal for either.

IRELAND

Why now? Explore by train, with fewer people and less precipitation.

The Emerald Isle isn't short of rain (how'd you think it got its nickname?) but, oddly, April is one of the driest months. Also, being after St Patrick's Day and before peak season, all the big attractions are open but it's still pretty quiet. That makes it a great time to travel around by train – a green option for a green island. Irish Rail can get you to many key locations: from Dublin, trains fan out to Sligo (hometown of WB Yeats), the craic-filled bars of Galway, colourful Killarney (and the surrounding national park), historic Cork and down to Rosslare, via the scenic east coast line. There are plenty of smaller stop-offs that might be made en route – or simply enjoy the views of spring-flush Ireland unrolling past the window.

Trip plan: A week-long rail loop from Dublin might include Westport (in Mayo), Galway, Limerick, Killarney, Cork, Waterford and back to Dublin; from here you could add on Sligo (good surf in April) or Belfast.

Need to know: Buy single tickets (cheaper when bought in advance) or consider a rail pass – for instance, the Irish Rail Explorer covers five days unlimited travel within 15 days for around €160.

Other months: Nov-Mar – wettest, some attractions close; May & Sep-Oct – mild, uncrowded; Jun-Aug – warm, long days, busiest.

Find gorgeous spots like Cork's Cobh on a round-Ireland rail trip

NEW HAMPSHIRE
USA

 Why now? For the sweetest springtime.

This pretty pocket of New England shakes off winter in fine fashion: in April, temperatures begin to rise (average highs of 21°C/70°F), snow disappears and wildflowers flourish. April also catches the tail end of maple sugaring season, when the trees squeeze out their last delicious dregs and the sugar shacks are still open for tours, tastings, wagon rides and pancake breakfasts. The landscape feels alive too. All that snow melt tops up the state's 100-plus waterfalls, from 43m-high (141ft) Arethusa to Flume Gorge. Some cascades can be seen via scenic drives – try the Kancamagus Scenic Byway, which passes through the heart of the White Mountains, or enjoy alternative watery views on a loop of Lake Winnipesaukee. Others require a wilderness walk to reach; plot a hike around Crawford Notch State Park and you could tick off ten falls in one day.

Trip plan: Hire a car. From state capital Concord, head north to the Lakes region, the Great North Woods (for Moose Alley and Beaver Brook Falls) and the White Mountains. Allow seven to 10 days.

Need to know: Two Amtrak train services (the Downeaster, which connects to Boston, and the Vermonter, which runs to Washington DC) stop at cities in New Hampshire.

Other months: Nov-Feb – snow, cold; Mar & May – quiet, warming, waterfalls; Jun-Aug – hottest, busy; Sep-Oct – fall foliage.

Fresh fish for sale in beautiful Bologna

© Susan Wright / Lonely Planet

EMILIA-ROMAGNA ITALY

 Why now? Hit a succession of sites in top touring weather.

It's time to hit the road. A really, really old one. The Roman-built Via Emilia was completed in 187 BCE, linking the city of Piacenza, on the Po River, to Rimini on the Adriatic coast – and it remains pretty much unchanged, providing a dramatic 260km (162 miles) drive through 2000 years of history. Mild April is ideal because there will be lots of sightseeing involved: ten unmissable cities and numerous Unesco sites lie en route. Take a spring stroll around Bologna's Piazza Maggiore, ancient university and bountiful markets. Visit the Unesco-listed centre and Ferrari Museum of Modena. Eat famed ham in Parma (a designated Creative City of Gastronomy), admire Forlì's Romanesque and Renaissance architecture, visit Forlimpopoli's 14th-century castle and seek out Cesena's thriving food and wine scene. Finish beside the sea in Rimini – it's a bit chilly for swimming, but you'll have the beaches largely to yourself.

Trip plan: Start in Piacenza (70km/43 miles from Milan) and drive eastwards. Allow plenty of time for stops – at least a week. The route can also be traced by train.

Need to know: Beware ZTLs (limited traffic zones), areas in the centre of Italian cities where traffic is restricted. Fines apply for driving into one without authorisation.

Other months: Nov-Feb – cold, damp; Mar & May – mild, uncrowded; Jun-Aug – hot, muggy, busy; Sept-Oct – warm, rainier.

BHUTAN

→ **Why now? Fabulous flowers and full-on festivals.**

Bhutan – a country that gauges its prosperity in terms of Gross National Happiness rather than material wealth – is always a jolly place to visit. But springtime is extra cheery. Pre-monsoon, the weather is dry and clear, ideal for comfy sightseeing and uninterrupted views of the snow-dusted Himalaya. Plus the birds are in song and the valleys are radiant with rhododendrons – the flower even has its own festival, held at Dochula's Lamperi Royal Botanical Garden in April. Early April is also when the country's biggest shindig – Paro Tshechu – is usually held, a colourful flurry of masked dances held at the Rinpung *dzong* (fortress). Combine festival fun with explorations of Bhutan's great outdoors: hike to cliff-teetering Tiger's Nest Monastery; take day-hikes in the pristine Punakha Valley (perhaps to Chimi Lhakhang Monastery); or try a longer route such as the seven-day Jhomolhari Trek, which ventures deep into the mountains.

Trip plan: Allow 10-12 days to include Paro, Thimphu and Punakha, longer to head to Bumthang or include a multi-day hike.

Need to know: Book early for visits coinciding with Paro Tshechu (note, dates shift depending on the lunar calendar).

Other months: Dec-Feb – cold; Mar & May – flowers, warm; Jun-Sep – wet; Oct-Nov – cooler, clear, dry.

(A) Traditional archery in Paro; (B) Up high at Tiger's Nest Monastery

© Angelo Cavalli / Getty Images

© Apisak Kanjanapusit / Shutterstock

© M Swiet Productions / Getty Images

YUCATÁN MEXICO

Sugar sands and clear
waters at Tulum beach

→ Why now? Balmy beaches, brilliant ruins.

The Yucatán ticks a lot of boxes. The beaches here – Caribbean-lapped lovelies, all white sand and palm trees – are idyllic. The hinterland is fantastic too, an adventure playground of thick jungle and cool *cenotes* (sinkholes), perfect for swimming. And it's historically fascinating. The Maya civilisation, which flourished from 2000 BCE until the 17th century, made quite a mark, building some of their most impressive temples here,

from mighty Chichén Itzá to lesser-known Uxmal, from the well-preserved pyramids of Ek Balam to cliff-top Tulum, right by the sea. Warm, dry April offers perfect beach weather and warm, calm seas – great for watersports and super for snorkelling – and, as peak season tails off, you can roam the ancient sites with smaller crowds.

Trip plan: Avoid the all-inclusives in places such as Cancún (though the resort's airport is a useful gateway). Instead, seek out community-based tour operators and

homestays that benefit the indigenous Maya, where you might sleep in hammocks, eat traditional food and visit off-the-beaten track *cenotes*.

Need to know: March to early April is when masses of US college students descend on the region for Spring Break. Check the dates and, if necessary, stay away from the Riviera Maya's party hotspots.

Other months: Nov-Mar – warm, dry; May-Jun – hotter, wetter; Jul-Oct – hurricane season.

103

May

WHERE TO GO WHEN

I WANT TO

CHALLENGE MYSELF

TAKE ME OUT FOR...
- FOOD
  - MURCIA, SPAIN P122
  - BALI, INDONESIA P110
- DRINK
  - MOLDOVA P110

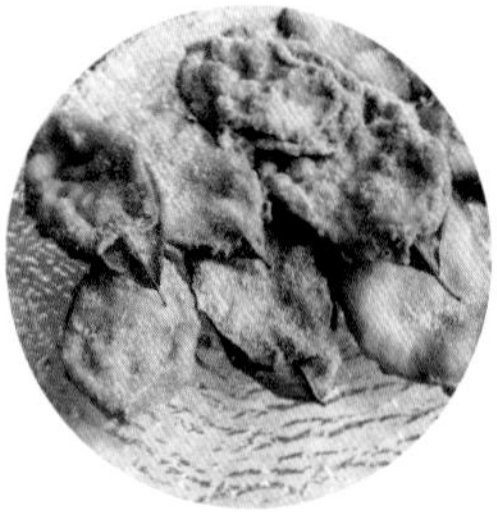

Munch your way through Murcia sampling local delights like *paparajotes* – fried lemon leaves

Drink in Moldova's millennia-old wine scene and hearty cuisine

TAKE ME SOMEWHERE...
- WARM
  - BELFAST & THE CAUSEWAY COAST, NORTHERN IRELAND P125
- WARMER
  - MEMPHIS, USA P127

Dive into Belfast's Titanic Museum and explore sights along the Causeway Coast

RELAX/ INDULGE

Find free-flowing waterfalls in late-spring Samothraki

TAKE ME TO THE BEACH
- REV UP
  - SPLIT & ŠIBENIK, CROATIA P110
- CHILL OUT
  - SAMOA P113
  - SAMOTHRAKI, GREECE P111

Sun-seek in Samoa and take a swim in Upolu's To Sua Ocean Trench

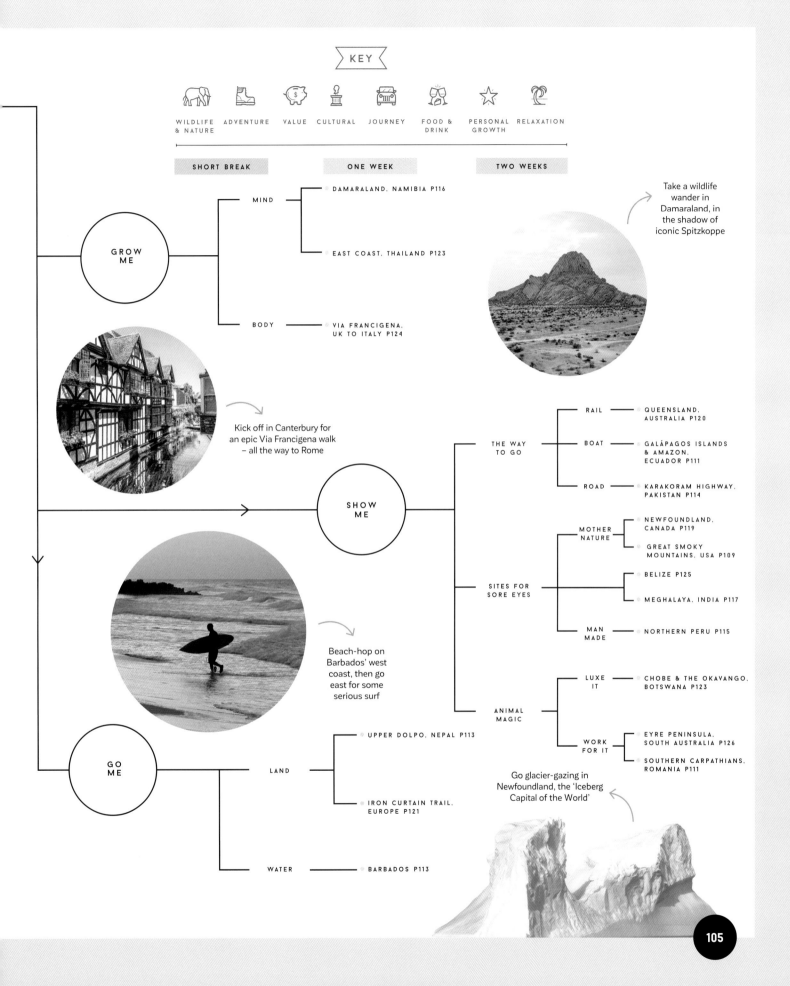

WILDLIFE & NATURE   ADVENTURE   VALUE   CULTURAL   JOURNEY   FOOD & DRINK   PERSONAL GROWTH   RELAXATION

SHORT BREAK   ONE WEEK   TWO WEEKS

GROW ME

MIND
- DAMARALAND, NAMIBIA P116
- EAST COAST, THAILAND P123

BODY
- VIA FRANCIGENA, UK TO ITALY P124

Take a wildlife wander in Damaraland, in the shadow of iconic Spitzkoppe

Kick off in Canterbury for an epic Via Francigena walk – all the way to Rome

SHOW ME

THE WAY TO GO
- RAIL — QUEENSLAND, AUSTRALIA P120
- BOAT — GALÁPAGOS ISLANDS & AMAZON, ECUADOR P111
- ROAD — KARAKORAM HIGHWAY, PAKISTAN P114

SITES FOR SORE EYES
- MOTHER NATURE
  - NEWFOUNDLAND, CANADA P119
  - GREAT SMOKY MOUNTAINS, USA P109
  - BELIZE P125
  - MEGHALAYA, INDIA P117
- MAN MADE — NORTHERN PERU P115

ANIMAL MAGIC
- LUXE IT — CHOBE & THE OKAVANGO, BOTSWANA P123
- WORK FOR IT
  - EYRE PENINSULA, SOUTH AUSTRALIA P126
  - SOUTHERN CARPATHIANS, ROMANIA P111

Beach-hop on Barbados' west coast, then go east for some serious surf

GO ME

LAND
- UPPER DOLPO, NEPAL P113
- IRON CURTAIN TRAIL, EUROPE P121

WATER
- BARBADOS P113

Go glacier-gazing in Newfoundland, the 'Iceberg Capital of the World'

EVENTS
IN MAY

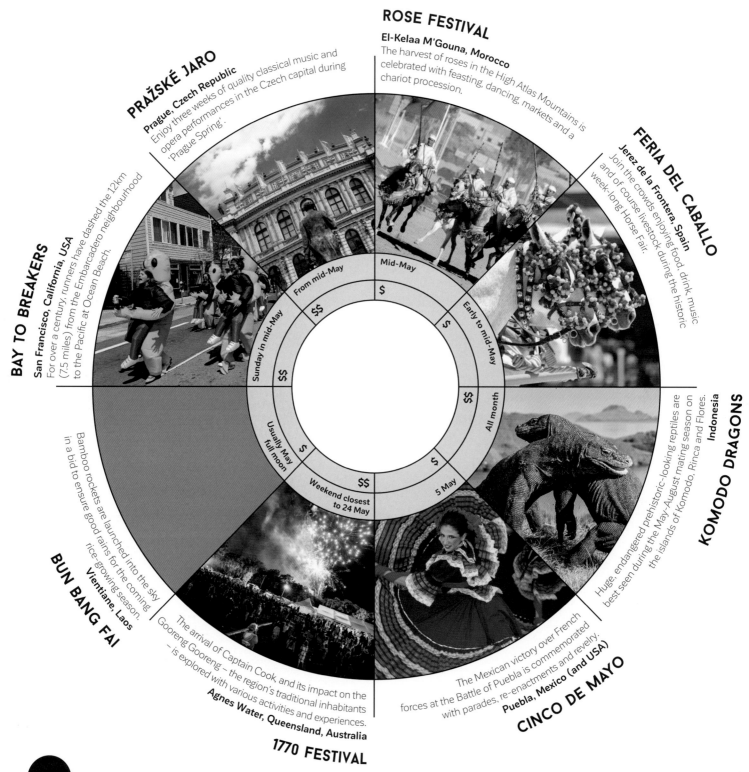

ROSE FESTIVAL
El-Kelaa M'Gouna, Morocco
The harvest of roses in the High Atlas Mountains is celebrated with feasting, dancing, markets and a chariot procession.

PRAŽSKÉ JARO
Prague, Czech Republic
Enjoy three weeks of quality classical music and opera performances in the Czech capital during 'Prague Spring'.

FERIA DEL CABALLO
Jerez de la Frontera, Spain
Join the crowds enjoying food, drink, music and of course livestock during the historic week-long Horse Fair.

BAY TO BREAKERS
San Francisco, California, USA
For over a century, runners have dashed the 12km (7.5 miles) from the Embarcadero neighbourhood to the Pacific at Ocean Beach.

KOMODO DRAGONS
Indonesia
Huge, endangered prehistoric-looking reptiles are best seen during the May-August mating season on the islands of Komodo, Rinca and Flores.

BUN BANG FAI
Vientiane, Laos
Bamboo rockets are launched into the sky in a bid to ensure good rains for the coming rice-growing season.

1770 FESTIVAL
Agnes Water, Queensland, Australia
The arrival of Captain Cook and its impact on the Gooreng Gooreng – the region's traditional inhabitants – is explored with various activities and experiences.

CINCO DE MAYO
Puebla, Mexico (and USA)
The Mexican victory over French forces at the Battle of Puebla is commemorated with parades, re-enactments and revelry.

Wheel labels (clockwise from top):
- Mid-May — $
- Early to mid-May — $
- All month — $$
- 5 May — $
- Weekend closest to 24 May — $$
- Usually May full moon — $
- Sunday in mid-May — $$
- From mid-May — $$

106

Snorkel the world's second-longest barrier reef in Belize

● BELIZE

● BELFAST & THE CAUSEWAY COAST, NORTHERN IRELAND

● EYRE PENINSULA, SOUTH AUSTRALIA

Swim amongst a mass migration of cuttlefish at the Eyre Peninsula's Point Lowly

Pay a May homage to rock'n'roll gods in Memphis

● MEMPHIS, USA

● GALÁPAGOS ISLANDS & AMAZON, ECUADOR

● NEWFOUNDLAND, CANADA

● EAST COAST, THAILAND

Slip from Split to Šibenik on a two-city Croatian odyssey

● SAMOA

● BALI, INDONESIA

Road-trip the Great Smoky Mountains before the summer crowds

● SAMOTHRAKI, GREECE

● SPLIT & ŠIBENIK, CROATIA

Take a cooking class in Ubud and make *babi guling* the Balinese way

● GREAT SMOKY MOUNTAINS, USA

● BARBADOS

● MURCIA, SPAIN

● DAMARALAND, NAMIBIA

Spy elephant, rhino and lion at Damaraland waterholes

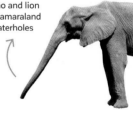

● QUEENSLAND, AUSTRALIA

Swish through Queensland in style aboard the vintage Savannahlander

● NORTHERN PERU

● SOUTHERN CARPATHIANS, ROMANIA

Discover Peru's isolated Caral, the oldest civilisation in all South America

Climb the Carpathians to track bison and bear, wild cats and wolves

● CHOBE & THE OKAVANGO, BOTSWANA

● MOLDOVA

● KARAKORAM HIGHWAY, PAKISTAN

● IRON CURTAIN TRAIL, EUROPE

● UPPER DOLPO, NEPAL

● MEGHALAYA, INDIA

Cross a living root-bridge in Meghalaya

Make like a pack pony on the remote trekking trails of Nepal's Upper Dolpo

● VIA FRANCIGENA, UK TO ITALY

GREAT SMOKY MOUNTAINS USA

→ **Why now? Glimpse a dazzling natural display, before the crowds arrive.**

The Smokies are truly on fire this month. This spectacular subrange of the Appalachian chain, on the border of North Carolina and Tennessee, is home to huge numbers of *Photinus carolinus* (synchronous fireflies) and May/June is typically when they put on their magical en-masse mating display: a forest-full of males flashing in unison. This natural wonder is the icing on the cake of a springtime road trip through the mountains. The USA's most popular national park is quieter at this time. Take scenic drives via its misty ridges, hike wildflower-flush trails, look out for the diverse wildlife – from groundhogs and chipmunks to salamanders and black bears – and soak up the strong Southern Appalachian culture: log cabins, mills and churches built by early settlers have been preserved here.

Trip plan: Start in Washington DC. Hire a car and drive through Shenandoah National Park and along the scenic Blue Ridge Parkway to the Great Smoky Mountains. Finish in Nashville or Atlanta. Allow two weeks.

Need to know: Due to high demand, seeing the fireflies at the national park's Elkmont viewing area is managed by a lottery process. The ballot usually opens in late April. Note that many picnic areas, campsites and visitor centres are closed November to early May.

Other months: Dec-Apr – cold, some facilities close; Jun – quiet, wildflowers, fireflies; Jul-Aug – warmest, busiest, most expensive; Sep-Nov – fall colours.

Sunset scenery in Great Smoky Mountains National Park

SPLIT & ŠIBENIK
CROATIA

→ **Why now? For exciting cities and empty islands.**

To see Split in spring is to see it at its best. Croatia's second-largest city, set between mountains and the Adriatic Sea, always has a buzz but in May it's dialling up: there are few tourists, but air and sea temperatures are rising – warm enough for hitting the beach – and, on 7 May, there's an explosion of local fervour as Split celebrates its patron saint, Domnius, with music, processions and rowing competitions. Visit St Domnius Cathedral and the shops and bars tucked inside the remains of Diocletian's Palace. Then hop along the coast to Šibenik, a city with a magnificent medieval centre and many fine seafood restaurants. Šibenik also offers easy access to the wonderful waterfalls of Krka National Park (cheaper to visit in May than in peak season) and the uninhabited Kornati Archipelago, 140 low-lying islands where you can play castaway for a day or a week.

Trip plan: Spend a few days in Split then travel to Šibenik. From there, frequent daily buses run year-round to Skradin and Lozovac (entrances to Krka) and boats run to the Kornati islands; take a day-trip or arrange to stay overnight in an off-grid cottage.

Need to know: Bus journeys between Split and Šibenik take around 1hr 15min.

Other months: Nov-Mar – cool, off-season; Apr – warm, good for activities; Jun-Aug – hottest, busiest; Sep-Oct – quieter, warm seas.

BALI
INDONESIA

→ **Why now? Eat your way into the local culture.**

Bali in May? Delicious. Dry, hot and sunny days, peak season crowds yet to descend and – as always – a relaxed vibe. Nowhere is the latter more true than in Ubud, the artsy, hippie highlands town with a good line in galleries and museums, ancient temples and a thriving food scene. Ubud, which is surrounded by lush forests, paddy fields and leafy plantations, has several world-class restaurants and fancy cocktail lounges as well as low-key food stalls and cafes serving Balinese specialities – *gado gado* salad, satay, *injin* porridge, *babi guling* (suckling pig). It's a great place to take a cookery course; as well as learning how to create zingy dishes, you might head to the market with a chef to select the best ingredients, play with exotic spices and find out more about Balinese food culture.

Trip plan: You could spend a day, a week or a month in Ubud. As well as cooking classes, it's a popular place for yoga and wellness retreats. More active possibilities include countryside hikes, hilly bike rides and whitewater rafting.

Need to know: Ubud is 35km (22 miles) from Bali's Denpasar Airport. Direct taxi transfers take around 40min; cheap local buses around 1hr 30min.

Other months: Jan-Apr & Oct-Nov – wet, though rain sporadic; Jun-Sep – dry season, busiest (peak months Jul-Aug)

MOLDOVA

→ **Why now? Toast spring and Victory Day.**

A two-for-the-price-of-one surprise package, former Soviet republic Moldova is as tasty as it is curious. Beneath capital Chișinău's Brutalist blocks you'll find bazaars, churches and cultural showcases (don't miss the National Art Museum or the Moorish-style Ethnographic and Natural History Museum) but also great wine, produced here for several millennia; Pinot Noirs, Cabernets and local varietals such as Fetească Neagră go down a treat with the hearty cuisine, blending Balkan, Turkish and Russian influences. There are more treats for the tastebuds in Transdniestr, a would-be breakaway republic still clinging to ties with Russia. Sample *divin* (cognac-style brandy) at the Kvint distillery, caviar at a sturgeon farm or Moldovan-Russian-Ukrainian cuisine in a local restaurant, and time your visit for 9 May to witness the bombastic Victory Day Parade, when tanks and troops rumble through capital Tiraspol.

Trip plan: Explore Chișinău, allowing time for tastings in nearby wineries and a visit to the cave monastery at Orheiul Vechi, then head east to Transdniestr to sample brandy, caviar and Tiraspol's Victory Day parade.

Need to know: Transdniestran rubles can be exchanged only with Moldovan leu, and only in-country. A visa isn't usually required; complete a migration card at the border. Check your government's advice on the security situation in Transdniestr before visiting.

Other months: Dec-Feb – often sub-zero; Apr & Nov – chillly; Jun-Oct – warm and bright but often rainy.

GALÁPAGOS ISLANDS & AMAZON
ECUADOR

➡️ **Why now?** To combine two watery wildlife wonderlands.

Ecuador offers an embarrassment of wildlife riches. Within its borders lies 2% of the Amazon Basin, which sounds paltry but is still loads, plus the jungle is relatively quick and easy to access here compared to, say, Brazil. Ecuador also has the matchless Galápagos archipelago, with its abundance of strange, unique, fearless creatures. May is a good time to combine both. In the Galápagos the weather is cooler, the water is at its clearest (great for snorkelling with marine iguanas, penguins and sea lions), turtles are hatching and blue-footed boobies are doing their comical courtship dance. In the Amazon, it's not the wettest (though, of course, it's always pretty damp), making it a good time for visiting a community-run ecolodge and taking boat trips and jungle hikes with the tribes that know the area best.

Trip plan: From capital Quito, fly to the Galápagos and explore the islands by expedition cruise (usually four or eight days). Return to Quito to access the Amazon – fly to Coca and take a road transfer and boat ride along one of the Amazon's tributaries to reach a jungle lodge.

Need to know: Quito sits at almost 3000m (9842ft) above sea level – you may feel the effects of the altitude.

Other months: Jan-Apr – Galápagos hot, Amazon wettest; Jun – drier and cooler; Jul-Sep – busy, rougher seas; Oct-Dec – cooler, cloudier.

SAMOTHRAKI
GREECE

➡️ **Why now?** To get there before the Greeks.

Lurking out in the northeast Aegean, Samothraki (Samothrace) also lurks off most foreign tourists' radars – and is all the more alluring for it (though it's popular among Greeks, so best avoided July and August). The island is home to abundant forests, streams and waterfalls – especially lush and full-flowing in spring – and 1664m (5459ft) Mount Fengári, the highest peak in the region, where it's said Poseidon sat to watch the Trojan War. This makes it a natural-adventure playground, great for hiking, rafting and canyoning, as well as a place to chill – the best beaches are at Pachia Ammos, Vatis and Kipos. If the sea still feels chilly in May, go to Thermá, to dip in the village's warm natural mineral springs. Other must-sees include the ancient ruins of the Sanctuary of the Great Gods and the pretty hilltop town of Chora, where you can kick back in tavernas and visit the folklore museum.

Trip plan: Ferries run at least daily year-round between Samothraki and the mainland port of Alexandroúpolis (2hr). Spend a week on the island.

Need to know: Public transport and car hire on Samothraki is limited. Consider hiring a car on the mainland and bringing it over. There is only one, expensive petrol station on Samothraki – fill up in Alexandroúpolis.

Other months: Nov-Mar – cool, wettest; Apr & Jun – warm, green; Jul-Aug – hot, busiest; Sep-Oct – warm, quieter.

SOUTHERN CARPATHIANS
ROMANIA

➡️ **Why now?** To put extra spring in your wildlife-tracking.

Things are afoot in the Romanian mountains. The rugged Southern Carpathians represent one of Europe's largest, most pristine, best protected wildernesses, home to swathes of old-growth forest and species that are rare elsewhere, including wolves, bear, wild cat, Eurasian lynx and, since 2014, the continent's only free-roaming bison herd. Bison disappeared from Romania around 200 years ago but have been reintroduced by conservation not-for-profit Rewilding Europe. As well as aiming to restore the region's biodiversity, Rewilding Europe supports community-based rural tourism enterprises, including safari companies. May, when the snow has gone, temperatures are mild, the wildflowers are out and the bears are active, is a lovely time to explore with expert guides and track the bison and other animals on foot.

Trip plan: It's a 3hr drive from Timişoara Airport to the Bison Visitor Centre in Armeniş, from where multi-day safaris head into the Tarcu Mountains Natura 2000 site – bison country. Accommodation is in tented camps or simple guesthouses.

Need to know: When tracking, wear neutral colours and odour-free mosquito/tick repellent. Pack binoculars.

Other months: Oct-Apr – snowy, winter wildlife tracking; Jun & Sep – warmer, good for hiking and tracking; Jul-Aug – hottest, storms possible.

© Theodor Negru / Shutterstock

111

(A) Upolu coastline, Samoa; (L) Stupa at Saldang, Upper Dolpo (R) Barbados beach at sunset

112

© Zzvet / Shutterstock

SAMOA

→ **Why now? Drier, cheaper days in paradise.**

Simmering away in the tropical South Pacific, the Samoa archipelago is a remote piece of paradise still embracing its traditional roots. The islands' culture – dominated by the tenets of Fa'a Sāmoa (the Samoan Way) – is as interesting as its seas are blue and its volcanic interior exotically profuse. Samoa is hot year-round (around 25-30°C/77-86°F), with consistent trade winds providing cooling late-afternoon breezes. What does change is the rain: May to October offer a significantly drier experience. As a shoulder month, May offers good weather at cheaper prices than the June-to-September peak. That's more money to spend on exploring the islands, from the rainforest, beaches and lagoons of Upolu to tiny, car-free Manono or the lava fields of Savai'i. Essential experience? Stay in an open-sided beach *fale* and snorkel the balmy blue – the water is a tasty 28°C (82°F) all year round.

Trip plan: Fly to Faleolo Airport on Upolu. Visit capital Apia's market and south-coast beaches. Bigger Savai'i (1hr 30min by ferry) is home to the ancient Polynesian mound of Pulemelei and volcanic action.

Need to know: Samoa is a 5hr flight from Sydney, 3hr 30min from Auckland, and 5hr from Hawaii.

Other months: Nov-Apr – wetter; Jun-Oct – drier.

UPPER DOLPO
NEPAL

→ **Why now? Easier access to a restricted mountain realm.**

Upper Dolpo, tucked into Nepal's northwest, between the Tibetan Plateau and the Dhaulagiri range, is about as remote as the country gets. One of the last remaining enclaves of pure Tibetan culture, the region only opened to outsiders in the late 1980s and still requires a special permit to visit. Treks here are long, tough, high and wild but worth it – you'll see few other trekkers but perhaps wolves, vultures, blue sheep and snow leopard tracks. From the airstrip at Juphal, hikes lead through Shey Phoksundo National Park, home of the nomadic Dolpo-pa people, taking in sacred Phoksundo Lake, 800-year-old Shey Gompa monastery, remote villages and multiple passes topping 5000m (16,404ft). Which is why May is an ideal month – by late spring, the snows have melted at higher altitudes, allowing easier access to this inaccessible-seeming place.

Trip plan: Allow 25-30 days, including transfer and contingency time. Most trekkers fly in to Juphal and out of Jomsom, in the Lower Mustang region. Independent trekking is not allowed.

Need to know: Upper Dolpo sits in the rain shadow of the Himalaya, so it's possible to trek here during the monsoon. However, as weather can disrupt flights to Juphal/Jomsom, late spring and late autumn are better choices.

Other months: Dec-Feb – cold; Mar-Apr – warm, dry, green; Jun-Sep – warmer, wet elsewhere in Nepal; Oct-Nov – dry, clear, busiest.

BARBADOS

→ **Why now? Sun's out, surf's up.**

Hear the word 'Barbados' and, immediately, Technicolour images of white sand, palm trees and umbrella-ed rum cocktails come to mind. This is your grade-A tropical paradise, prime for beach lazing, sun-soaking and shooting the sea breeze. But it's also one of the best islands in the Caribbean for surfing, especially on its Atlantic-facing south and east coasts. Conditions are usually good and consistent from November right through to June; the advantage of May is that, while there might be a little more rain than in the preceding months, it's still super sunny and prices are lower too. Top spots for catching waves include Freights Bay (good for beginners), South Point and Soup Bowl, a world-class wave near laidback Bathsheba that has hosted international competitions. Brandons, a glorious beach near capital Bridgetown, is popular too.

Trip plan: To access multiple surf beaches, hire a car. The small east coast fishing community of Bathsheba is more rum bars and local guesthouses than glitzy resorts, and provides a relaxed base.

Need to know: Swimming at Bathsheba can be dangerous due to rip tides and undertows. Seek local knowledge before entering the water.

Other months: Dec-Apr – dry, busy; Jun – quieter, hotter; Jul-Oct – hurricane season; Nov – shoulder month.

© travelview / Shutterstock

KARAKORAM HIGHWAY & THE HINDU KUSH PAKISTAN

Karakoram Highway views near Karimabad

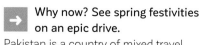

➜ **Why now? See spring festivities on an epic drive.**

Pakistan is a country of mixed travel fortunes: beloved of '60s Hippie Trailers; largely avoided post 9/11. But one thing's for sure, when it *is* safe to visit, there's arguably nowhere better. Fascinating culture, extraordinary mountains, overwhelming hospitality, few tourists, epic journeys – not least the drive up the legendary Karakoram Highway to lush Shangri-La-like Hunza. May is a fine time to take to the road. Warming temperatures see apple and apricot trees in bloom, provide clear views of the astonishing peaks and – hopefully – ensure a snow-free Shandur Pass (3700m/12,139ft), in order to travel west between Gilgit and Chitral. The month also heralds the Chilam Joshi Festival in the Kalash Valleys, when the pagan Kalash people celebrate spring with music, dance and wine.

Trip plan: For an overland loop north of capital Islamabad, including the Karakoram Highway, Hunza, Gilgit, Chitral, the Kalash Valleys, Swat Valley and ancient archaeological site of Taxila, allow two weeks. A guided trip with a knowledgeable tour operator is recommended.

Need to know: Read up on cultural etiquette before travelling – dress modestly. Take a bandana to cover your face when travelling on dusty roads.

Other months: Nov-Mar – cold, snow in mountains; Ap & Jun – spring, warm; Jul-Aug – hot and wet in Islamabad, warm in highlands; Sep-Oct – cooler.

Kuélap, Peru's high-mountain Chachapoyan fortress

NORTHERN PERU

→ Why now? Great sites in green landscapes.

If it was a region in any other country, northern Peru would likely be a tourist honeypot. But having to compete with the south – home to bucket-list-topper Machu Picchu – it's shamefully overlooked. And yet, it's where you'll find archaeological treasures left by civilisations far older than the Inca: the ancient site at Caral (dated to around 2600 BCE); the vast adobe citadel of Chan Chan, founded by the pre-Columbian Chimú Empire; the Moche-built burial site of Sipán and complex of El Brujo (the 'Temple of the Wizard'); and the 3000m-high (9842ft) mountaintop fortress of Kuélap, constructed by the Chachapoyan civilisation from 500 CE. May is a marvellous month to explore, with the wet season over and average highs of 24°C (75°F) but landscapes still green and 771m-high (2530ft) Gocta Falls (one of the world's tallest cascades, 105km/65 miles from Kuélap) in full post-rains flow.

Trip plan: A two-week trip north of Lima, using a few internal flights, could combine a range of ancient sites with the port of Trujillo (home to a fascinating archaeology museum), the Spanish colonial city of Cajamarca and a trek to Gocta Falls.

Need to know: Some of the sites are in remote areas; road journeys can be long and bumpy.

Other months: Nov-Feb – rainy season, hot; Mar-Apr – rains abate; Jun – lush, dry, bright; Jul-Aug – driest, cool; Sep-Oct – warm, sunny, showers.

© NiarKrad / Shutterstock

115

Track black rhino from
a community-run
Damaraland camp

DAMARALAND
NAMIBIA

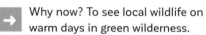

→ **Why now? To see local wildlife on warm days in green wilderness.**

Even in a country as sparse as Namibia – the second least-populated place on earth – Damaraland stands out as especially empty. Sprawling across north-central Namibia, it's a wilderness of craggy mountains, dry riverbeds and desert-adapted animals, including elephant, rhino and lion. May, when days are warm and dry and the landscape is still tinged green, is a great time to seek out these species as they gather around waterholes. Better still, the country is a pioneer in community-driven ecotourism, with large areas run as communal conservancies that empower local people. In Damaraland you'll find several award-winning, community-run camps that use solar energy, recycle water and employ former poachers as rangers and guides. Head out to track rare black rhino on foot, spot gemsbok, kudu, zebra and elephant, get involved with community projects and gaze at some of the most sparkling dark skies.

Trip plan: Southern Damaraland is around 560km (348 miles) from capital Windhoek (6hr drive). Alternatively, it's possible to fly in to some lodges. Allow at least three or four days in the area; combine it with the Atlantic Coast and Etosha National Park.

Need to know: Twyfelfontein, close to the Damaraland town of Khorixas, is home of one of Africa's largest concentrations of prehistoric petroglyphs.

Other months: Jan-Apr – peak rains, hot; Jun – dry, greener, cheaper; Jul-Sep – dry, peak season; Oct-Dec – hot, early rains.

MEGHALAYA INDIA

Meghalaya's mighty
Nohkalikai Falls

→ **Why now? A monsoon appetiser in the world's wettest place.**

It rains *a lot* in the northeast Indian state of Meghalaya (aka 'the abode of clouds'). The towns of Cherrapunjee and Mawsynram are among the wettest places on the planet, especially when the monsoon really kicks in, from July to September. Things are getting damper by May but that means impressive waterfalls, luxuriant hills, atmospheric mists and experiencing a taste of what makes Meghalaya tick. It's

not too hot, either (15-25°C/59-77°F), so a welcome respite from the soaring temperatures elsewhere in India. Plot adventures into the cave-riddled Garo, Khasi and Jaintia hills and soak up the culture of the Khasi people – although largely converted to Christianity, they've retained many old traditions, not least spirited festivals and the creation of living bridges, woven from fig-tree roots.

Trip plan: Guwahati, in neighbouring Assam, is a handy access point. A week-

long trip might include the lively city of Shillong (don't miss frenetic Iew Duh market), Sohra (for cliffs and cascades), the Khasi Hills and the living root bridge of Nongriat.

Need to know: Festivals such as Chad Sukra (when the Jaintia people mark the start of sowing season) are held April/May.

Other months: Dec-Mar – cold, misty; Apr & Jun – pleasantly cool, damp; Jul-Sep – heaviest rains, very hot; Oct-Nov – warm, humid.

117

NEWFOUNDLAND
CANADA

→ Why now? Watch an onslaught of icebergs.

They call the waters off Newfoundland and Labrador 'Iceberg Alley'. In spring, great hunks of Arctic ice – mostly cast-offs from the glaciers of western Greenland – float down the Atlantic coast past Canada's easternmost province. They usually arrive in April and May, peaking mid-May and June. You can stand onshore and watch these white titans drift by or take a boat trip for a closer look. Good spots include St Anthony, Twillingate, Bonavista and St John's/Cape Spear. Seabirds also start to show up in May, while by the end of the month the first whales appear.

Trip plan: From capital St John's follow the Atlantic coast north to the Bonavista Peninsula (home to pretty Trinity) and Twillingate (the 'Iceberg Capital of the World'). Veer west to the fjord-cut mountains of Gros Morne National Park, then north to northernmost Newfoundland, for St Anthony and the 1000-year-old Viking site of L'Anse aux Meadows.

Need to know: Newfoundland has its own time zone, which is 30min ahead of Atlantic Standard Time.

Other months: Apr – mild, icebergs, whales arrive; Jun-Aug – warmest, peak whales; Sep-Oct – autumn colours, cooling; Nov-Mar – cold, snow activities possible.

(L) Sperm whale fluke off the Newfoundland coast; (R) Twillingate iceberg

QUEENSLAND
AUSTRALIA

 Why now? Ride vintage rails through the tropics.

Slow travel is the best travel, which makes this classic Queensland rail ride great indeed, as it's certainly in no rush. The silver-bullet-style 1960s rolling stock of the Savannahlander train chugs unhurriedly between Cairns and Forsayth, through the rainforest-cloaked Kuranda range to the Outback. It's a leisurely journey, with no fixed seating and a laidback schedule – it's not uncommon for the driver to stop for cattle on the line or to admire wildlife spotted outside the window. The Savannahlander makes its 850km (528 miles) return trip once a week between March and November – though May is a first-class choice, being the start of the dry season: little rain, fractionally cooler climes (28°C/82°F) but landscapes that are still rampantly green.

Trip plan: The Cairns-Forsayth round trip takes four days, including optional side tours to Undara Lava Tubes, Cobbold Gorge and the Chillagoe Caves. It's possible to combine the Savannahlander with the 1950s carriages of the Gulflander (aka the 'Tin Hare'), which runs Normanton-Croydon (bus transfers link the two train routes).

Need to know: There are no sleeping cars on the Savannahlander – passengers spend nights in towns along the line (Almaden, Forsayth and Mt Surprise) while the train waits at the station.

Other months: Nov-Apr – hot, wet; Jun-Oct – drier, cooler.

Crossing Queensland aboard the Savannahlander

Cold War memorial along
the EuroVelo route at
Mikulov, Czech Republic

© Vladiczech / Shutterstock

IRON CURTAIN TRAIL EUROPE

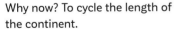

→ Why now? To cycle the length of the continent.

The Iron Curtain – the ideological barrier erected in the aftermath of WWII – cut Europe into East and West for almost 50 years, running from the Black Sea to the Barents Sea. Now, the 9950km-long (6183 miles) EuroVelo 13 cycle trail retraces this divide, providing a slowly unfurling history lesson and a whole lot of scenery as it winds up from Bulgaria and the Balkans through Austria, the Czech Republic and Germany, into the Baltics

and Finland, finishing in the Arctic Circle – in total it passes 20 countries. It's a huge challenge, so best to set off in the best weather: heading north in spring will ensure you reach the Arctic before the snow starts.

Trip plan: The southern trailhead is at Rezovo, near the Turkish border, on Bulgaria's Black Sea coast. The route finishes at Grense-Jakobselv, near the Norwegian town of Kirkenes. Allow three months. Interesting shorter, fully waymarked sections include the 400km (248 miles) Austrian route, which includes

Cold War reminders, the Danube, Bratislava (Slovakia) and Sopron (Hungary).

Need to know: For inspiration, read *The Cyclist Who Went Out in the Cold*, Tim Moore's account of riding the Iron Curtain Trail (he set out, southbound, in the Arctic winter).

Other months: Oct-Mar – very cold in far north, snow; Apr & Jun – spring, warm, good for starting northbound ride; Jul-Sep – hottest, best start window for southbound cycle.

121

MURCIA
SPAIN

→ **Why now? To eat *really* well.**
As you might expect from the name, there isn't really a bad time to visit the Costa Cálida (the 'Warm Coast'). But balmy, sunny May, with average highs of around 25°C (77°F), is a good time to get a real flavour of the place before summer crowds arrive. And the flavours are exceptional: surrounded by hills, vineyards, olive groves, fertile gardens and rich seas, the region is renowned for its quality meat, fruit, veg and fish – so much so it was designated Spanish Capital of Gastronomy 2021. Regional specialities to look out for include *caldero del mar menor*, a cauldron-cooked rice stew traditionally made by fishermen from catch too small to sell; and *paparajotes*, battered and fried lemon leaves. Tapas trails can be followed in both regional capital Murcia and the historic port of Cartagena (also home to a Roman theatre and museum of underwater archaeology).

Trip plan: Spend a week grazing around Murcia and Cartagena as well as hiking and biking the forest trails in Sierra Espuña Regional Park and relaxing on the Costa Cálida's long, sandy beaches.

Need to know: Buses (45min) and trains (1hr) connect the two cities.

Other months: Dec-Mar – mild; Apr & Jun – sunny, warm; Jul-Aug – hot, busy; Sep-Nov – mild, quiet.

CHOBE & THE OKAVANGO
BOTSWANA

→ **Why now? For a dry, healthy wildlife wonderland.**

May means all change in northern Botswana. It's the start of the dry, cool season, when the landscape is still verdant from the previous months' rains but the skies are increasingly cloud-free. Also, the wildlife – looking fit and healthy, thanks to all the water – gradually becomes more active as temperatures drop. Prices and numbers of tourists are lower than the coming peak months too, adding extra attraction to *mokoro* (traditional canoe) trips along the fingery tributaries of the Okavango Delta and game drives in Chobe National Park, where wildlife, including huge herds of elephants, is starting to gather at the riverbanks.

Trip plan: Chobe and the Okavango make a good combination. Allow at least ten days to make the most of both, taking boat, canoe and 4WD safaris, learning to fish and visiting local villages. Consider staying on a private concession in the Okavango, where more activities (including night drives and walking safaris) will be permitted.

Need to know: Floodwaters begin to fill the northwest of the Okavango Delta from April and steadily flow southeast – some areas don't see water until August, which effects *mokoro* trips in those areas.

Other months: Dec-Mar – wet, hot; Apr – some rain, green, hot; Jun-Aug – dry, cool; Sep-Nov – dry, hot.

EAST COAST
THAILAND

→ **Why now? Relax on the right coast.**

May in Thailand is marvellous for crowd-free beach escapes, so long as you pick wisely. The west coast – including Phuket and Krabi – can be damp, as the southwest monsoon starts. But over on the east, the likes of Ko Samui, Khanom and Ko Pha-Ngan are hot, largely dry and free of crowds: just right for a restorative break. Thailand in general and Ko Samui in particular – with its gentle vibe, spiritual heritage, healthy food and glorious nature – has garnered quite a reputation for quality wellness retreats; the offerings vary but range from pilates and meditation to Thai boxing and sleep therapy. In mid-season May you might find cheaper prices at high-end places. Or book a simple bungalow and put together your own wellness stay: visit the Big Buddha at Bo Phut; swim at Na Muang waterfall; cruise around Ang Thong Marine National Park; and do yoga on the beach.

Trip plan: Flights from Bangkok to Ko Samui take from 1hr 15min. Alternatively, take a sleeper train to Surat Thani and a bus to Don Sak, from where ferries run to the island.

Need to know: Add on Ko Tao, for excellent diving; the catamaran from Samui to Ko Tao takes about 2hr.

Other months: Oct-Dec – northeast monsoon, wettest; Jan-Apr – warm, dry, peak season across Thailand; Jun – hot, dry across Gulf, wet elsewhere; Jul-Sep – rains peak elsewhere, drier across Gulf.

Elephans bathe in an Okavango Delta tributary near Chobe, Botswana

© LouieLea / Shutterstock

123

VIA FRANCIGENA
UK TO ITALY

→ **Why now? To make a historic walk with the weather.**

Setting off on the Via Francigena – the 2000km (1243 mile) Christian pilgrimage trail linking Canterbury and Rome – requires serious planning. Longer and less-trodden than Spain's busy Camino de Santiago, the journey follows in the footsteps of Bishop Sigeric the Serious, who walked the route in the 10th century. It leaves England's White Cliffs for the Somme battlefields and Champagne vineyards of France, Lake Geneva and the Swiss Alps, and covers half the length of Italy. It'll be a challenge no matter what – it takes most hikers around 100 days – but starting in late May should help a little: spring-time climes to begin, summer and snow-free passes in the mountains, hot but eventually turning autumnal in Italy.

Trip plan: The route starts at Canterbury Cathedral and finishes at St Peter's Basilica in Rome. It uses mostly well-defined paths, and is signposted the whole way. There is a variety of accommodation en route, from campsites to monasteries.

Need to know: Order a pilgrim passport from the Confraternity of Pilgrims to Rome and collect stamps as you go; you'll need this document to stay at pilgrim accommodation and to qualify for a certificate on completion.

Other months: Nov-Mar – cold, snow in mountains; Apr & Jun – warm, best starting window; Jul-Aug – hot; Sep-Oct – warm, too late for full route.

Via Francigena passing through Aosta Valley, Italy

© Ken Scicluna / AWL Images Ltd

© milosk50 / Shutterstock

Xunantunich, just one of Belize's impressive Maya ruins

BELIZE

Why now? Encounter marine giants and Maya monuments in dry weather.

Diminutive Belize packs a big punch. Only about 290km (180 miles) long, and with English the official language, it's a cinch to hop between its ancient Maya ruins, wildlife-rich tropical forests, living Maya communities and the cays and atolls of the world's second-longest barrier reef, offering gorgeous beaches and fabulous snorkelling. May's a sweet spot for weather and wildlife, when the sun shines, whale sharks – the world's biggest fish (growing to 12m/39ft long) – cruise near Gladden Spit, and nesting green, hawksbill and loggerhead turtles lumber onto beaches on Glover's Reef and Ambergris Caye. In the north, explore relatively little-visited temples at jungle-set sites such as Xunantunich and Lamanai; today, the descendants of the ancient Maya who built these monuments live in villages around Toledo, where they welcome visitors to immersive homestays.

Trip plan: From Belize City, head west to explore Maya sites such as Lamanai and Xunantunich, veer south to spot wildlife in Cockscomb Basin Forest Reserve and meet the modern Maya around Toledo, then snorkel, dive and chill on Glover's Reef and Ambergris Caye.

Need to know: The famous Blue Hole – a perfectly round sinkhole in the sea beyond the cays – offers amazing diving, but is really suitable only for scuba enthusiasts with experience of deep dives.

Other months: Dec-Apr – relatively dry, warm, whale sharks arrive Apr; Jun-Nov – wetter but still warm.

BELFAST & THE CAUSEWAY COAST
NORTHERN IRELAND

Why now? Rowdy times, both arty and avian.

Belfast is buzzing. In the past few decades, the industrial city has had a makeover: its old docks have been transformed (and are now home to the striking Titanic Museum) and its Cathedral Quarter has been rebranded as a cultural hub – especially in May, when a ten-day Arts Festival brings masses of music, drama, street theatre and more to the district. Mild, spring-flush May is also a good time to take in the popular sights of the Causeway Coast, before the school holidays begin in June. Make a road trip via the remarkable rocks of the Giant's Causeway, Glenarm and Dunluce castles, the Carrick-a-Rede Rope Bridge and tiny Rathlin Island where, from April to July, puffins join a host of other seabirds.

Trip plan: Spend two days in Belfast – soak up culture in the Cathedral Quarter, sink a few pints in the fine Victorian pubs, visit the Ulster Museum and Botanic Gardens, and climb Cave Hill. Then head north, for five or so days on the Causeway Coast.

Need to know: Belfast to Ballycastle is a 1hr 10min drive. Ferries from Ballycastle to Rathlin take from 25min; cars are restricted on the island – travel as a foot passenger or with a bike.

Other months: Oct-Mar – cool, damp; Apr & Jun – spring, warm, fairly dry, birds; Jul-Sep – warmest, busiest.

EYRE PENINSULA
SOUTH AUSTRALIA

Lake MacDonnell in the pink, thanks to salt-loving algae

➜ **Why now? To be part of the wildest gathering.**

The odds of exceptional wildlife encounters are high on the Eyre Peninsula, the wild cape dangling down at the eastern end of the Great Australian Bight. It's dotted with national parks and conservation areas where there are few people but *a lot* of creatures – from yellow-footed rock wallabies and wedge-tailed eagles to sea lions and dolphins. The local population is bolstered in May, when southern right whales start migrating past the coast and giant cuttlefish arrive – this is the only spot on the planet where these massive molluscs are known to gather en masse. Swim with them at Whyalla before continuing around the peninsula, stopping to meet great white sharks at Port Lincoln (the only place in the country where you can cage dive, if you dare), be dazzled by magenta-pink Lake MacDonnell, take eco-boat trips into Baird Bay and whale-watch at the Head of Bight.

Trip plan: Whyalla is a 4hr drive from Adelaide. A full Eyre roadtrip, from Whylla to the Head of Bight, will take at least eight days.

Need to know: More than 65% of Australia's seafood comes from the waters off the Eyre Peninsula. Eat exquisite oysters, and tour the oyster beds, at Coffin Bay.

Other months: Dec-Feb – hot, busiest; Mar-Apr – mild, quieter, cuttlefish (May-Aug); Jun-Aug – cool, whales; Sep-Nov – warm.

© f11photo / Shutterstock

Memphis' Sun Studios, birthplace of American rock'n'roll

MEMPHIS USA

 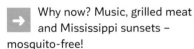

→ **Why now? Music, grilled meat and Mississippi sunsets – mosquito-free!**

Memphis is less like a city, more like a religion. People come to pay homage in the spiritual home of the blues, rock'n'roll, Elvis Presley and Memphis-style barbecue. In short, it's a feast for ears, bellies and souls. Spring sees the Tennessee city at its tastiest: good weather, before summer's sticky, buggy heat; plus the Memphis in May festival, incorporating the Beale Street Music Festival, the World Championship Barbecue Cooking Contest, the Great American River Run and more. There are sites aplenty: take a tour of legendary Sun Studio; visit the National Civil Rights Museum (part housed inside the Lorraine Motel, where Martin Luther King Jr was shot in 1968); and, of course, make a pilgrimage to Graceland, Elvis' uber-kitsch home. Also, explore once down-at-heel neighbourhoods like South Main and Crosstown, where quirky stores, microbreweries and hipster hangouts are injecting new life.

Trip plan: Allow three days in the city. The centre is compact – walk or use the vintage Main Street Trolley. Combine Memphis with Nashville and New Orleans on a week-long musical road trip.

Need to know: Graceland is 15km (9 miles) south of downtown Memphis on US 51 (aka Elvis Presley Blvd). A free shuttlebus runs there from Sun Studio.

Other months: Mar-Apr & Sept-Oct – mild; Jun-Aug – hottest, humid; Nov-Feb – cooler, wettest.

127

June

WHERE TO GO WHEN

I WANT TO

CHALLENGE MYSELF →

TAKE ME OUT FOR...

FOOD
- • SICILY, ITALY P133
- • CAPE COD, USA P135

Find food heaven in Sicily, from ricotta-filled *cannoli* to chickpea *panelle*

DRINK — • SHETLAND, SCOTLAND P138

Banish the Shetland breezes with a wee dram of fine whisky

TAKE ME SOMEWHERE...

WARM — • GDAŃSK, POLAND P135

WARMER — • AVEIRO & COIMBRA, PORTUGAL P149

Enjoy architecture and urban verve in Gdańsk

Find Polynesian paradise in tropical Bora Bora

RELAX/ INDULGE

Dive into a protected underwater wonderland in the Bazaruto Archipelago

TAKE ME TO THE BEACH

REV UP
- • PAYS DE LA LOIRE, FRANCE P141
- • TORRES STRAIT ISLANDS, AUSTRALIA P139

CHILL OUT
- • BAZARUTO ARCHIPELAGO, MOZAMBIQUE P140
- • BORA BORA, FRENCH POLYNESIA P137

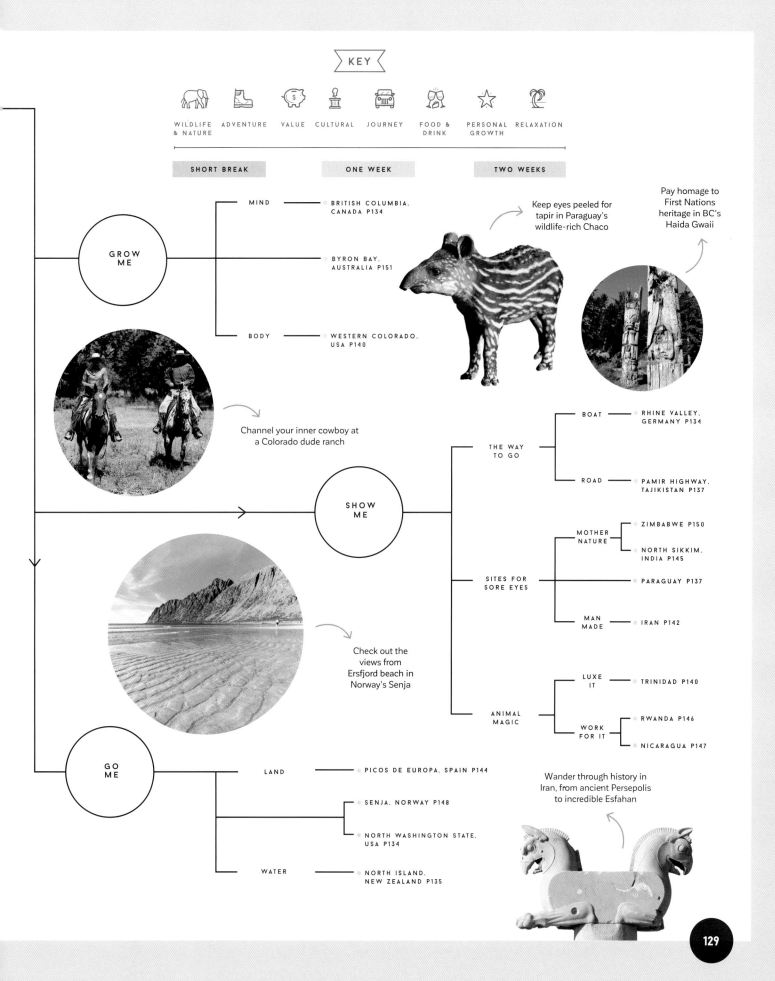

WILDLIFE & NATURE   ADVENTURE   VALUE   CULTURAL   JOURNEY   FOOD & DRINK   PERSONAL GROWTH   RELAXATION

SHORT BREAK   ONE WEEK   TWO WEEKS

GROW ME

MIND — BRITISH COLUMBIA, CANADA P134

BYRON BAY, AUSTRALIA P151

BODY — WESTERN COLORADO, USA P140

Keep eyes peeled for tapir in Paraguay's wildlife-rich Chaco

Pay homage to First Nations heritage in BC's Haida Gwaii

Channel your inner cowboy at a Colorado dude ranch

SHOW ME

THE WAY TO GO
BOAT — RHINE VALLEY, GERMANY P134
ROAD — PAMIR HIGHWAY, TAJIKISTAN P137

MOTHER NATURE
ZIMBABWE P150
NORTH SIKKIM, INDIA P145

SITES FOR SORE EYES — PARAGUAY P137

MAN MADE — IRAN P142

ANIMAL MAGIC
LUXE IT — TRINIDAD P140
WORK FOR IT
RWANDA P146
NICARAGUA P147

Check out the views from Ersfjord beach in Norway's Senja

GO ME

LAND — PICOS DE EUROPA, SPAIN P144

SENJA, NORWAY P148

NORTH WASHINGTON STATE, USA P134

WATER — NORTH ISLAND, NEW ZEALAND P135

Wander through history in Iran, from ancient Persepolis to incredible Esfahan

EVENTS
IN JUNE

BOI-BUMBÁ

Parintins, Brazil
A local legend about a resurrected cow is retold competitively during three days (and nights) of music, dance, parades and partying.

FESTA DO SÃO JOÃO

Porto, Portugal
Thousands flock to the centre of Portugal's second city for a midsummer festival with music, dancing, sardine-snacking and fireworks.

WORLD FESTIVAL OF SACRED MUSIC

Fez, Morocco
World-renowned musicians and poets perform in the extraordinary medieval city, exploring traditions of spirituality and art.

INTI RAYMI

Sacsayhuamán, Peru
All hail the sun god! This annual festival re-enacts five-century-old Inca traditions among vast, ancient ruins on the outskirts of Cusco.

OKAVANGO FLOODS

Okavango Delta, Botswana
Rains in the Angolan highlands surge south into Botswana – making this the best time for mokoro (dugout canoe) safaris amid profuse wildlife.

QUEENSTOWN WINTER FESTIVAL

Queenstown, New Zealand
A packed schedule of snowsports and other more unusual activities, plus free music and full-on partying.

REGATTA OF ST RANIERI

Pisa, Italy
Crews representing the four quarters of this historic Tuscan city compete in a boat race in honour of Pisa's patron saint.

DRAGON BOAT FESTIVAL

China
Enjoying a public holiday, Chinese people feast on zongzi (rice dumplings), drink xionghuangjiu (realgar wine) and – yes – race dragon boats.

Last weekend in June · $$

24 Jun · $

May to Aug, depending on rains and location · $$$

Late June · $$

23 and 24 June · $

Mid-June · $$

June (date varies) · $$

17 June · $$

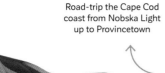

BYRON BAY, AUSTRALIA

Road-trip the Cape Cod coast from Nobska Light up to Provincetown

CAPE COD, USA

WESTERN COLORADO, USA

Strike a (yoga) pose on the sand or have a swell time out on Byron Bay's breaks

Look beyond the Loire's chateaux to less visited spots like Guérande

PAYS DE LA LOIRE, FRANCE

BRITISH COLUMBIA, CANADA

PICOS DE EUROPA, SPAIN

NORTH WASHINGTON STATE, USA

Hike summertime Picos de Europa trails and spot birds of prey on the way

AVEIRO & COIMBRA, PORTUGAL

NORTH ISLAND, NEW ZEALAND

Paddle out into orca territory from Washington's San Juan Islands

Survey Coimbra from its hilltop university

TRINIDAD

BORA BORA, FRENCH POLYNESIA

SENJA, NORWAY

GDAŃSK, POLAND

SICILY, ITALY

NICARAGUA

TORRES STRAIT ISLANDS, AUSTRALIA

Seek out squawking seabird colonies in Shetland

Savour authentic *arancini* in sun-soaked Sicily

Go off-grid in the pristine Torres archipelago

SHETLAND, SCOTLAND

ZIMBABWE

BAZARUTO ARCHIPELAGO, MOZAMBIQUE

Go big in Zimbabwe, from game-spotting to mighty Victoria Falls

PARAGUAY

IRAN

Write yourself into a Rhine Valley fairytale at stately Schloss Stolzenfels

NORTH SIKKIM, INDIA

Espy iconic Islamic architecture in Iran's Esfahan

RWANDA

RHINE VALLEY, GERMANY

PAMIR HIGHWAY, TAJIKISTAN

SICILY ITALY

Why now? Feast on fine food and wine.

The largest Mediterranean island is – excuse the travel cliché – a true cultural crossroads: ancient Greeks and Arabs, medieval Normans, Spanish and English conquerors, colonisers and visitors all left their marks here. This mixed heritage is evident in Sicily's extraordinary historic sites: the ancient Hellenic and Roman monuments of Agrigento, Siracusa and Taormina; Palermo's Norman palace and nearby cathedral at Monreale – all less crowded before the peak of July and August, yet delightfully warm for wandering. But it also inflects the island's distinctive cuisine. On a culinary circumnavigation, savour hints of North Africa in oranges and couscous. Devour tuna, anchovies and sardines, and snack on *arancini* (filled, fried rice balls), *cazzilli* (potato croquettes) and *panelle* (chickpea fritters). Look for teardrop-shaped *caciocavallo* and sheep's milk ricotta cheeses, the latter stuffed into pastry tubes for sweet *cannoli*. And sip excellent Corvo, Regaleali and sweet Malvasia and Marsala wines.

Trip plan: Airports at Palermo, Catania, Trapani and Comiso receive international flights, or arrive by train across the Strait of Messina. Buses (and slower, less widespread trains) serve most coastal destinations; exploring is easier with a car. Allow at least a week to get a taste of the island.

Need to know: Ferries to the Aeolian Islands, with their rich culinary pickings, sail frequently from Milazzo.

Other months: Nov-Feb – cool, quiet, many coastal resorts closed; Mar-Apr – spring, almond blossoms, pleasant; May – warm, prices moderate; Jul-Aug – hot, beaches and historical sites crowded; Sep-Oct – getting cooler, good value.

(L) Monreale and its Norman cathedral; (R) Ricotta-filled *cannoli*

RHINE VALLEY
GERMANY

→ **Why now?** Sail beneath rock-top bastions, vineyards and medieval villages in the sunniest month.

On a castles-per-kilometre basis, few journeys hold a candle to the Rhine – particularly the gorge between Bingen and Koblenz. This most dramatic stretch is guarded by a succession of medieval fortifications in various states of romantic decay and magnificent restoration. There's Schloss Stolzenfels, a near-Neuschwanstein fairytale confection of turrets and crenellated walls; the mid-river toll-castle, Pfalzgrafenstein; ruined Burg Rheinfels, with its labyrinthine tunnels; and Burg Rheinstein, with its drawbridge and portcullis. Between them lie postcard-pretty villages of half-timbered houses – Rüdesheim, Bacharach, St Goar, Boppard – and the Lorelei rock, of singing siren fame. Sure, you won't be alone in June – but with the sun sparkling on the water, and a glass of local Riesling in hand, why worry?

Trip plan: Rhine cruises take about a week to sail between Basel and Amsterdam via Strasbourg, Speyer, Mainz, the gorge, Koblenz and Cologne.

Need to know: The Moselle, a tributary of the Rhine, is also lined with vines and studded with castles, but less touristed – hiking, cycling or navigating its course is a good alternative or addition. If a full-on multi-day cruise isn't for you, buy a hop-on-hop-off one-day ticket for KD Line (k-d.com) boats sailing between between Mainz and Koblenz, and fill in the gaps with efficient trains.

Other months: Nov-Mar – cold, often grey, some tourist facilities closed; Apr-May & Oct: mild, quiet; Jul-Sep – warm, busy, festivals.

BRITISH COLUMBIA
CANADA

→ **Why now?** Absorb authentic First Nations experiences.

Warm, pre-peak-season June is Canada's National Indigenous History Month, culminating with Indigenous Peoples Day on the 21st – visit now to immerse yourself in the cultural heritage of its First Nations, Inuit and Métis peoples. Indigenous tourism is burgeoning wonderfully in Canada, not least in British Columbia: there are more than 200 First Nations communities that call the province home, and a multitude of ways of discovering their cultures, from stays at Indigenous-owned wilderness lodges to traditional wellness breaks and Pow Wows (in situations when visitors are welcomed). The remote, mystical Haida Gwaii archipelago, off the far northern coast, is the place to engage with Haida people: stay at a float lodge amid the forest, walk to age-old totem poles with Haida elders, visit the Haida Heritage Centre and watch for whales – numbers peak here in early June.

Trip plan: Ferries run to Haida Gwaii from Prince Rupert on the BC mainland (6hr). There are also flights between Vancouver and Sandspit on Haida Gwaii (2hr). Join a tour with an Indigenous-owned operator or hire a car.

Need to know: Add on Indigenous experiences in Vancouver – explore sprawling Stanley Park (former site of the Xwayxway First Nations village), visit the Museum of Anthropology and shop at the Bill Reid Gallery of Northwest Coast Art.

Other months: Dec-Mar – freezing; Apr-May – warming, uncrowded; Jul-Aug – warmest, busiest; Sep-Nov – quiet, autumn colours.

NORTH WASHINGTON STATE USA

→ **Why now?** Kayak with killer whales and trek epic trails in an adventure-seeker's nirvana.

This month in Washington the stars align – the sun shines more, the days are longer and warmer (around 22-25°C/72-77°F) and cetacean sightings soar, yet trails and accommodations are yet to get summer-busy. And some of those constellations shine from below: the bioluminescence that sparkles in the waters of the Salish Sea in summer months is one more reason to take to the waters around the San Juan Islands. Join a sea-kayaking tour for the best chances of paddling alongside orca foraging for salmon in these nutrient-rich waters, not to mention porpoises, seals and bald eagles; minke and humpback whales fin here, too. Back on land, hikers are spoilt for choice among the old-growth temperate rainforest, ice-scoured peaks and wild coast of Olympic National Park, spanning over 3700 sq km (1428 sq miles).

Trip plan: From Seattle, head west to explore the wilds of the Olympic Peninsula before recrossing Puget Sound to paddle the San Juan Islands; add more time on the trails around glaciated volcanic Mt Baker in the North Cascades, and toast your trip among the craft breweries of lively student town Bellingham.

Need to know: Bioluminescence in the Salish Sea is most commonly encountered after hot, sunny days and around full moon.

Other months: Oct-Apr – cool, rain peaking midwinter; May – warmer, drier, still lush; Jul-Sep – busier, hotter.

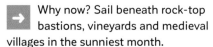

© Markus Thompson / 500px

NORTH ISLAND
NEW ZEALAND

→ **Why now? Warm up in natural hot springs on a winter road trip.**

New Zealand in winter, without the skiing – why? Trust us: the North Island has not just one but a string of secret weapons that make an off-season road trip a treat. There's the geothermal activity which has created bubbling, steaming pools in which to soak. There's the surf, at its biggest and most reliable at Raglan. Caves don't care about winter – the temperature's the same year-round, and Waitomo's famous constellations of glowworms keep a-glowing. For a handy join-the-dots route between North Island hotspots, drive the Thermal Explorer Highway between Auckland and Napier. Detouring to ride the left-hand break at Raglan and float through the Waitomo Caves, browse your way through Hamilton, discover Māori culture and take a hot-spring dip in Rotorua, gawp at Orakei Korako's cave and geothermal park, admire Napier's Art Deco architecture and taste the finest drops from the Hawke's Bay wineries – all without the crowds of summer.

Trip plan: Allow at least four days for the drive from Auckland to Napier, plus extra for detours.

Need to know: Most New Zealand ski areas open in July, but Happy Valley on Mt Ruapehu welcomes snowhounds from early June.

Other months: Dec-Feb – warm, drier, very popular; Mar-May – autumn colours, cooler weather, lower prices; Jul-Aug – cold, more rain (snow on mountains), skiing, crowds and prices fall; Sep-Nov – warming, good rafting and trekking weather.

CAPE COD
USA

→ **Why now? Celebrate sun, sea and sand (and seafood).**

If you're fond of sand dunes and salty air, try New England's favourite seaside destination. The flexed arm of Cape Cod is lined with beaches, cutesy towns, oysters, clams and lobster rolls – no wonder millions flock here each year. Most, though, come in July and August; after Memorial Day the crowds thin, making June a delicious month to visit, with more chance of bagging accommodation and finding space on a beach. Not that it's too quiet: the month is peppered with events celebrating the arts (including Provincetown International Film Festival). Trace an arc around the Cape by car, pausing at the pretty harbours and heading out on a whale-watching cruise; or cycle the 40km (25 miles) Cape Cod Rail Trail between South Dennis and Wellfleet.

Trip plan: Cape Cod is easiest to access from Boston: flights serve Provincetown and Hyannis, fast ferries connect Boston and Provincetown several times daily in summer, and buses and a weekend train link Boston with Hyannis.

Need to know: Even in June, it pays to book accommodation well in advance.

Other months: Jul-Sep – summer; Oct-Nov & Apr-May – shoulder season; Dec-Mar – winter, cheaper, some facilities closed.

GDAŃSK
POLAND

→ **Why now? Discover golden treasures galore: sands, amber and rich history.**

Perched in a sheltered spot on the Baltic at the mouth of the Vistula River, the city currently known as Gdańsk has attracted visitors – welcome and otherwise – for over 1000 years: Bohemians, Teutonic Knights, the Hanseatic League, and Prussians (later, Germans) who knew it as Danzig. They left a magnificent historic core, packed with Renaissance architecture lovingly restored after WWII devastation: stroll the Royal Way to admire magnificent townhouses, city gates and churches, and shop for some of the fine amber for which the city has long been famous. That gold-tinged jewellery isn't the only thing that glints in warm June sunshine. The sandy beaches of Sopot, the leisure element of the tri-city conurbation of Gdańsk, beckon from just a few kilometres to the north, together with a host of lively bars and nightclubs – still fairly calm before the densest crowds of high summer arrive.

Trip plan: Spend a couple of days exploring the city's old sections, plus a day (and night) at the coast in Sopot. If possible, add more days to explore northern Pomerania – at least as far as the enormous fortress at Malbork, Europe's largest Gothic castle.

Need to know: Don't leave Gdańsk without tasting its most unusual drink – Goldwasser, an aniseedy liqueur gleaming with flecks of real gold leaf.

Other months: Dec-Feb – very cold, picturesque in snow; Mar-Apr & Oct-Nov – cool, quiet; Jun-Sep – warm, busy events calendar.

BORA BORA
FRENCH POLYNESIA

Why now? Relax in a tropical paradise in the balmiest season.

Blue, turquoise, azure, teal, indigo… there aren't enough words to describe the hues of the Pacific Ocean around French Polynesia on a clear, calm, sunny day. And there are plenty of those in June, the start of the driest season, when the main island of Bora Bora and its *motu* (ringing islands) bask in temperatures of around 25-30°C (77-86°F). This is the stuff of movies, with luxurious resorts perched over the crystal waters, shaded by swaying palms – and you need to be a film star to afford the prices at the very top hotels and resorts, though more modest accommodation can be found. As if the scenery wasn't paradisiacal enough, the snorkelling and diving, over coral gardens and with sharks and rays, is spectacular.

Trip plan: Bora Bora receives several flights daily from Tahiti, and a few from Huahine, Mo'orea, Maupiti and Ra'iatea. Try to get a seat on the left of the plane for the best views.

Need to know: Book well at this busy time of year. Later in July (when the traditional Heiva i Bora Bora festival is held) and August, are the most popular months.

Other months: Jul-Aug – driest, busiest; May & Sep-Oct – higher humidity, better availability, lower prices; Nov-Apr – wet season, high humidity.

(A) Idyllic Bora Bora bungalow; (L) Pamir Highway views; (R) Ruined Jesuit mission in Trinidad, Paraguay

PAMIR HIGHWAY
TAJIKISTAN

Why now? Drive one of the world's greatest but least-travelled road trips.

The 'Stan that travel (mostly) forgot is a land of snow-leopard-prowled, sky-scraping peaks (over 90% of Tajikistan is mountainous) and of Silk Road-era fortifications. Visit while it's still a tourism *terra incognita* to enjoy its epic landscapes and historic sites by yourself, traversing the prosaically named M41 road – better known as the Pamir Highway. Devised as part of the 'Great Game' political shenanigans between Britain and Russia in the 19th century, this unforgettable high-level odyssey snakes roughly east from capital Dushanbe through its namesake Pamir Mountains, past ancient ruby mines, canyons and lakes, fortresses of the Panj Valley and remote villages – homestays provide insights into the culture of Persian-speaking Tajik people. By June the mountain air is clear and cool, wildflowers bloom and snow's cleared from trekking trails.

Trip plan: Dushanbe receives few long-haul flights, most usefully from Moscow, İstanbul and Dubai. Hire a local guide, driver and 4WD vehicle, allowing at least a week to drive the Pamir Highway.

Need to know: Some border regions sometimes suffer security problems – check the current situation, and visa requirements, with your government and tour operator. Bring clothing for all weather conditions, which change rapidly.

Other months: Dec-Feb – very cold; Mar-May – wildflowers, pleasant in valleys, still snow in mountains; Jul-Sep – Pamirs comfortable, roads clear, lowlands scorching; Oct-Nov – snow may close mountain roads, lowlands pleasant with autumn colours.

PARAGUAY

Why now? Discover South America's wild, historic heart.

Leave any preconceptions about Paraguay at the check-in desk – if you have any: few people know much about this diverse landlocked nation, and fewer still have visited. Today, though tourism infrastructure is still sparse, this friendly country is emerging from a period tainted by a reputation for poverty, crime and unrest. June, when the climate is dry, temperatures moderate and before July heralds holiday season, is the time to explore the Spanish colonial architecture of capital Asunción and to delve into the Chaco. A vast, semi-arid region of marshes, saltwater lagoons, palm forests and savannah punctuated by cacti the size of houses, this 'Green Inferno' is home to native Guaraní people, Mennonite communities and a dizzying array of birdlife; if you're lucky, you might also spot caiman, tapir and giant anteater. In the south, tour the historic towns and ruined red sandstone *reductions* (missions) of San Ignacio Guazú, Trinidad and Jesús, founded by Jesuits in the 17th and 18th centuries.

Trip plan: From Asunción, book a guided tour north to the Chaco then sweep back south to explore the Jesuit Missions. Allow a week to ten days.

Need to know: Although Iguazú Falls – by some measures, the world's largest, sweeping in a 2.7km-wide (1.6 miles) arc – straddles the Brazilian-Argentine border, it's easily accessed from Paraguay via the crossing at Encarnación, providing a dramatic climax to a trip.

Other months: Dec-Feb – very hot, humid; Mar-May – temperatures dropping; Jul-Sep – relatively cool; Oct-Nov – getting hot.

Bring binoculars
to zoom in on
Shetland puffins

© Mark Caunt / Shutterstock

SHETLAND SCOTLAND

➜ **Why now?** Roam the UK's northernmost wilds and sip Scotch in endless summer days.

Closer to Bergen than Edinburgh, the 100-plus Shetland Islands in the North Atlantic have a distinctly Nordic flavour – indeed, they were Norwegian till 1469. Come in June, when the sun barely sets, to hike windswept hills and coast; to discover the deafening seabird colonies of Sumburgh Head, Fair Isle, Foula and Noss, bustling with thousands of breeding puffins, kittiwakes, guillemots, gannets and more; and to explore the islands' 5000 years of human occupation at the enigmatic *broch* (stone tower) of Mousa and turf-clad ruins of Jarlshof. The weather can turn without warning but if clouds gather, retreat to sparky capital Lerwick's fine museum or one of its tempting bars – a

traditional fiddle tune and a dram of local whisky should warm your cockles: Shetland Reel, on Unst, is Scotland's northernmost (legal) distillery.

Trip plan: Sumburgh Airport receives flights from mainland Scottish cities and Kirkwall in Orkney. Ferries sail to Lerwick from Aberdeen and Kirkwall, as well as between islands in the archipelago. Hire a car or join a guided tour to explore, allowing at least a week.

Need to know: Though not quite as plagued by midges as some mainland spots, Shetland's biting population can be voracious in summer when the wind drops. Bring repellent.

Other months: Nov-Mar – cold, dark, short, often wet days. Apr-May – warmer, dry-ish; Jul-Aug – long days, balmy, busiest; Sep-Oct – cooler, wetter.

TORRES STRAIT
ISLANDS AUSTRALIA

→ **Why now?** Discover a unique culture and art, and relax on peaceful beaches.

Sprinkled across the strait separating Papua New Guinea from the Cape York Peninsula lie dozens of tropical specks; most are uninhabited, and even those with permanent populations could hardly be called bustling – perfect for getting off-grid and discovering a unique indigenous heritage. Make the hop across from Queensland in the balmy days of June to explore the archipelago's pearl-fishing history, hike among WWII fortifications on Horn and Goods islands, visit Gab Titui Cultural Centre – showcasing the Torres Strait Islands' Melanesian-inflected art and culture – and laze on unspoilt beaches lapped by pellucid waters. A favourite spot for lounging is the sweep of sand at the western tip of Friday Island, where you can enjoy some of the archipelago's renowned fishing and visit Kazu Pearl Farm to savour great Japanese food. Cool off with a beer at Australia's northernmost bar, the Torres Hotel on Thursday Island.

Trip plan: Horn Island is served by flights from Cairns, while boats sail (usually daily during the Dry) from Seisia on Cape York to Thursday Island. Ferries link Horn and Thursday, and water taxis zip between other islands.

Need to know: Though English is widely spoken, you'll also hear words of Torres Strait Creole – *eso* means thank you, *wa* is yes, and *gud lak* is the equivalent of 'cheers!'

Other months: Nov-May – the 'Wet', humid, very hot, cyclones possibly (mainly Jan-Mar); Jun-Oct – the 'Dry', cooler.

Reef-fringed islands in the Torres Strait archipelago

TRINIDAD

→ **Why now?** Watch rare sea turtles nest on Caribbean shores.

Though the leatherback is the planet's heftiest turtle, weighing up to 700kg (1543lb), it's defenceless against the egg collection and fisheries bycatch that have ravaged populations – it's now classed as Vulnerable. So meeting this ancient creature is always special – and seeing dozens of females lumbering onto shore to lay hundreds of eggs is simply magical. During the peak nesting season (Mar-Jun), the beaches of Matura, Fishing Pond and, particularly, Grande Riviere in northern Trinidad host up to 500 egg-laying females each night – and in June (when World Sea Turtle Day is celebrated on the 16th) the hatchlings start to emerge, scuttling down to the sea to start the cycle again. Make a turtle encounter the centrepiece of a trip to this southeast Caribbean island, where, even though the rainy season is beginning, you can also enjoy plenty of warm sunshine, lively nightlife and festivals, and often lower prices (less so in Grande Riviere). Birdwatchers are in paradise, too, with several hotspots for spotting rare species.

Trip plan: From Piarco Airport, southeast of capital Port of Spain, head northeast to Matura and Grande Riviere, or trace the northwest coast for waterfalls, soft sand and bake'n'shark (fried fish and flatbread) at Maracas Beach. Veer north of Piarco into the Northern Range hills to Asa Wright Nature Centre (check opening details) for hummingbirds and west to Caroni Swamp for scarlet ibis.

Need to know: You'll need a permit for nighttime beach access at Grande Riviere, available locally.

Other months: Jan-May – warm, dry; Jul-Dec – rain, usually in afternoon downpours.

WESTERN COLORADO USA

→ **Why now?** Saddle up for ranch life and ecological renewal.

Whether the young you thrilled to the movies of Johns Ford and Wayne, hummed the themes of *Rawhide* or *Bonanza*, rooted for *Young Guns* or pondered the themes of more recent revisionist Westerns, the thrill of donning chaps, mounting a mustang and herding steers remains elemental for many of us. But like the themes and attitudes of those films and TV shows, ranching's evolved over the years. Today many outfits not only host urbanites looking to play out cowboy fantasies in 'dude ranches' – offering activities such as yoga, rafting, birdwatching, writing workshops and mountain-biking as well as the more-usual riding, hunting and fishing – but also embrace modern ideas of conservation and sustainability. Beat the high summer heat with a June vacation at one of Colorado's innovative ranches – perhaps Zapata or Chico Basin, where you can get hands on with the nitty-gritty of raising cattle and bison and learn how habitats are managed to protect biodiversity.

Trip plan: Ranches hosting guests are scattered throughout the mountains west of Hwy 25. Check eco and conservation credentials before booking.

Need to know: The level of riding and involvement with cattle varies between ranches and and time of year. The Colorado Dude & Guest Ranch Association website (coloradoranch.com) has details of member properties across the state.

Other months: Oct-Mar – cold, snow possible, many ranches close; Apr-May – cool, quiet; Jul-Sep – warm, most popular.

BAZARUTO ARCHIPELAGO MOZAMBIQUE

→ **Why now?** Dive and snorkel clear, warm, turquoise waters.

Are these the most beautiful tropical islands on Earth? The Bazaruto Archipelago faces stiff competition from other Indian Ocean destinations (and Mozambique's own Quirimbas Archipelago) – but wriggle your toes into the silky sand on a glorious June morning (prime dry season), or gaze through your mask at impossibly colourful reef fish, and maybe a humpback whale migrating past, and they could stake a fair claim. Much of this chain of five islands off Mozambique's southeastern coast is protected as a national park, conserving dolphins, dugongs, sea turtles and around 2000 fish species. Oh, and Nile crocodiles – but perhaps you're not so keen to see those. This is a paradise for divers, but also for anyone seeking a truly barefoot beach holiday.

Trip plan: Several islands have airstrips, and access is usually by plane or helicopter, speedboat or dhow from the mainland port of Vilankulo. Day trips from Vilankulo are possible but most visitors arrive on a package to one of the luxury lodges with an upmarket tour operator, often incorporating South Africa's Kruger National Park.

Need to know: Humpback whales migrate past the archipelago from June or July to September or October.

Other months: Jul-Oct – dry; Apr-May & Sep-Nov – best diving; Nov-Mar – rains build.

Ride the Grand Éléphant
at Les Machines de
l'Île de Nantes

PAYS DE LA LOIRE FRANCE

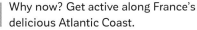

→ **Why now? Get active along France's delicious Atlantic Coast.**

The Loire? It's all chateaux and Chenin Blanc, right? Well, not quite. Head west and you'll discover another sparkling treat: the Atlantic, washing some 450km (280 miles) of coastline – about half of which comprises sandy beaches. Roam the shore of the Pays de la Loire in the warm, dry days of June, before the crowds of high summer descend, and you'll discover charming seaside villages such as Piriac, Guérande's medieval walled town, the cultural hub of Nantes – now famed for its huge puppet-automata machines – and, yes, chateaux. But you'll also find activities: sand-yachting at Saint-Jean-de-Monts, canoeing the Vendée marshes, snorkelling around Île d'Yeu, and foil-surfing and superb sailing at Les Sables d'Olonne, renowned as the startpoint of the Vendée Globe round-the-world solo race. Make time to sample the oysters of Île de Noirmoutier and sardines of Saint-Gilles-Croix-de-Vie, washed down with a fine Loire Muscadet.

Trip plan: Spend a day or two discovering Nantes' cultural gems, then head down the coast to try watersports and gorge on seafood.

Need to know: La Vélodyssée (cycling-lavelodyssee.com) is a cycle route of over 1200km (746 miles) along France's entire west coast, from Roscoff to Hendaye. The stretch through Loire Atlantique, around 330km (205 miles) from Nantes to La Rochelle, would make a fine tour of a week or so.

Other months: Dec-Feb – cool, quiet; Mar-May – warming, still relatively untouristy; Jun-Sep – warm, dry, busy (especially Aug); Oct-Nov – cool, some rain, peaceful.

© Jean-Dominique Billaud

141

IRAN

Why now? Explore ancient cities before the heat builds.

The land once called Persia is where misconceptions come to die. Political posturing wins column inches, but there are so many treasures that really deserve the headlines: the extraordinary Islamic architecture of Esfahan, with its intricate blue-patterned tiles; the huge, bustling bazaars of Tehran, Esfahan, Shiraz or Tabriz; the magnificent remains at Persepolis, dating back two-and-a-half millennia; the deserts; the poems; the food; and – most of all – the people. By June the mercury is rising fast at lower altitudes, but prices and crowds are dropping. Summer is also the season for hiking in the Alborz Mountains, particularly the ascent of Mt Damavand, a true icon of Iran.

Trip plan: Fly to Tehran, head south to the desert city of Yazd, the ancient ruins at Persepolis, sophisticated Shiraz and majestic Esfahan, before scooting up to the Alborz Mountains to tackle Mt Damavand and roam among the Castles of the Assassins.

Need to know: Most visitors require a visa – apply well before you intend to travel. Females over the age of nine should wear a headscarf in visa application photos. Check entry requirements and your government's travel advice well in advance.

Other months: Mar-May – spring, cool, biggest crowds and highest prices; Jul-Aug – hot in lower regions, best for mountains; Sep-Oct – cooler, lower prices; Nov-Feb – cold.

Do look up in Esfahan's Kakh-e Ali Qapu

PICOS DE EUROPA
SPAIN

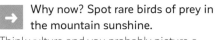

→ **Why now? Spot rare birds of prey in the mountain sunshine.**

Think vulture and you probably picture a bald, wrinkly, squabbling specimen. The bearded vulture, though, is altogether different: with a 3m (10ft) wingspan, orange chest, black facemask and red eye-rings, plus that characteristic 'beard', the raptor also known as a lammergeier is mesmerising. Long persecuted, bearded vultures are resurgent in the Picos de Europa thanks to a novel reintroduction project – and June is a wonderful time to spot them soaring above the gleaming limestone crags of this spectacular national park in northern Spain. Watch for them as you hike the trails, or visit the open-air vulture feeding site above Covadonga, a small town renowned as the site of the 8th-century battle that began the so-called 'reconquest' of Spain. Look for other birds of prey – griffon and Egyptian vultures, honey buzzards and golden eagles – as well as (if you're incredibly lucky) wolves. You'll want to work up a hunger (and a thirst): the food and drink of the Asturias region are tremendous, particularly traditional *queso azul* (blue cheese), *fabada* (pork and bean stew) and *sidra* (cider).

Trip plan: Santander and Asturias are the nearest airports, and Santander is also accessible by ferry from Cork (Ireland), Plymouth and Portsmouth (UK). Public transport within the Picos is limited; hiring a car (or hiking) is the best option.

Need to know: Another good place to spot bearded vultures is Ordesa y Monte Perdido National Park, over to the east in the Aragon Pyrenees.

Other months: Dec-May – snow on higher trails; Jul-Sep – warm, dry; Oct-Nov – cooler, wetter.

© Justin Folkes / Lonely Planet

A typical Picos view, characterised by limestone crags and placid lakes

© Himadri & Chandrani / 500px

NORTH SIKKIM INDIA

Hilltop Lachung in
northeast Sikkim

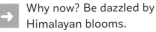

Why now? Be dazzled by Himalayan blooms.

Sikkim is truly a land apart. Formerly an independent kingdom, this sparsely populated Himalayan region has been a state of India only since 1975; even today its jagged peaks, Tibetan-style Buddhist monasteries and Bhutia, Lepcha and Nepali villages seem distinct from neighbouring areas. June, after Bengali holidaymakers have mostly departed but before the heaviest rains set in, is a wonderful time to enjoy floral fireworks displays: perhaps 4000 species of flowering plants have been recorded here, including around 40 rhododendrons and hundreds of orchids that spangle the forested hillsides and valleys east of Kanchenjunga – at 8586m (28,169ft), the planet's third-highest mountain. Following in the footsteps of renowned 19th-century botanist-adventurer Sir Joseph Dalton Hooker, venture to the remote settlements of Lachung and Lachen, delving into the lush Yumthang Valley and visiting the Shingba Rhododendron Sanctuary.

Trip plan: Bagdogra Airport, a little south of Darjeeling, is the gateway for Sikkim.

Allow at least a week to travel north via Kalimpong and Gangtok to explore the high valleys east of Kanchenjunga.

Need to know: In addition to a tourist visa, special permits may be required to visit some or all of Sikkim – check the latest information with the Indian consulate in your home country.

Other months: Dec-Feb – very cold, snow in many areas; Mar-May – warmer, rhododendrons start to bloom, rain begins to build; Jul-Sep – warm, wet; Oct-Nov – drier, cool, peak trekking season.

Mountain gorilla close
encounter, Volcanoes
National Park

RWANDA

 Why now? To see eye to eye with a silverback gorilla.

That something so huge (a male gorilla can top 180kg/397lb) can be so vulnerable is hard to understand. Yet only 1000 or so endangered mountain gorillas survive in two isolated subpopulations. June, the beginning of Rwanda's dry season, is the time to venture to Volcanoes National Park to track one of its 10 habituated groups; prepare for muddy, steep trails, heady altitude (around 3000m/9850ft) and the heart-melting sight of a precious primate family. A gorilla encounter is far from the only reason to come to Rwanda. The calm, neat capital, Kigali, is a fine place to start, redolent with the aroma of Rwanda's great coffee; Nyungwe Forest harbours large populations of chimpanzees and Ruwenzori colobus monkeys; while to the east Akagera National Park is a pretty mix of savannah, hills and valleys, with giraffe, zebra, elephant and some shy lions.

Trip plan: Fly to the capital, Kigali. Independent travel is fairly straightforward, with a good minibus service, though it's easiest to book a tour (including gorilla tracking) with an international operator.

Need to know: Book your gorilla-tracking permit (currently US$1500, but subject to change) well in advance for this popular season.

Other months: Jul-Aug – driest season, gorilla-trekking easiest; Mar-May & Nov – heaviest rain; Sep-Oct & Dec-Feb – damp, possibly cheaper, better gorilla-permit availability.

© Eric Lafforgue / Lonely Planet

Palm-lined beachfront on
Little Corn Island

NICARAGUA

→ **Why now? Spot jungle wildlife and snorkel dazzling reefs in the lushest season.**

The start of the rainy season, from the middle of the year, may make beach-lounging on Nicaragua's Pacific coast a little less appealing – but it also augurs outstanding birdwatching and snorkelling. Visit in June, before the heaviest downpours set in, to delve into Reserva Biológica Indio Maíz: walk and kayak its emerald jungle to spot diverse avian species including manakins, toucans, tanagers, trogons and, if you're fortunate, scarlet macaws, watching out too for howler monkeys, sloths, colourful tree frogs and caiman. This is also the ideal time to fin through clear, warm waters off the laid-back Corn Islands or Pearl Cays, swimming above beautiful coral reefs alongside reef and nurse sharks, eagle rays and possibly hammerhead sharks.

Trip plan: From capital Managua, head south to admire the pastel-hued historic architecture of Granada, then sail across Lake Nicaragua to the twin-volcano Ometepe Island. Skirt the south of the lake and follow the San Juan River to the Reserva Biológica Indio Maíz. Continue up the Caribbean coast to Bluefields for the hop to the Corn Islands. The Pearl Cays are accessible from Pearl Lagoon (1hr) or Little Corn Island (2hrs).

Need to know: Local currency is the córdoba, though US dollars may be accepted; bring cash to remote areas such as the Corn Islands, where ATMs are limited.

Other months: Nov-Apr – dry, warm; May – hot, rains begin; Jul-Oct – wet (heavy rains may disrupt travel Sep-Oct).

147

Hike up to spiky
Segla for superlative
Senja views

SENJA NORWAY

→ **Why now?** Hike mountain trails and paddle Arctic fjords under the Midnight Sun.

Wilder, bigger and emptier than the more touristed (and photographed) Lofotens, Norway's second-largest island dials up the scenic splendour – and in June, you've endless hours to drink it all in: on Senja, 322km (200 miles) above the Arctic Circle, the sun never sets between mid-May and mid-July. A handy National Tourist Route (Road 86/862) follows the most dramatic sweeps and inlets of the north and west coast, visiting quiet fishing villages and remote beaches. But you'll see more on foot or at sea-level than behind the wheel. Lace up hiking boots to climb Barden for widescreen vistas across dino-fin mountain Segla. Rock-hop to the end of the Skøyteneset Peninsula beneath soaring white-tailed eagles. Amble through moose-browsed birchwoods to the turf-bark-and-branch home of Sami man Nikolai Olsen Kaperdal. And kayak around the Bergsøyan archipelago from Hamn i Senja to complete your Arctic epic.

Trip plan: The nearest airport is at Tromsø. Public transport is sparse; exploring is easiest with your own transport. Stop at idyllic Sommarøy to hike around Hillesøya, catch the ferry from nearby Brensholmen to Botnhamn on Senja, then trace the fractal coast west and south, returning to the mainland via the bridge at Finnsnes. Allow at least a week.

Need to know: June is peak season – book accommodation well in advance.

Other months: Nov-Apr – dark, very cold; May & Jul-Oct – reliably above freezing; snow melts on peaks from June.

AVEIRO & COIMBRA
PORTUGAL

→ **Why now? Discover culture, canals, crooners and delicious cuisine.**

Portugal's brightest minds have studied – and celebrated – in Coimbra for over seven centuries, since its venerable hilltop university opened in 1290. By June, though, the youngsters have ebbed away, leaving the cobbled streets echoing with the soul-stirring tones of the city's distinctive style of *fado* music. Once you've admired the magnificent Romanesque 12th-century Sé Velha (Old Cathedral) and climbed the 180 steps of the the Torre da Universidade for city views, make the short hop north to Aveiro, the so-called 'Venice of Portugal'. Glide along its canals aboard a colourful *moliceiro* (traditional seaweed-harvesting boat), strolling streets lined with elegant Art Nouveau villas and absorbing the action at the Mercado do Peixe (Fish Market) – around which, of course, you'll find the freshest seafood. Then slip across to the sand and surf at Praia de São Jacinto or Praia da Costa Nova before holidaymakers arrive in force in July.

Trip plan: Aveiro is just over 30min by train from Porto, which has the nearest airport; Coimbra's another 30min further south. Buses and trains between the two take around 45min. Spend a night or two in each.

Need to know: Seek out Aveiro's sweet speciality, *ovos moles* – shell-shaped egg-and-sugar delicacies typically displayed in wooden barrels.

Other months: Nov-Mar – cool, wet; Apr-May – warm, end-of-term festivities in Coimbra; Jul-Aug – hot, dry; Sep-Oct – warm, quieter.

Swish through Aveiro aboard a traditional *moliceiro* boat

PRINCESA SANTA JOANA

02-AL

149

(T) Living life on the edge in the Devil's Pool; (B) Hwange giraffe

ZIMBABWE

 Why now? Marvel at thundering falls and big game.

The indigenous people who dubbed Africa's most iconic cataract Mosi-oa-Tunya – 'The Smoke that Thunders' – weren't kidding: the vast volume of water plummeting 108m (354ft) down Victoria Falls creates an extraordinary noise and spray that can obscure views around the end of the wet season. In June, after both rains and heat have eased, the falls are still impressive but more accessible (particularly the hair-raising natural tub called Devil's Pool at the very edge), and dropping river levels make rafting and kayaking past hippos and crocs feasible. This is also prime time for game-viewing in Hwange National Park, where outstanding guides lead 4WD and thrilling walking safaris for the best chances of spotting lion, elephant, leopard, cheetah, buffalo, giraffe, zebra, various antelopes, African wild dog and even elusive pangolin.

Trip plan: Fly into Victoria Falls Airport, spend two or three days around the cataracts, then transfer to Hwange National Park for several days of superb game-viewing. If time permits, add a three-day fly-in visit to Mana Pools National Park for more excellent wildlife watching.

Need to know: Many nationalities require a visa. The KAZA Univisa, available on arrival at selected airports and border crossings, permits entry to both Zimbabwe and Zambia, plus day-trips into Botswana, allowing multi-country travels.

Other months: Nov-Mar – hot, heaviest rains; Apr-May – cooling, fresher, lush landscapes; Jul-Aug – mild, dry, busier; Sep-Oct – heating up, stretches of Victoria Falls may dry up.

© Camila Se / Shutterstock

BYRON BAY AUSTRALIA

Winding up a day on the
surf at Byron Bay beach

→ **Why now? Enhance your wellbeing on a yoga retreat.**

The June solstice sees adherents across the globe celebrate the International Day of Yoga. Though Byron Bay may no longer be the preserve of backpackers and hippies, having evolved into a stylish, upmarket destination, it retains a decidedly laidback air and alternative scene – an ideal place to recharge your spiritual and physical batteries at one of the excellent yoga retreats and studios. Of course, yoga sessions don't take all day – and, though you could spend the rest of your time meditating, why would you when there's such a wealth of beaches and activities on hand? Don mask and snorkel to encounter subaquatic marvels at Julian Rocks – watch for wobbegong sharks, sea turtles, rays and kaleidoscopic fish – or grab your surfboard and shorty wetsuit to catch the reliable winter swells. This is the time to watch for whales, too: thousands of humpbacks migrate through the waters off Byron between June and October; spot them from shore at Cape Byron or join a dedicated whale-watching boat tour.

Trip plan: Spend a few days surfing, diving, snorkelling, wildlife-watching, kayaking and feasting, each topped and tailed with yoga sessions.

Need to know: For more alternative-lifestyle action, make the 1hr drive inland to Nimbin, famed as the region's New Age hub since 1973.

Other months: Dec-Feb – hot, humid, busy; Mar-May – warm, rainy, getting quieter; Jul-Sep – mild, clear water; Sep-Nov – warming up, increasing rainy days.

151

July

WHERE TO GO WHEN

CHALLENGE MYSELF

I WANT TO

TAKE ME OUT FOR...

FOOD ● SASKATOON, SASKATCHEWAN, CANADA P165

DRINK ● VIENNA, AUSTRIA P174

Imbibe craft beers and delve into the food scene of super-cool Saskatoon

Sip house-made wines in the courtyard of a Viennese Heurigen

TAKE ME SOMEWHERE FOR...

WILD DAYS ● DARWIN & LITCHFIELD NATIONAL PARK, AUSTRALIA P159

WILD NIGHTS ● AARHUS & JUTLAND, DENMARK P161

Check in to the hopping cafes, cocktail bars and clubs of Aarhus

RELAX/ INDULGE

Stroll Stone Town's alleys and Old Fort before hitting the Zanzibar beaches

TAKE ME TO THE BEACH

REV UP ● ANDROS & BIMINI, BAHAMAS P159

WISCONSIN, USA P172

CHILL OUT

ZANZIBAR, TANZANIA P158

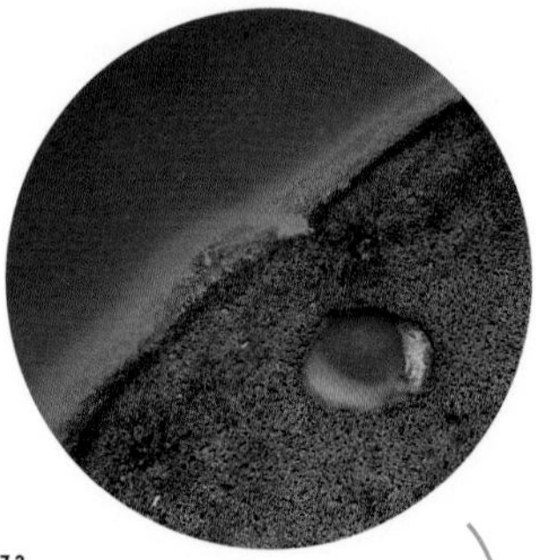

Dive blue holes and rich reefs in the Bahamas' Andros and Bimini

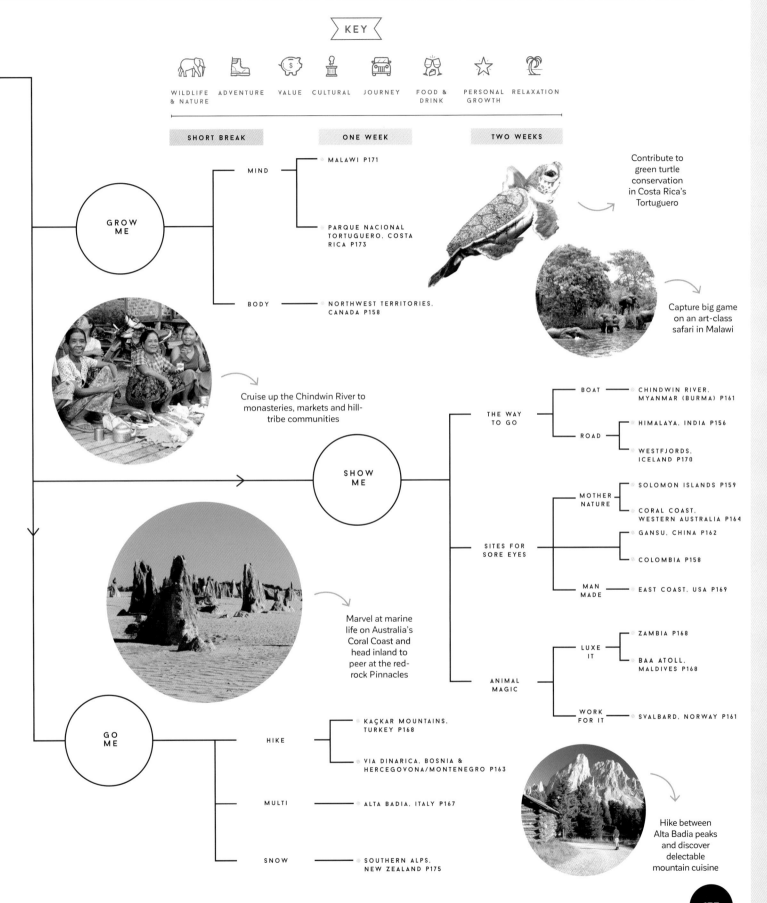

WILDLIFE & NATURE   ADVENTURE   VALUE   CULTURAL   JOURNEY   FOOD & DRINK   PERSONAL GROWTH   RELAXATION

SHORT BREAK   ONE WEEK   TWO WEEKS

GROW ME

MIND
- MALAWI P171
- PARQUE NACIONAL TORTUGUERO, COSTA RICA P173

BODY
- NORTHWEST TERRITORIES, CANADA P158

Contribute to green turtle conservation in Costa Rica's Tortuguero

Capture big game on an art-class safari in Malawi

Cruise up the Chindwin River to monasteries, markets and hill-tribe communities

SHOW ME

THE WAY TO GO
- BOAT — CHINDWIN RIVER, MYANMAR (BURMA) P161
- ROAD — HIMALAYA, INDIA P156
- WESTFJORDS, ICELAND P170

SITES FOR SORE EYES
- MOTHER NATURE
  - SOLOMON ISLANDS P159
  - CORAL COAST, WESTERN AUSTRALIA P164
  - GANSU, CHINA P162
  - COLOMBIA P158
- MAN MADE — EAST COAST, USA P169

ANIMAL MAGIC
- LUXE IT
  - ZAMBIA P168
  - BAA ATOLL, MALDIVES P168
- WORK FOR IT — SVALBARD, NORWAY P161

Marvel at marine life on Australia's Coral Coast and head inland to peer at the red-rock Pinnacles

GO ME

HIKE
- KAÇKAR MOUNTAINS, TURKEY P168
- VIA DINARICA, BOSNIA & HERCEGOVONA/MONTENEGRO P163

MULTI
- ALTA BADIA, ITALY P167

SNOW
- SOUTHERN ALPS, NEW ZEALAND P175

Hike between Alta Badia peaks and discover delectable mountain cuisine

EVENTS
IN JULY

NAADAM
Ulaanbaatar, Mongolia
Contestants compete in the 'three manly sports' of horse racing, archery and Mongolian wrestling in the country's most-watched festival.

11–15 July
$$

GION MATSURI
Kyoto, Japan
For well over a millennium the city has celebrated with elaborately decorated float processions, street parties and feasting on traditional snacks.
All month
$$$

MEDIEVAL DAYS
San Marino
Residents don medieval costume and practice historic activities during high summer – watch out for crossbow bolts.

REGGAE SUMFEST
Montego Bay, Jamaica
The biggest music festival in Jamaica brings a week of shows by great reggae and dancehall acts from across the Caribbean.
Late July
$$

Third week in July
$$

ZANZIBAR INTERNATIONAL FILM FESTIVAL
Zanzibar, Tanzania
A showcase for the arts and cultures of the Dhow Countries (in Africa, the Gulf States, Iran, India, Pakistan and the Indian Ocean).
First two weeks of July
$$

BIRD COURTSHIP
Galápagos Islands, Ecuador
Blue-footed boobies perform their peculiar hopping courtship during the breeding season for many seabirds in the 'enchanted islands'.
All month
$$$

WIFE-CARRYING WORLD CHAMPIONSHIPS
Sonkajärvi, Finland
Men lug spouses over an obstacle course in a hilarious and surprisingly nailbiting competition.
First weekend in July
$$

CALGARY STAMPEDE
Calgary, Alberta, Canada
Rodeo action, country music, fireworks, food, drink and the big Stampede Parade celebrate the cowboy culture of the Canadian prairies.
From first Friday after Canada Day
$$

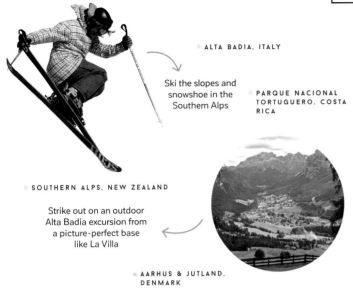

○ ALTA BADIA, ITALY

Ski the slopes and
snowshoe in the
Southern Alps

○ PARQUE NACIONAL
TORTUGUERO, COSTA
RICA

○ SOUTHERN ALPS, NEW ZEALAND

Strike out on an outdoor
Alta Badia excursion from
a picture-perfect base
like La Villa

○ AARHUS & JUTLAND,
DENMARK

○ EAST COAST, USA

○ CORAL COAST,
WESTERN AUSTRALIA

Take an East
Coast road
trip through
America's
history

○ ZANZIBAR, TANZANIA

Soak up sights, scents
and succulent Spice
Island seafood
in Zanzibar

Dive the Bahamas
for close
encounters with
dolphins and
manta rays

○ WISCONSIN, USA

○ ANDROS & BIMINI, BAHAMAS

Kayak to coastal caves
on Wisconsin's island-
spangled Great Lakes

Drive the
Westfjords Way
to the wilds of
Hornstrandir
Nature Reserve

○ ZAMBIA

○ DARWIN & LITCHFIELD
NATIONAL PARK, AUSTRALIA

○ NORTHWEST
TERRITORIES,
CANADA

Road-trip from
Darwin in the
Dry to dip in
Litchfield's
waterfalls

○ WESTFJORDS, ICELAND

○ SOLOMON ISLANDS

○ GANSU, CHINA

Behold big
Buddhas in Gansu's
Mogao Grottoes

○ MALAWI

○ CHINDWIN RIVER,
MYANMAR (BURMA)

○ SVALBARD, NORWAY

○ VIENNA, AUSTRIA

○ COLOMBIA

Discover coffee
country and San
Agustín's statuary
in Colombia

Lace up your
boots for summer
trekking in the
Kaçkar mountains

○ BAA ATOLL,
MALDIVES

○ KAÇKAR MOUNTAINS,
TURKEY

○ HIMALAYA, INDIA

Hike through
some of the
Balkans' best
bits on the Via
Dinarica trail

○ SASKATOON, SASKATCHEWAN,
CANADA

○ VIA DINARICA, BOSNIA &
HERCEGOVONA/MONTENEGRO

HIMALAYA INDIA

→ **Why now? Snowless roads for a magnificent drive.**

There are breathtaking road trips, and there are literally breath-taking road trips. The Khardung La is both. This 5600m (18,373ft) pass near Leh, amid the Indian Himalaya, was a key thoroughfare on the Silk Road and is now one of the world's highest motorable highways. Crossing it by bus is an adventure; crossing it astride a classic Enfield Bullet motorbike even more so. Either way, both mountain views and soaring altitudes will leave you gasping. The roads here are only open for a few months a year, so make the most of the warm, snow-free conditions. Bikers could zigzag up from Manali (Himachal Pradesh) to Leh (Ladakh) – one of the world's best mountain rides. Or fly from Delhi to Leh to visit the town's Tibetan-style palace and stupas before taking the Khardung La into the isolated Nubra Valley. The high road west into Kashmir, via Lamayuru Monastery and Zanskar, is an excellent add-on; finish with a houseboat stay on the lake at Srinagar.

Trip plan: Fly from Delhi to Leh, explore the Indus and Nubra valleys, head west into Kashmir, then fly back to Delhi from Srinagar.

Need to know: Before visiting Srinagar, in a sometimes volatile region, check the security situation and your government's advice on visiting.

Other months: Aug-Sep – roads passable; Oct-Apr – cold/very cold, roads impassable; May-Jun – warming slowly.

Heady Himalaya views along the Khardung La

ZANZIBAR
TANZANIA

→ **Why now?** Delve into Stone Town and the Indian Ocean under blue skies.

The spice island Unguja – known to most as Zanzibar – is a scent sensation. Stroll the maze-like alleys of old Stone Town on a warm evening and you'll catch whiffs of nutmeg, clove and cinnamon in the Darajani bazaar, frying seafood at stalls in Forodhani Gardens, and the aroma of black coffee in Jaws Corner, where old men gather to watch TV and gossip. Zanzibar's historic heart, with its crumbling palaces and heartrending slavery-era relics, is just one gem of this treasure-trove island, at its best in July, in the middle of the dry season. Board a dhow to snorkel off the west coast, watching for dolphins; sniff the leaves and buds of a spice plantation; and find your own patch of coral-sand perfection on one of the wonderful beaches.

Trip plan: Spend at least a couple of days wandering the labyrinthine alleys of Stone Town and visiting a spice plantation before heading to a beach – Nungwi is a good base for dives off Tumbatu and Mnemba islands.

Need to know: Incidence of malaria has dropped in recent years, but consult a physician for the latest advice before you travel.

Other months: Jun & Aug-Oct – cool, dry; Nov-Dec & Mar-May – rainy; Jan-Feb – hot, dry.

NORTHWEST TERRITORIES
CANADA

→ **Why now?** Run the river wild to immerse yourself in Indigenous culture.

This vast region of tundra and taiga is as empty as it is wild, with a population smaller than the tiniest Caribbean nation scattered across a land nearly as large as Mongolia. To discover the natural and cultural wonders of the Northwest Territories, take a river journey into its untamed heart, possible for just a few weeks from late June when temperatures are (relatively) balmy and days stretch forever. Canoe a stretch of Canada's longest river, the Deh Cho (Mackenzie); raft the South Nahanni from thundering, 96m-high (315ft) Virginia Falls in the sky-piercing Mackenzie Mountains; or enjoy a gentle kayak on Great Slave Lake, North America's deepest. En route, learn about the traditional culture of the Dene peoples who have adapted to this challenging environment over tens of millennia, and watch for caribou, Dall sheep, black bear, moose and wood bison – the continent's largest land mammal.

Trip plan: Fly to Yellowknife and join a river adventure led by expert local guides – perhaps a nine- or 10-day canoe trip along the Deh Cho/Mackenzie from Fort Providence to Fort Simpson, or a week's paddle downstream from Virginia Falls on the South Nahanni.

Need to know: When driving from Yellowknife to Fort Providence, watch for wood bison alongside (or even on) Hwy 3.

Other months: Nov-Mar – dark, brutally cold, Northern Lights; Apr-May – nudging above freezing, many parts still snowy; Jun & Aug – warmer, very long days; Sep-Oct – getting colder and darker.

COLOMBIA

→ **Why now?** Wake up and smell the coffee in a mini dry season.

Caribbean beaches, mountains, plains, jungle, desert: Colombia encompasses an astonishingly diverse array of landscapes, with correspondingly varied climates. July and August bring a period of drier weather perfect for touring *fincas* (coffee farms) amid the beautiful, rolling hills of the Zona Cafetera; admiring dazzling birdlife in Reserva Ecologica Rio Blanco; sleeping beneath the stars among the cacti and otherworldly rock formations of the Tatacoa Desert; hiking the lush highlands around Popoyán; and discovering the pre-Columbian tombs, petroglyphs and huge carved heads around San Agustín and Tierradentro. Also visiting this month are giants: between June and November, humpbacks calve off Colombia's Pacific coast – join a whale-watching tour in Nuquí or from Buenaventura into Bahía Málaga to spot breaching behemoths. It's also the driest month to spy sloths and pink river dolphins in Colombia's slice of the Amazon.

Trip plan: Complete a loop from Bogotá, heading west to the coast for whale-watching, south through the Zona Cafetera to Cali, then through the pre-Columbian archaeological sites at San Agustín and Tierradentro, and north via a night in the Tatacoa Desert. Fly to Leticia for a few days delving into the Amazon rainforest.

Need to know: The security situation can be volatile, particularly in border regions; check government advice before travel. Fares and accommodation prices can rise in July and August – book ahead.

Other months: Dec-Mar – drier; Apr-Jun – wetter; Aug – drier; Sep-Nov – wetter.

SOLOMON ISLANDS

→ **Why now?** Dive among WWII wrecks and swim with dugongs.

Time didn't exactly forget these 1000 or so islands scattered across the South Pacific. But it certainly slowed to a crawl, particularly since this nation between New Guinea and Vanuatu emerged from the shadow of bloody WWII fighting and later political turbulence. The few intrepid travellers who do venture here encounter unique cultural, historical and natural spectacles in blissful peace. Visit in cooler, drier July for the most comfortable conditions. On lush, wild Tetepare Island, snorkel with dugongs and watch leatherbacks nest. On Skull Island, see the remains of revered chiefs and vanquished warriors harvested by headhunters. On rugged Malaita, glide past stone-built artificial islands in Langa Langa Lagoon. On Kolombangara, tackle the two-day hike up the extinct volcanic cone of Mt Veve, past Japanese wartime relics. And at Marovo Lagoon and other spectacular scuba sites, dive past sunken ships, sharks, turtles and manta rays, diminutive pygmy seahorses and nudibranchs, schooling barracuda and jacks, all populating some 500 species of coral.

Trip plan: Capital Honiara on Guadalcanal receives international flights from Brisbane and Port Moresby; domestic flights and boats link other islands. Liveaboard package tours enable divers to discover a range of sites.

Need to know: Mosquitoes are rife, with malaria and dengue fever present; use insect repellent and cover arms and legs. Attacks by saltwater crocodiles are not unknown; check local advice.

Other months: Dec-May – wet, hot (risk of cyclones Jan-Apr); Jun & Aug-Nov – cooler, drier, less humid.

ANDROS & BIMINI
BAHAMAS

→ **Why now?** Alternate activity with indolence on and under the water.

The Bahamas are so almost the Caribbean yet, crucially, not quite. True, this speckle of islands and cays between Cuba and Florida boasts limpid waters and beautiful beaches. But summer here, though 'rainy', is less afflicted by the storms that often hit other islands. July brings calm, clear, warm seas, ideal for enjoying superb diving and snorkelling off tourist-light Andros; its east coast is protected by the world's third-longest barrier reef, stretching more than 270km (170 miles). Divers plunge into the brine to fin alongside spectacular elkhorn corals and lofty walls, and into canyons, caves and blue holes. Hop across to Bimini for manta ray encounters (peaking in July, when sharks are less prevalent) and the chance to come face to smiling beak with an Atlantic spotted dolphin, the curious, agile species that skims boat bow-waves in these parts. Add mangroves, excellent fishing, thriving birdlife and white-powder beaches, but subtract crowds – Andros is even quieter and better value in July.

Trip plan: Regular flights from Nassau serve Andros and Bimini, which also receives flights from Fort Lauderdale. Ferries sail Nassau-Andros in about 4hr.

Need to know: Bahamas' Independence Day, 10 July, is celebrated with parades, exhibitions and fireworks over the preceding days.

Other months: Nov-May – dry, cooler, busy; Jun & Aug – hotter and a little wetter, uncrowded; Sep-Oct – hot, humid, storms more likely, some accommodation closes.

DARWIN & LITCHFIELD NATIONAL PARK AUSTRALIA

→ **Why now?** Get a taste of the Top End in the Dry.

You know the seasons are serious when they're divided simply into the Wet and the Dry. When planning a visit to the Northern Territory's tropical Top End, it pays to pick Dry – at least, if you want to get out and explore. July brings clear skies and dry days, so it's ideal for enjoying Darwin's largely outdoor attractions: amble through Bicentennial Park; browse the stalls at Mindil Beach Sunset Markets or pick up a souvenir at one of the other weekend bazaars; or catch a classic movie at the Deckchair Cinema. It's worth taking one of several easy escapes from the city for a day at least – cooling off under Wangi Falls in nearby Litchfield National Park, or discovering the unique Indigenous culture of the Tiwi Islands.

Trip plan: Fly to Darwin from most Australian cities plus Bali, Singapore and Kuala Lumpur; or ride the Ghan railway from Alice Springs and Adelaide. Day tours run from Darwin to the Tiwi Islands and Litchfield National Park.

Need to know: Beware of box jellyfish when sea swimming – a bigger problem in the Wet, but check local information before diving in during the Dry.

Other months: May-Jun & Sep-Oct – the Dry (less rain, slightly cooler); Nov-Apr – the Wet (hot, wet).

(A) Canalside life
in easygoing Aarhus;
(L) Boating up
the Chindwin; (R)
Mother walrus
and her pup in the
Svalbard archipelago

AARHUS & JUTLAND
DENMARK

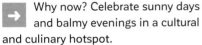

→ **Why now?** Celebrate sunny days and balmy evenings in a cultural and culinary hotspot.

Reinforcing the theory that second cities are often more creative and captivating than capitals, Denmark's number-two burg is buzzier than a beehive. Founded by Vikings some 13 centuries ago, today perky Aarhus is eminently contemporary, with its groundbreaking ARoS art museum, rejuvenated waterfront cultural centre, Dokk1, and innovative Iceberg apartment blocks. Even the Moesgaard Museum, home of the 2000-year-old bog-preserved Graubelle Man, offers a cutting-edge tour through the past – and Den Gamle By's open-air historical re-creation never goes out of fashion. Come evening, the city reveals its true colours, with cafes, cocktail bars and clubs showcasing that quintessentially Danish blend of smiles and smarts. High summer brings a host of festivals celebrating flowers, jazz, Viking heritage and more, plus warm sun (nudging 20°C/68°F) for basking on sandy Baltic beaches: try Den Permanente near the centre, silky-soft Bellevue just to the north, and the blissfully empty strands of eco-island Samsø, just a short ferry ride away.

Trip plan: Regular buses link Aarhus Airport with the city in 45min. The flat terrain is easily explored on foot or by bike.

Need to know: The AarhusCARD (visitaarhus.com/aarhuscard), valid for 24, 48, 74 or 120 hours, covers public transport and admission to museums and other cultural attractions – worthwhile if you'll be visiting two or more sites.

Other months: Nov-Mar – chilly (Christmas markets Dec); Apr & Oct – quieter, cooler; May-Jun & Aug-Sep – warmer, busy festival calendar.

CHINDWIN RIVER
MYANMAR (BURMA)

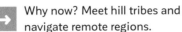

→ **Why now?** Meet hill tribes and navigate remote regions.

In general, the sticky, hot, wet monsoon season is seen as, well, rather putting a damper on travel in Asia. Not so for voyages up the Chindwin River: it's only after the rains really set in that the upper reaches of this snaking, 1200km-long (746-mile) waterway are typically navigable, opening up a remote region of wild beauty, populated with cultures barely touched by foreign visitors. In July the water is high and cruise vessels sail upstream from the confluence with the Ayeyarwady, Myanmar's largest (and much more-frequented) waterway, to encounter Buddha-lined caves and *payas* (temples) around Monywa, the ancient teak Kyi Taung Oo monastery at Mingkin, and WWII-era heritage at tiny Sittaung. As the boat follows the Chindwin's meanders north, the backdrop of forested hills becomes loftier and less populated; around Homalin (the furthest point upstream most vessels can navigate), Shan and Naga people live in villages studding the flanks of ridges topping 2700m (8858ft).

Trip plan: Mandalay receives international flights. Some Chindwin cruises depart from Mandalay; others sail upstream from Monywa or downstream from Homalin. It's possible to continue to the temples of Bagan or further up the Ayeyarwady River.

Need to know: Political upheavals periodically cause disruption and security concerns in some or all of Myanmar – check the latest advice from your government before travelling.

Other months: Oct-Apr – dry (coolest and busiest Dec-Feb); May-Jun & Aug-Sep – rainy, hot.

SVALBARD
NORWAY

→ **Why now?** Admire bright light, big bears, clear seas.

In the high Arctic, the window of opportunity for cruising is open only briefly: the northernmost shores and most remote fjords of the chilly Svalbard archipelago are accessible by sea for only a month or two each summer. But it's a window worth seeking out. In July, the seas are mostly clear of ice, the temperature 'soars' to a (relatively) balmy 5°C (41°F) and the sun shines for weeks on end – morning, noon and (mid)night – enabling 24-hr sightseeing. Expedition cruise vessels plough past the islands' jagged mountains and creaking glaciers, while expert guides keep watch for wildlife: walrus colonies, herds of reindeer, Arctic foxes, seals, whales of all sorts and, of course, polar bears. Perhaps 3000 of the huge white predators stalk Svalbard and the surrounding Arctic region; in summer, when the ice breaks up, the bears stay close to the coast. Board a small Zodiac boat and explore the shoreline for the chance of a close encounter.

Trip plan: Fly via Oslo to Longyearbyen on Spitsbergen, Svalbard's main island, from where one- or two-week cruises depart; itineraries and activities are dictated by weather and sea conditions.

Need to know: For the more adventurous, tall-ship vessels glide around Svalbard under sail. It's also possible to cruise from mainland Norway to Spitsbergen.

Other months: Sept-Mar – Northern Lights (Nov-Mar very cold); Apr-Jun & Aug – Midnight Sun (boat trips May-Sept).

Devotees spin prayer wheels at the Labrang Monastery *kora*

GANSU CHINA

 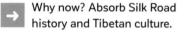

→ **Why now? Absorb Silk Road history and Tibetan culture.**

While lowland regions of China swelter in summer heat, summer is the time to explore the high Tibetan plateau, when temperatures are pleasant and trails are free of snow. Cupping the northeastern arc of the plateau, Gansu province is popular with domestic tourists, renowned as the gateway of the ancient Silk Road and the home of jaw-dropping grottoes, notably at Mogao near Dunhuang. But away from those hotspots you'll find peace, along with rich Tibetan culture and wild landscapes, particularly in Gannan prefecture south of provincial capital Lanzhou. Here, the chants of lamas waft across Xiahe from Labrang Monastery – one of the six great monasteries of Tibetan Buddhism; walk the 3.5km (2-mile) *kora* (pilgrimage circuit) around reputedly the world's longest stretch of prayer wheels,

before refuelling on *momos* (Tibetan steamed dumplings). Continue south to admire Buddhist sculptures and frescoes in the grottoes of Bǐnglíng Sì, far quieter than Mogao; to roam mountain meadows and yak-grazed prairies; and to stroll among stupas in Tibetan mountain villages such as Langmusi.

Trip plan: From Lanzhou, delve south into Gannan to explore Tibetan-style Buddhist monasteries, then west along the Silk Road corridor to discover cave art, grotto temples and ancient fortifications.

Need to know: Most visitors to China need a visa; if you plan to visit the Tibetan Autonomous Region, you'll almost certainly need to arrange additional permits – check the latest situation well in advance.

Other months: Nov-Mar – very cold; Apr & Oct – cool, quiet; May-Jun & Aug-Sep – warm.

Lake Orlovačko in Sutjeska National Park, Bosnia & Hercegovina

VIA DINARICA
BOSNIA & HERCEGOVINA/ MONTENEGRO

Why now? Hike the spine of the Balkans.

Parts of the former Yugoslavia have developed rapidly since its breakup: Croatia's much-vaunted coast, for example, bustling in summer. Yet in hamlets speckling the remote higher reaches of the Dinaric Alps, time seems to have stood still. The best way to immerse yourself in traditional mountain culture is to trek the relatively new Via Dinarica. Its 1200km-long (746-mile) waymarked White Trail snakes southeast from Slovenia through Croatia, Bosnia & Hercegovina, Montenegro and into Albania's Accursed Alps, conquering the highest peaks en route. Sunny summer days, when snow's melted from the loftiest sections, beckon hikers through the uplands south of Sarajevo, past the glacial lakes and forested ridges of Sutjeska National Park (the country's oldest and largest) across the border into Montenegro, skirting Tara Canyon (Europe's deepest) and through Unesco-listed Durmitor National Park, meeting shepherds and bedding down in isolated mountain huts en route.

Trip plan: Depending on your start point, access the trail from Split (Croatia), Sarajevo or Podgorica. Experienced, fit hikers cover the 400km (248 miles) or so between shepherd-village Lukomir and the trail's endpoint, Valbona (Albania), in about two weeks. Alternatively, plan a Bosnia loop from Sarajevo, visiting Lukomir, Sutjeska National Park and climbing Maglić (2386m/7828ft), the highest peak in Bosnia & Hercegovina.

Need to know: Mostar, named for its vertiginous 16th-century Ottoman bridge, is close to the endpoint of Stage 31 – a good spot to break the trail.

Other months: Nov-Mar – winter, snow at higher altitudes; Apr-Jun & Aug-Oct – warm, mostly dry.

© Slavenko / Shutterstock

163

CORAL COAST
WESTERN AUSTRALIA

→ **Why now?** Meet charismatic sea creatures, roam red-rock canyons and wander among wildflowers.

Stretching over 1000km (621 miles) between Cervantes and Exmouth, the 'Coral Coast' of Western Australia encapsulates much of the country's appeal in miniature, making this relatively little-touristed stretch ideal for a winter road trip through empty expanses. Here you'll discover dramatic rock formations – the Pinnacles, limestone needles punching through the sand near Cervantes – and russet Tumblagooda Sandstone gorges in Kalbarri National Park. You'll experience surfing and subaquatic adventures along the world's largest fringing reef – 300km (186 miles) of coral that's home to some 500 fish species. And you'll meet miraculous wildlife, like when whale sharks gather in their hundreds on Ningaloo Reef (March to July), along with manta rays – more numerous off Exmouth May to September – and humpbacks arrive to join the fun, too. Further south, dolphins flit through the waters of Shark Bay, and from July to October, more than 12,000 species of wildflowers festoon Kalbarri.

Trip plan: Allow at least a week – ideally, two – for the drive north from Perth to Exmouth, with time to explore the Pinnacles, Geraldton, Kalbarri, Shark Bay and Coral Bay.

Need to know: Public transport is limited along the coast. For maximum flexibility, hire a car or join a hop-on-hop-off bus tour (largely aimed at backpackers).

Other months: Nov-Feb – very hot; Mar-May – hot, some rain; Jun & Aug-Sep – pleasantly warm.

© SammyVision / Getty Images

The Coral Coast reef stretching toward the horizon at Exmouth

SASKATOON, SASKATCHEWAN CANADA

A green summer scene in the 'Paris of the Prairies', Saskatoon

→ Why now? For tasty times on the prairie.

Peak summer typically means peak crowds – but on Canada's endless prairie, it's not hard to lose the hordes. Landlocked Saskatchewan is a landscape of space and silence – indeed, an audio-ecologist deemed its Grasslands National Park one of the world's quietest places. It's also a great place to eat and drink. The province is the breadbasket of Canada, encompassing 50% of its arable farmland, not to mention a heap of extremely photogenic grain silos.

Super-cool Saskatoon, which sits amid all this fertility, has become one of the country's hottest foodie spots. A raft of distillers, craft brewers, artisan bakers and cocktail shakers have popped up in the small-but-mighty 'Paris of the Prairies'. Take a foodie tour and cooking class, and visit nearby farms to meet producers. July also sees the sweet, nutty Saskatoon berries ripen – try them in everything from pies to wine.

Trip plan: Explore foodie Saskatoon on foot – hit venerable local institutions such as 9 Mile Legacy brewery, Baba's Perogies, the Berry Barn and celeb chef Dale MacKay's restaurants. And make time for paddleboarding on the South Saskatchewan River and visiting Wanuskewin Heritage Park.

Need to know: Saskatoon is on VIA Rail's Toronto-Vancouver Canadian service, which runs three times a week in summer (twice-weekly in other seasons).

Other months: Nov-Mar – freezing; Apr-Jun – mild, variable; Aug – hot, dry, sunny; Sep-Oct – often warm.

© Scott Prokop / Shutterstock

165

ALTA BADIA
ITALY

> **Why now? Sample superb cuisine amid marvellous mountains.**

If the Dolomites are the Alps at their most magnificent, the Alta Badia valley in South Tyrol promises the Dolomites at their tastiest. This jagged array of deep valleys, high plateaus and piercing pinnacles in northern Italy echoes with poignant history: between 1915 and 1918, Italian and Austro-Hungarian forces fought amid these unforgiving peaks, and today you can hike routes such as the Kaiserjäger to discover their trenches and gun emplacements. Alta Badia is renowned for its skiing, but in summer the cable cars and mountain huts reopen to serve hungry hikers, cyclists, paragliders and trail-runners instead. The region is spangled with Michelin stars, but even simple refuges dish up good-value but top-notch cuisine (think mountain cheeses, pasta and strudels). For an extra adrenaline buzz, tackle the challenging via ferrata climbs, a method of traversing vertiginous rock faces via rungs and cables.

Trip plan: The nearest airports are at Innsbruck, Verona and Venice. La Villa, San Cassiano (St Kassian) and Corvara make excellent bases from which to explore the peaks and valleys.

Need to know: The South Tyrol region was part of the Austro-Hungarian empire till WWI. Many place-name signs are in both Italian and German, and you'll hear those languages spoken plus, possibly, a third: Ladin, a venerable Romance tongue descended from ancient Latin.

Other months: Dec-Mar – great skiing; Apr-May & Oct – quieter, less accessible; Jun & Aug-Sep – warm, best for hiking and outdoor pursuits.

A land of contrasts:
(L) Lago di Carezza;
(R) Val di Funes

©Matt Munro / Lonely Planet

167

BAA ATOLL
MALDIVES

→ **Why now? Swim with giants in bath-warm waters.**

Chances are, you haven't given much thought to plankton. You should – particularly if you're a snorkeller or diver – as these tiny ocean-drifting organisms feed the bigger sea creatures that make underwater adventures so thrilling. Knowing the where and when of plankton 'blooms' is the way to max your marine megafauna moments – particularly in the Maldives. July is one of the rainier months in this nation of nearly 1200 islands scattered across the Indian Ocean; and in Baa Atoll, it's plum snorkelling season, when burgeoning plankton attracts not just dozens but hundreds of huge manta rays and whale sharks – the world's largest fish, reaching 10m (33ft) long. You'll encounter countless dazzling fish and other marine creatures on and around reef walls and *thilas* (pinnacles) – but head for Hanifaru Lagoon to swim with the most numerous congregations of rays and sharks. As a bonus, prices tend to be lower in 'rainier' months, punctuated by typically short downpours.

Trip plan: Malé international airport has domestic connections to Dharavandhoo in Baa Atoll; seaplanes and speedboats link to other islands. Choose between a liveaboard package or land resort – most offer direct access to spectacular snorkelling and diving.

Need to know: Scuba diving isn't currently permitted in Hanifaru Lagoon – snorkellers only. Divers head to the cleaning station at nearby Dharavandhoo Corner.

Other months: Mid-Dec-Apr – driest; May-Jun & Aug-Nov – showers, lower prices.

KAÇKAR MOUNTAINS
TURKEY

→ **Why now? Trek dramatic mountain trails in warm weather.**

The Kaçkar Mountains loom inland from the Black Sea in Turkey's far northeast. Climbing from forest-cloaked valleys onto upper slopes glistening with glaciers and alpine lakes, trekking routes – many open only for a few months or weeks each year, most reliably in July and August – meander up to stone villages and *yayla* (summer pastures) where shepherds tend livestock in a way of life little changed in centuries. Among several tempting trails are two long-haul traverses: the southern trans-Kaçkar route including the conquest of its namesake 3937m (12,917ft) peak (testing but non-technical), and the Trans-Altiparmak trek in the north; both take about three days. As an alternative, base yourself in a mountain village like Barhal, with its 10th-century Georgian church, and enjoy day walks around tarns, waterfalls and wildflower-strewn meadows, absorbing the local culture and cuisine (especially baked treats) of the Hemşin people around Ayder.

Trip plan: Approach the mountains from the south via Erzurum or the west from Trabzon; both have airports served by flights from İstanbul, with international connections. Ayder (2hr from Trabzon) is the main hub for tourism and trekking. Hire a local guide or book a tour – trails aren't all clear.

Need to know: The highest paths may be free from snow from only a few weeks, from mid-July to mid-August.

Other months: Oct-Apr – paths may be covered in snow, very cold (commonly below freezing Nov-Mar); May-Jun & Aug-Sep – trails clear, warmer.

ZAMBIA

→ **Why now? Enjoy a sensational safari on a clear, balmy day.**

Encountering a lion on foot might be the most electrifying moment of your life. And it's almost inevitable in Zambia, birthplace of walking safaris – best undertaken in the cooler, drier days of the southern winter. Accompanied by an expert guide and scout, stroll between stylish lodges and bushcamps, absorbing not just the sights but also the sounds, smells and tastes of the wilderness. South Luangwa National Park is the heartland of strolling safaris, its mix of grassland, riverine and mopane woodland home to most of the Big Five plus specialities including Thornicroft's giraffe. Elsewhere, Zambia's other national parks offer diverse experiences. Spot unwieldy-looking shoebill storks and black lechwe in Bangweulu Wetlands; kayak among chuckling hippos and past elephants, buffalo and dazzling birdlife in Lower Zambezi; track predators across vast Kafue; and follow the huge wildebeest migration in little-visited Liuwa Plain.

Trip plan: Focus on one or two areas – South Luangwa and Lower Zambezi for safari first-timers, Liuwa and Kafue in the west for subsequent visits, Bangweulu and Kasanka in the central north for shoebill and bat connoisseurs. Allow at least a week, ideally longer.

Need to know: Though many bushcamps close during the rainiest months – when trees and flowers bloom, birds sport breeding plumage, and many creatures give birth – some offer 'emerald season' discounted packages.

Other months: Nov-Mar – wet, hot; Apr-May – rains ease, heat recedes; Jun-Aug – cool, dry, popular; Sep-Oct – heat rising, game gathers around receding waterholes.

© SeanPavonePhoto / Getty Images

Stroll key city sights like
the Old State House on
Boston's Freedom Trail

EAST COAST USA

→ **Why now? Drive a revolutionary road in Independence month.**

Two and a half centuries ago, America fought for – and finally won – its liberty. Independence Day, 4 July, is a great excuse for an east-coast road trip stitching together major locations in the Revolutionary War. Sure, you won't have historic sites to yourself in this sunny, warm month, but then this is a story of togetherness and joint endeavour. Start at the beginning in Virginia, genning up on early colonial life at the Jamestown Settlement living history museum, Colonial Williamsburg and the interactive American Revolution Museum at Yorktown. Scoot north through Washington DC (gawping at the Declaration of Independence) via George Washington's home at Mount Vernon, revealing important truths about the lives of enslaved people as well as the first president. Philadelphia is packed with treasures, including the famously cracked Liberty Bell, while Valley Forge and Washington Crossing national historic parks provide insights into the Patriots' military exploits. Boston's Freedom Trail illuminates key episodes preceding Paul Revere's ride on 18 April 1775; follow his galloping route to Lexington and Concord, sites of the war's first clashes, to round off a truly revolutionary road.

Trip plan: The drive between Virginia and Concord covers about 1368km (850 miles), depending on exact routings – allow at least a week.

Need to know: The Colonial Parkway in Virginia is a truck-free scenic byway linking historic sites of Jamestown, Williamsburg and Yorktown.

Other months: Dec-Feb – cold, quiet; Mar-May & Sep-Nov – reasonable weather and prices; Jun & Aug – warm, busy, costs highest.

WESTFJORDS
ICELAND

→ **Why now? Drive Iceland's oldest region on endless days.**

Iceland's far northwest is crowned by a rack of gnarled reindeer antlers: the Westfjords, its spectacular fjords, glacial valleys and sheer scarps ice-scoured over millennia. The completion of the Dýrafjörður Tunnel in 2020 made possible a new road trip: the Vestfjarðaleiðin (Westfjords Way), a 950km (590 mile) circular drive with branches reaching the wildest highlights, offering a peaceful alternative to the popular Ring Road. Get behind the wheel in high summer, when roads are clear and night never comes, and when breeding puffins and other seabirds throng the soaring seacliffs of Látrabjarg. Of course, you'll want to park up to explore on foot, too – to spot Arctic fox among the orchid-specked wilds of Hornstrandir Nature Reserve, to join seals on the pink-sand beach of Rauðasandur, to soak in Drangsnes geothermal pool, to gawp at Drangajökull glacier and the seven tiers of Dynjandi Falls, and to meet the smiling, independent people of this long-isolated region.

Trip plan: The Vestfjarðaleiðin peels off from Route 1, the main ring road, 111km (69 miles) north of Reykjavík, a little further from Keflavík International Airport. Allow at least a week to circuit the Westfjords and enjoy the various activities and cultural attractions.

Need to know: Weather can change rapidly year-round – bring clothes for all conditions.

Other months: Oct-Apr – dark, cold, some roads snow-blocked, Northern Lights possible (backcountry skiing popular Mar-Apr); May & Sep – pleasant, some accommodation closed; Jun & Aug – warm, long days.

Multi-tiered Dynjandi Falls, one of many Westfjords highlights

© Reto Buhler / Shutterstock

© gualtiero boffi / Shutterstock

MALAWI

Take a wildlife art
class in Malawi

→ **Why now? To get artistic in picture-perfect Africa.**

What a palette Malawi has: the turquoise shallows and deep blues of Lake Malawi, the purple-tinged escarpments of the Rift Valley, the wildflower-dotted Nyika Plateau, the lush greens of the forests and riverbanks, the warm yellows of the savannah, rainbow-bright cichlids, iridescent kingfishers, black-and-white striped zebra. This compact yet diverse African country is as pretty as a picture – and a great spot for trying to paint one of your own. Going on an expert-led art safari, learning to draw in the wilderness, forces you to really see; you get all the thrills of a wildlife-watching trip but an additional deeper level of immersion and creativity. And July is ideal for hours spent at the easel: the skies are dry but the land is still green, and the animals – from elephant herds to chortling hippo – are active and healthy. Liwonde National Park, where the palm-lined Shire River weaves through game-rich grasslands, is especially picturesque.

Trip plan: Malawi's main international airport is in the capital, Lilongwe. Join an organised art-focused trip that combines multiple locations in order to capture different landscapes. Allow ten days.

Need to know: Bilharzia (schistosomiasis) is present in Lake Malawi – the risk is greatest in areas close to villages.

Other months: Dec-Apr – wet, flooding possible, good birding; May-Jun & Aug – dry, cool, lush; Sep-Nov – dry, hotter, vegetation more parched.

Coastal caves on Devils Island in Lake Superior's Apostle chain

WISCONSIN
USA

→ Why now? Cool off with a great lake break.

In Wisconsin's warmest month, with temperatures hitting 25°C or so (around 77°F), the shores of lakes Michigan and Superior lure hordes of heat-fleeing urbanites. Unsurprisingly, the pretty waterfront villages and beaches of Door County, dubbed the 'Cape Cod of the Midwest', bustle with vacationers, though there's still peace to be found on Washington Island and in Newport State Park. For a real retreat, head northwest to the shore of Lake Superior – stopping en route to dip or fish in one of the glacial lakes peppering Vilas and Oneda counties. Charming Bayfield, its streets lined with Victorian buildings, is likeable enough in itself but, more importantly, it's the jumping-off point for the Apostle Islands, a mostly still-wild archipelago of 22 russet-fringed emerald specks. Pitch your tent at one of the simple campsites, admire the sandstone cliffs and caves from a kayak or on one of the many hiking circuits – or just find an empty beach and loll in the sunshine.

Trip plan: Door County is 64km (40 miles) from Green Bay, 241km (150 miles) from Milwaukee; Bayfield is 354km (220 miles) from Minneapolis.

Need to know: Feeling fruity? Door County is renowned for its cherries and apples, while Bayfield is surrounded by berry farms and orchards – make time for farm visits and fruit feasts.

Other months: Dec–Mar – very cold, dipping below freezing; Apr-Jun – spring, snow lingers; Aug – warm, sunny; Sep-Nov – cool to cold, autumn colours from Oct.

Green turtle
nesting on the
Tortuguero sands

PARQUE NACIONAL TORTUGUERO COSTA RICA

 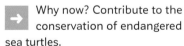

→ **Why now? Contribute to the conservation of endangered sea turtles.**

Lying on a flourishing floodplain chequered by canals on the Caribbean coast, the 'mini-Amazon' Tortuguero is a biodiversity hotspot. Take to the waterways to spot more than 400 bird species plus caiman and crocodiles, howler monkeys, sloths, river otters and manatees; the park is also home to jaguar, though you'd be fortunate indeed to encounter one. Crucially, it's an important nesting site for the endangered green turtle, perhaps 40,000 of which nest

here each year between June and October (leatherbacks and critically endangered hawkbills arrive earlier in the year). Though you'll likely experience afternoon rain showers during this 'green season' month, in truth it's a fine time to visit Tortuguero – and better still to join a volunteer project helping secure a future for the charismatic reptiles, threatened by habitat loss, fisheries bycatch, hunting and egg-harvesting. Typically you'll patrol nesting beaches, possibly assisting with turtle research projects and other conservation work including biodiversity surveys – and

you'll thrill to the sight of a huge female lumbering onto the beach at night to dig her nest and lay some 100 eggs in the sand.

Trip plan: Book a placement with an established volunteer organisation; plan well ahead, allowing time to process permits for wildlife research. Alternatively, tour operators in San José offer short packages to Tortuguero.

Need to know: Beware of swimming in the sea here – sharks and crocs lurk.

Other months: Dec-Apr – hot, drier; May-Jun & Aug-Nov – hot, wetter.

173

VIENNA AUSTRIA

→ **Why now?** Wander between wineries and taverns during the longest days.

A local tavern serving its own vintages in a grape-shaded courtyard, rustic snacks on the side? This vine idea took fruitful root in Vienna centuries ago: Heurigen (wine taverns) have been refreshing thirsty patrons here since the Middle Ages. Unsurprisingly, the Heuriger concept became hugely popular, and today dozens still tempt locals and visitors for a cool *viertel* (quarter-litre) on a warm afternoon – never warmer than July, when a stroll between outlying taverns provides the ideal way to escape the busy central sights. Grinzing, northwest of the city, is the best-known district for Heurigen and Weingüter (wineries), and is renowned for live music – fun but a little touristy. Stretch your legs a little further to discover less-vaunted areas such as Sievering, Neustift, Nussdorf, Stammersdorf and Streberdorf in the north, and Mauer in the southwest, freshening up with a walk along the verdant trails of the Wienerwald (Vienna Forest).

Trip plan: Vienna's excellent public transport system reaches most Heurigen districts. The 38 tram runs to Grinzing (as does the kitsch but fun Heurigen Express road train); take 31 to Stammersdorf, D to Nussdorf, 60 to Mauer.

Need to know: Traditionally, Heurigen are identified by a wreath or a pine branch hung above the door.

Other months: Dec-Feb – very cold, often grey; Mar-Apr – cool, quieter; May-Jun – heating up, rainy; Aug – warm, city busy; Sep-Nov – cooling, often crisp days.

(T) Grinzing is home to a host of Heurigen; (B) Grapes on the vine

Surveying the
snowbound scene
in the Southern Alps

SOUTHERN ALPS NEW ZEALAND

→ Why now? Snowshoe across white wilds.

Queenstown could never be accused of letting adrenaline levels flag. And in midwinter, when snow cakes the surrounding Remarkables, skiers flock here to swoosh down the slopes at Treble Cone. But downhill's not the only game in (or around) town. In July, the coldest month of the year, with temperatures reliably dipping below freezing at night, opportunities for tobogganing, dog-sledding and, particularly, snowshoeing abound. Activity specialists offer half- and full-day

snowshoe tours involving a short walk or gondola ride to reach the powder. For a real wilderness fix, plot an overnight or multi-day adventure staying in the backcountry huts – some managed by the Department of Conservation, others privately owned and used by tour groups – that stud the high levels of the Southern Alps. Tours into the Two Thumb Range from Lake Tekapo traverse the Aoraki Mackenzie International Dark Sky Reserve, rewarding trampers with spectacular stargazing. Perhaps the finest routes climb into the Pisa Range south of Wanaka, where first-timers and

experienced backcountry wilderness snowshoers can both enjoy a fix.

Trip plan: Base yourself in Queenstown (busier) or Wanaka, and plan either a series of day excursions or multi-day tours staying in backcountry huts, led by experienced local guides. Snowshoe hire and helihiking opportunities are available.

Need to know: Some resorts get busy with families during July school holidays.

Other months: Nov-Mar – warm, great hiking; Apr-May – pleasant weather, less busy; Jun & Aug-Oct – cold, snow on mountains.

August

WHERE TO GO WHEN

CHALLENGE MYSELF →

I WANT TO

TAKE ME OUT FOR...
- FOOD —— SINGAPORE P193
- DRINK —— PORTLAND, OREGON, USA P197

Learn to tango like a local in Buenos Aires

Dig in to some hawker market comfort-food favourites

TAKE ME TO THE...
- CAPITAL
  - LUXEMBOURG P185
  - BUENOS AIRES, ARGENTINA P192
- COUNTRY SIDE —— CHAMONIX, FRANCE P183

Hit the slopes – in your running shoes – around Chamonix

RELAX/ INDULGE

Snorkel in Borneo's warm waters

TAKE ME TO THE BEACH
- REV UP —— BORNEO, MALAYSIA P199
- CHILL OUT
  - NORTHEAST SRI LANKA P185
  - NORTHEAST BRAZIL P183

Surf til the sun sets in Arugam Bay, Sri Lanka

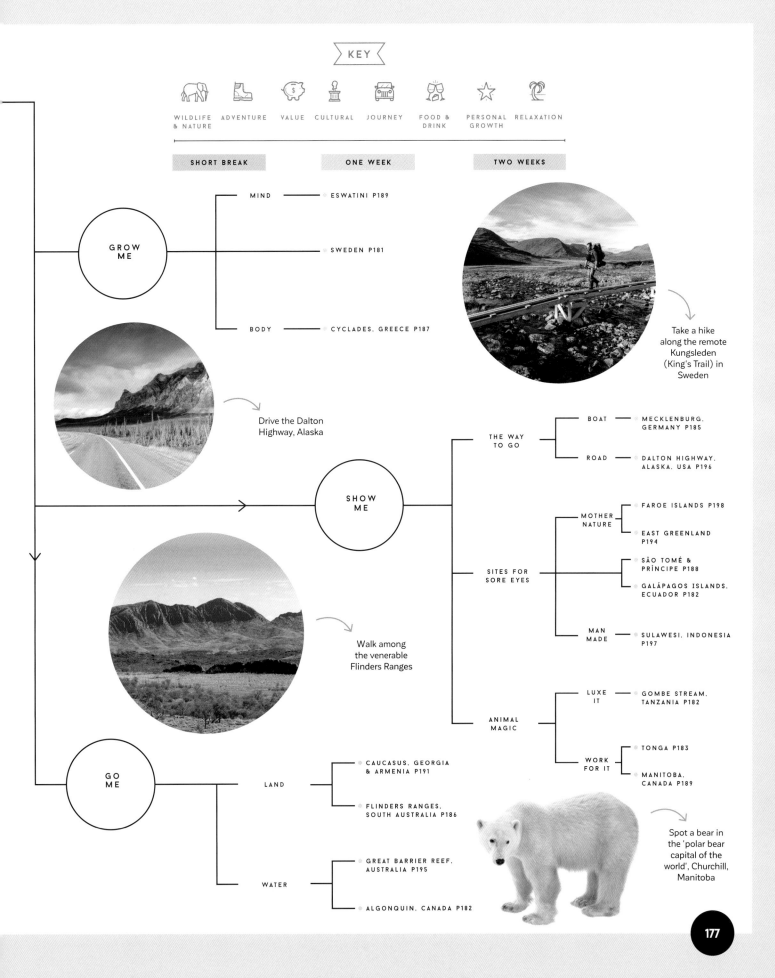

SHORT BREAK | ONE WEEK | TWO WEEKS

GROW ME

MIND — ESWATINI P189

SWEDEN P181

BODY — CYCLADES, GREECE P187

Take a hike along the remote Kungsleden (King's Trail) in Sweden

Drive the Dalton Highway, Alaska

SHOW ME

THE WAY TO GO
- BOAT — MECKLENBURG, GERMANY P185
- ROAD — DALTON HIGHWAY, ALASKA, USA P196

SITES FOR SORE EYES
- MOTHER NATURE — FAROE ISLANDS P198
- EAST GREENLAND P194
- SÃO TOMÉ & PRÍNCIPE P188
- GALÁPAGOS ISLANDS, ECUADOR P182
- MAN MADE — SULAWESI, INDONESIA P197

Walk among the venerable Flinders Ranges

ANIMAL MAGIC
- LUXE IT — GOMBE STREAM, TANZANIA P182
- WORK FOR IT — TONGA P183
- MANITOBA, CANADA P189

GO ME

LAND
- CAUCASUS, GEORGIA & ARMENIA P191
- FLINDERS RANGES, SOUTH AUSTRALIA P186

WATER
- GREAT BARRIER REEF, AUSTRALIA P195
- ALGONQUIN, CANADA P182

Spot a bear in the 'polar bear capital of the world', Churchill, Manitoba

EVENTS
IN AUGUST

LA TOMATINA

Buñol, Spain
Grab as many tomatoes as you can, cram yourself among tens of thousands of fruit-wielding combatants, hurl and repeat.

CROP OVER

Barbados
Months of intermittent partying come to a climax with glittery Carnival processions and noisy revelry to the rhythms of soca and steel bands.

MAHERERO DAY

Okahandja, Namibia
Thousands of Herero people don colourful costumes and gather to commemorate tribal chiefs who died leading the revolt against colonial German forces.

JAGUAR SPOTTING

Pantanal, Brazil
As water bodies dry up in South America's greatest tropical wetland, sightings of the continent's biggest cats peak.

ST DOMINIC'S FAIR

Gdánsk, Poland
For over seven centuries, traders, artisans, food stalls, entertainers and fun-seekers have packed Gdánsk's streets and squares each summer.

MT HAGEN CULTURAL SHOW

Mt Hagen, Papua New Guinea
Cultural groups from across the western highlands gather for PNG's most renowned singsing, with dances, feasting and rituals.

INTERNATIONAL CAMEL DERBY

Maralal, Kenya
Camel jockeys ride their lumbering steeds through town, watched by traditionally clad Samburu tribespeople.

AMISH ACRES ARTS & CRAFTS FESTIVAL

Nappanee, Indiana, USA
Discover the works of hundreds of artists and craftspeople in this celebration of Amish heritage and creativity.

Last Wednesday in August · $

Ends early August · $$

Usually 26 August · $$

Three weeks in early August · $

August (date varies) · $$

First weekend in August · $$

Usually August, occasionally September · $$

All month · $$$

178

VERY
FAMILY
FRIENDLY

GREAT BARRIER REEF,
AUSTRALIA

BORNEO, MALAYSIA

Look out for
orangutans in Borneo's
rainforests

Swim with turtles on
Lady Elliot Island,
Great Barrier Reef

NORTHEAST BRAZIL

Plunge into clear
pools at Lençóis
Maranhenses
National Park,
Brazil

TONGA

MECKLENBURG, GERMANY

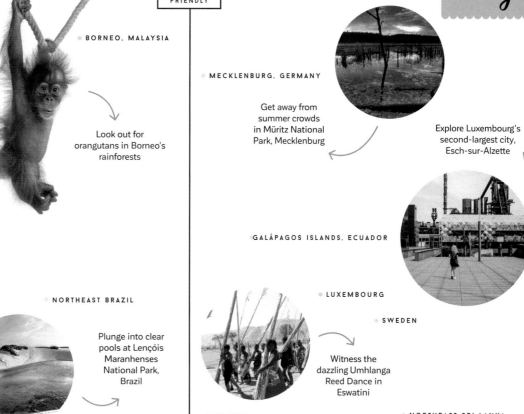

Get away from
summer crowds
in Müritz National
Park, Mecklenburg

Explore Luxembourg's
second-largest city,
Esch-sur-Alzette

GALÁPAGOS ISLANDS, ECUADOR

LUXEMBOURG

SWEDEN

Witness the
dazzling Umhlanga
Reed Dance in
Eswatini

ESWATINI

NORTHEAST SRI LANKA

EXPENSIVE
WORTH IT

GOOD
VALUE

SINGAPORE

ALGONQUIN, CANADA

Canoe the paddle-
friendly waters of
Algonquin

GOMBE STREAM, TANZANIA

CYCLADES, GREECE

FAROE ISLANDS

FLINDERS RANGES,
SOUTH AUSTRALIA

MANITOBA, CANADA

Dodge the crowds
in craggy-coasted
Iraklia, Cyclades

SULAWESI,
INDONESIA

CHAMONIX, FRANCE

BUENOS AIRES, ARGENTINA

Base yourself
between the
peaks in Tasiilaq,
Greenland

EAST GREENLAND

SÃO TOMÉ & PRÍNCIPE

PORTLAND, OREGON, USA

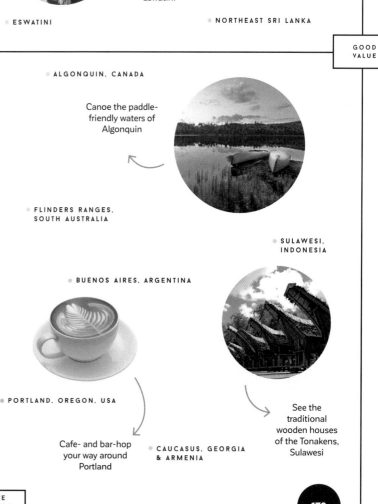

See the
traditional
wooden houses
of the Tonakens,
Sulawesi

Have a perfect beach day (or
two...) at Praia Banana,
São Tomé & Príncipe

DALTON HIGHWAY,
ALASKA USA

Cafe- and bar-hop
your way around
Portland

CAUCASUS, GEORGIA
& ARMENIA

LEAVE
THE KIDS
AT HOME

SWEDEN

→ **Why now? For a free foraging adventure.**

Allemansrätt is an amazing thing. This 'Right of Public Access', written into Swedish law, means everyone has the right to freely roam the countryside – that is, to visit any beach, swim in any lake, fish anywhere off the coast, put up a tent on (almost) any patch of ground and forage all over. And in a country with as much wonderful wilderness as Sweden, the possibilities are endless – even in peak-season August there's plenty enough space for everyone. Plus it's a great month for foraging: look out for wild mushrooms plus bushes heavy with blueberries, raspberries, lingonberries and cloudberries. But where to go? Perhaps a wild-camp kayaking expedition around the islands of the Stockholm Archipelago? Or a hike along the Kungsleden (King's Trail) in remote Swedish Lapland? Or how about berry-picking in the forests of Skuleskogen National Park?

Trip plan: For the Kungsleden, you can fly (1hr 30min) or take the train (16hr) from Stockholm to Kiruna, board a train to Abisko (70min) and start from there. For Skuleskogen, take the train from Stockholm to Örnsköldsvik (6hr) and then a bus to the park entrance.

Need to know: *Allemansrätt* states that you're allowed to access any area, except for private residences, within 70m (230ft) of a house or on cultivated land.

Other months: Nov-Apr – cold, snow; May-Jun – warm, long days; Jul & Sep – warmest, good foraging; Oct – cooling, fall colours.

Swedens wonderful, free-to-roam wilderness

GOMBE STREAM
TANZANIA

→ **Why now? To track down chimps.**
This tiny national park – the smallest in Tanzania – has a big reputation. Dr Jane Goodall founded the Gombe Stream Research Centre in 1965 to study the area's chimpanzees, and the conservation work hasn't stopped since. It's a fantastic spot to get up-close to the primates – there are around 150 habituated chimps here. Although chimp-trekking can be done year-round, the odds of finding them quickly are better later in the dry season (August-October), when the animals tend to stay on the lower slopes of the park's forested mountains. While you're here, keep an eye out for other primates, such as red-tailed colobus and vervet monkeys, as well as elephants and 200-plus species of birds. The park lies on the shore of Lake Tanganyika, where you can loll on soft sand and snorkel among colourful cichlids too.

Trip plan: Gombe makes a good two/three-day add-on to a traditional northern Tanzania safari. Or you could combine it with other little-visited areas in the west, such as Katavi (home to huge numbers of hippos) and Mahale Mountains (another chimp hotspot).

Need to know: The nearest town is Kigoma, which has a small airport. It's a 2hr 30min flight from Dar es Salaam.

Other months: Jan-Feb – dry, green, quiet; Mar-May – long rains, many lodges close; Jun-Jul & Sep-Oct – dry, cool, best for tracking; Nov-Dec – short rains, lush.

ECUADOR

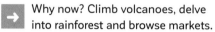

→ **Why now? Climb volcanoes, delve into rainforest and browse markets.**
Little Ecuador packs the best of South America into one handy-sized package. It has colonial architecture in Quito and Cuenca; Inca remains at Ingapirca; indigenous markets at Otavalo, Saquisil and Zumbahua; magnificent cones (including picture-perfect Cotopaxi) along the 'Avenue of the Volcanoes'; and profuse wildlife in the Amazon, the Galápagos and the northern cloud forests. Both highlands and rainforest are driest in August, so it's prime time for absorbing the cultural highlights and getting active on volcanoes and rafting whitewater rivers. Ecuador's a bargain, to boot, with great-value accommodation.

Trip plan: From capital Quito, head north to spot iridescent hummingbirds in Mindo cloud forest and on to the bustling market at Otavalo (pausing en route to hop back and forth across the equator). Then dip back south to hike on Cotopaxi or Chimborazo, soak in the thermal waters at Baños, explore the Inca remains at Ingapirca and admire historic Cuenca. It's worth spending time and money flying deep into the Amazon along the Napo River to stay in one of the wonderful community-run ecolodges.

Need to know: A Galápagos cruise is less appealing in August, with rough seas and more cloud.

Other months: Jan-May – cool, wet in highlands and Amazon; Jun-Jul & Sep – driest months in highlands and Amazon; Oct-Dec – wet in Amazon, dry in highlands.

ALGONQUIN
CANADA

→ **Why now? Paddle the great outdoors without the pesky bugs.**
Algonquin Provincial Park lies within easy reach of Toronto and Ottawa – two of Canada's biggest cities – but couldn't feel much more like proper wilderness. It's a sprawling expanse of craggy ridges, maple-cloaked hills, spruce bogs, lakes, ponds and streams that is roamed by moose, black bear and wolves. It's best explored by paddle: there are 2000km-plus (1243 miles) of canoe routes here, with options ranging from day trips to longer adventures and thrilling whitewater rivers. The Big Trout Lake Loop from Canoe Lake is a good mid-length backcountry expedition; each night you'll set up camp by a different lake, where you can listen for wolves and be awed by the stars (there's no light pollution out here). August is excellent because days are warm, evenings are cool and virtually all of the mosquitoes have buzzed off.

Trip plan: Canoe Lake is around 300km (186 miles) from both Toronto and Ottawa. An access road off Highway 60 leads to a permit office and Portage Store. Allow five days for the Big Trout Lake Loop.

Need to know: Weekends can get busy (more so later in July and August) – book camping spots well in advance and consider travelling midweek.

Other months: Nov-Apr – cold, lakes possibly icy; May – water cold, bug-free; Jun – warm, blackflies and mosquitoes; Jul – less buggy, humid; Sep-Oct – cold nights, quiet, autumn colours.

CHAMONIX
FRANCE

Why now? To run like *le vent*.
Chamonix is the de-facto capital of trail running. The town's lively centre is filled with stores selling Lycra accoutrements and grippy-soled running shoes, and people come from all corners of the globe to scamper the surrounding slopes – from here, at the foot of Mount Blanc, paths climb across France and into Switzerland and Italy. The crescendo of this mountain-running fervour is the UTMB (the Ultra-Trail du Mont Blanc), the Olympics of the ultra scene. Held at the end of August, the week-long festival of doing mad feats on foot includes various races, including a 170km (106 miles) loop around the highest peak in the Alps. Being in town for UTMB is a thrill – grab a cowbell and clang for the competitors. Or come earlier in the month, when the weather is relatively settled and warm, to join a trail running course, and learn how to jog around the mountains yourself.

Trip plan: Buses run from Geneva airport to Chamonix several times daily. Trains from Paris and Geneva stop at St-Gervais-Les-Bains, from where local trains serve Chamonix. Both guided and independent trail runs are possible.

Need to know: Many outdoors shops in town offer free guided trail runs – check for details.

Other months: Dec-Apr – snow, winter sports; May & Nov – off season, unpredictable weather; Jun & Oct – warm, mountains may be accessible; Jul & Sep – warmest, snow cleared, busiest.

TONGA

Why now? Swim with singing humpback whales.
Tonga welcomes various visitors throughout the year. There are surfers, who come here to ride 3m (10ft) swells and offshore reef breaks. There are game fishers, who come to reel in blue marlin. There are sun- and beach-lovers, who seek out their own untouched piece of paradise among the 170-plus islands. But the biggest fans of this gorgeous South Pacific archipelago are the humpback whales who migrate here from Antarctica between July and September each year to calve. This is one of the few places in the world where it's possible to swim with these melodic behemoths – select a responsible operator and be sure not to disturb the new families. With manta rays, dolphins, sea turtles and a host of dazzling marine life joining the underwater party, Tonga is a spectacular place to snorkel and dive, while kayaking is a great way to explore the atolls and islands. There's ancient history in the form of huge trilithons and the royal stone tombs around Mu'a, while getting to know today's laidback community is a treat.

Trip plan: Tonga's airport at Nuku'alofa is served by direct flights from Auckland, Fiji and Sydney, with lots of connections.

Need to know: Humpback whales gather around Tonga to calve from July to September.

Other months: Dec-Mar – wettest; Apr-Jul & Sep-Nov – drier.

NORTHEAST
BRAZIL

Why now? Dive into crystal-clear waters among rolling dunes.
Word got out about Jericoacoara (Jeri) a while ago, so this travellers' beach paradise, with its watersports, capoeira classes and laidback vibe, is now everyone's favourite secret. Yet the stretch of Brazil's north coast between São Luís and Fortaleza is still something special. There are dozens of places, including regional capital Fortaleza, at which to enjoy sea, sun, sand and sports such as surfing, windsurfing and kitesurfing. Then there's the remarkable Lençóis Maranhenses National Park, a vast expanse of folded dunes interspersed with limpid pools (full in August) just begging to be plunged into, plus mangroves, lagoons and turtles.

Trip plan: Explore the coast on a road trip between São Luís, with its pastel-hued colonial mansions, and Fortaleza, both accessible on flights from Rio de Janeiro and other Brazilian cities, pausing at Lençóis Maranhenses National Park and Jeri en route.

Need to know: The Pôr do Sol (sunset dune) at Jeri is reputedly one of the few places you can see the 'emerald flash' – a green spark as the sun dips into the ocean.

Other months: Jul & Sep-Feb – sunny, dry, best windsurfing (Dec-Feb: national holidays, beaches busy); Mar-Jun – rainy season.

(A) Boating around Malchow, Mecklenburg; (L) Fishers along the coast in northeast Sri Lanka; (R) Lush Müllerthal, Luxembourg

MECKLENBURG
GERMANY

Why now? For boating away from other people.

It may be peak summer holiday season in Germany but it's not hard to escape the crowds in the 'land of 1000 lakes'. The sleepy region of Mecklenburg, to the north of Berlin, is splattered with interconnected rivers, channels, *wasserstrasses* (waterways) and lagoons; much of the area falls into Müritz National Park and is a haven for wildlife – cormorants, storks and osprey might be spotted. It's also a delightful place for messing about in boats, which enables you to sail away from other people. Hire a motor cruiser, yacht or *penichette* (traditional barge) and float between medieval towns (such as Waren, Malchow and Templin), sites such as Schwerin Castle, forested banks and waterside *Fischerhütte*, where you can pick up some of the area's famed smoked fish. Temperatures hover around 25°C (77°F), ideal for lounging on deck and leaping off for refreshing swims.

Trip plan: The Mecklenburg region is easily accessible from Berlin – for instance, Rheinsberg is 70km (43 miles) north (2hr by train). Boats can be hired from a number of bases, including Wolfsbruch (near Rheinsberg), Lübz and Fürstenberg. Allow a week or more.

Need to know: Consider hiring extras: SUPs, bikes, angling gear (and fishing licenses) so you can catch your own suppers.

Other months: Nov-Mar – chilly, limited boat hire; Apr-May & Oct – warm, quiet; Jun-Jul & Sep – warmest, busiest, best for swimming.

NORTHEAST
SRI LANKA

Why now? Loll or surf at Indian Ocean beaches under the sun.

There's a triple whammy of good news about Sri Lanka's northeast in August: the weather is great, prices are low, and beaches are quiet. Unlike the southwest, which catches the rain now, the northeast coast this month has blue skies, warm waters and – at Arugam Bay particularly – fine surf. Civil war ensured this region was largely off limits till recently, so the coast is little-developed – you can still find an empty patch of sand at spots such as Nilaveli, Uppuveli and Passekudah. The centre is also pretty dry in August, good for visiting the rock fortress of Sigiriya and spiritual hub Kandy, which bursts into noisy, colourful life during the Esala Perahera celebrations honouring the Sacred Tooth relic of Buddha each summer. Be warned: spicy Sri Lankan food is addictive.

Trip plan: International flights serve Colombo; Trincomalee and the northeastern beaches are reached by train or bus and taxi.

Need to know: Dates for the 10-day Esala Perahera festival vary across July and August depending on how the month of Esala falls.

Other months: Feb-July & Sep – dry, warm; Oct-Jan – wet

LUXEMBOURG

Why now? The culture is just capital.

Compact little Luxembourg – just 82km (51 miles) long by 57km (35 miles) wide – is often overlooked in favour of neighbouring France, Belgium and Germany. Which makes it a good choice for high-summer August. Thanks to the long days and sunny weather, the streets of the Grand Duchy's cities are lively with outdoor concerts, festivals and pavement cafes – and nowhere more so, perhaps, than Esch-sur-Alzette. The country's second-largest city, known as the 'Metropolis of Iron' thanks to its industrial heritage, was named European Capital of Culture 2022, shining a spotlight on its attractions, from the National Museum of the Resistance to the old Belval blast furnaces, which have been restored and integrated into a new urban quarter. The city has plenty of green space too, where you can escape the summer heat. Or head further afield, to the trails of the Müllerthal gorges or the leafy Ardennes forest.

Trip plan: Trains (1hr 20min) and buses (30min) link Luxembourg City and Esch-sur-Alzette. Luxembourg City has an international airport and is well connected to other European hubs (Brussels is 3hr 30min by train).

Need to know: In 2020 Luxembourg became the first country in the world to offer free nationwide public transport for everyone.

Other months: Nov-Feb – winter, cold; May-Jul & Sep – pleasantly warm; Mar-Apr & Oct – cooler.

FLINDERS RANGES
SOUTH AUSTRALIA

Aerial view of the
Flinders Ranges

→ **Why now? Cool weather for walking.**

The craggy, saw-toothed Flinders Ranges are venerable indeed. Formed over 600 million years, they're home to some of the oldest multi-cellular fossils on earth – the region's Nilpena Ediacara National Park, designated in 2021, is arguably the world's richest and most intact paleontological site. Also, human activity here dates back 49,000 years, with Aboriginal stories seemingly woven around every rock and outcrop. August is a good time to plot your own Flinders walkabout: there's more rain, but it fills the creeks and pools, attracting wildlife. Animals are more active during the cooler winter days too – hikers might find themselves strolling with yellow-footed rock wallabies, emus, grey kangaroos and flocks of galahs. The rugged northern section of the 1200km (750 miles) Heysen Trail (which starts on the south coast) cuts through the region, finishing at Parachilna Gorge, winding via Mt Remarkable, Alligator Gorge and the crater-like bowl of Ikara (Wilpena Pound). Truly epic hiking country.

Trip plan: The Flinders Ranges are about 500km (311 miles) north of Adelaide. The Heysen can be walked independently by well-prepared, experienced hikers or via a guided tour; sections 38 to 61 cross the Flinders Ranges.

Need to know: August averages around 15°C (59°F) during the day but nights can drop to almost freezing so warm clothing is recommended.

Other months: Oct-Mar – very hot, fire danger, hikes not possible; Apr-May – warm; Jun-Jul – coolest, wildlife active; Sep – warming, wildflowers.

Crystal-clear waters of the Cyclades

CYCLADES
GREECE

→ **Why now? To swim between offbeat isles.**

OK, we won't lie: August across this magnificent Mediterranean archipelago is hardly castaway-quiet. The weather is too alluringly hot and sunny, and popular islands like party-central Mykonos and dreamy Santorini heave. However, smaller outposts – such as Schinousa, uninhabited Fidousa and craggy-coasted Iraklia – will be far less crowded. Plus there's a way to get away from everyone: jump in that crystal-clear blue sea. Book an open-water swimming holiday to hop between bays, coves and beaches under your own steam – rather than hordes of tourists, you'll see sea caves, rock arches, towering cliffs and colourful fish. You'll also pick up some new swimming techniques, explore with like-minded waterbabies, feel the health benefits of wild swimming and finish in local tavernas each night. Even better, the sea temperature is a delicious 23-27°C (73-80°F).

Trip plan: From Athens, flights connect to Cycladean islands such as Naxos (the nearest airport to Schinousa). Ferries run from Athens to Naxos and from Naxos to Schinousa. For safety it's best to join a swimming tour with a dedicated guide and support boat. Swims of various lengths are possible.

Need to know: Tinted googles, water shoes and waterproof sun cream are recommended.

Other months: May-Jul & Sep – hot (busiest Jul-Aug); Apr & Oct – mild; Nov-Mar – cool, quiet, some tourist facilities close.

(A) Towering Cão Grande; (B) Abandoned hospital-turned-open-air museum

© Justin Foulkes / Lonely Planet

SÃO TOMÉ & PRÍNCIPE

→ **Why now?** Explore volcanic peaks, whale-cruised seas, plantation history and one of Africa's most raucous festivals.

The tiny twin-island nation in the Gulf of Guinea typically receives most of its (admittedly few) visitors in August. Some arrive to experience the extraordinary spectacle of the Auto de Floripes – the uniquely loud, kaleidoscopic, modern take on a medieval morality play performed annually in the streets of self-proclaimed 'world's smallest capital', Santo António on Príncipe. Others are passing through – the humpback whales that migrate past between August and October offer fabulous whale-watching opportunities. Those rare human travellers who do make it here savour the empty, pristine beaches – notably Boi and Banana on Príncipe – gawp at majestic volcanic peaks such as Cão Grande, and roam the tumbledown remains of cacao plantations dating from the Portuguese colonial era, many still occupied by the descendants of imported labourers.

Trip plan: International flights, usually via Lisbon, serve São Tomé International Airport, from where regional flights make the 35min hop to Príncipe. Spend a couple of days on São Tomé.

Need to know: Malaria is present on São Tomé but rare on Príncipe. Cover arms and legs and use repellent in the evenings, and consider prophylaxis. Inter-island flights and the few accommodation options get booked out well in advance for the Auto de Floripes.

Other months: Oct-mid-Jan & mid-Feb-May – heavy downpours, flowers bloom; Jun-Jul, Sep & mid-Jan-mid-Feb – drier seasons, cloudier, rain always possible.

© Justin Foulkes / Lonely Planet

188

ESWATINI

→ **Why now? Big festivities in Africa's little culture capital.**

Landlocked Eswatini (known, until 2018, as Swaziland) has all the animal allure you'd expect from a wild tract of southern Africa. There are 17 game-packed protected areas spread across this pocket-sized nation's bushveld, highveld and subtropical forests – ranger-led walks in Hlane Royal National Park are a particular thrill. But arguably it's the human interactions here that'll leave the greatest impression. Ruled by one of the world's last remaining absolute monarchs, Eswatini has a uniquely well-preserved cultural heritage, displayed in most dazzling fashion in late August (also, handily, the height of the dry season) at the Umhlanga Reed Dance. This huge-scale event at Ludzidzini sees up to 40,000 exuberant, brightly dressed girls dance before the King and the Queen Mother, accompanied by poker-faced warriors – it's an unmatched eruption

Brightly dressed girls at the exuberant Umhlanga Reed Dance

© Homo Cosmicos / Shutterstock

of swaying, singing, ululating, colour and noise.

Trip plan: Allow 10-12 days to explore Eswatini, combining a handful of wildlife areas (Hlane, Malolotja, Mkhaya) with ancient San art (Nsangwini Rock Shelter) and stays at community-led tourism spots (such as Shewula Mountain Camp) to learn more about Swazi culture. Umhlanga

lasts eight days – visitors are only allowed to take photographs with prior permission from the Ministry of Information.

Need to know: Capital Mbazbane is a 45min flight or 4hr 30min drive from Johannesburg in South Africa.

Other months: Oct-Mar – rainy season, green, hot; Apr-Jul & Sep – dry, cool, best wildlife-watching.

MANITOBA CANADA

→ **Why now? For a convergence of creatures.**

The isolated outpost of Churchill is the self-proclaimed 'Polar Bear Capital of the World', and in October and November wildlife-lovers flock here to see the awesome ursine giants as they migrate to their winter hunting grounds. But come a little earlier in the year and not only is the weather warmer (with average highs around 15°C/59°F), but you might get even more bang for your buck. From June

to September the bears are still stalking the flower-flecked tundra, and can be seen on safaris with expert guides who lead trips on foot. Meanwhile, around 60,000 curious, snow-white beluga whales visit the Hudson Bay area to breed and calve; get up-close by boat, by kayak or by aqua-gliding – that is, clinging to a floating platform that's towed behind a vessel, putting you right at whale level. Keep an eye out for seals, Arctic hare, Arctic fox and over 200 species of birds too.

Trip plan: Book a trip with a specialist operator for a summer experience in the Churchill area. Allow five/six nights.

Need to know: Trains (45hr) and planes (4hr) connect Winnipeg, Manitoba's capital, and Churchill.

Other months: Oct-Nov – cold, polar bears; Dec-Mar – very cold, aurora, dog-sledding; Apr-May – cold; Jun-Jul & Sep – warmest, belugas, birds, bears.

CAUCASUS
GEORGIA & ARMENIA

→ Why now? Hike a spectacular, sustainable trail.

When completed, the Transcaucasian Trail will be a monster – a marvellous 3000km (1864 miles) monster, streaking across the little-visited mountains of Georgia and Armenia, from the Black Sea to the Caspian Sea. The project, begun in 2015, aims to safeguard the nature and culture of the Caucasus by creating a world-class hiking route and developing sustainable tourism initiatives along the way. Trekkers will be able to follow centuries-old shepherds' tracks, visit monasteries and medieval villages, stay in family guesthouses, feast on homecooked dishes and raise a glass or three of excellent local wine. Hundreds of kilometres have already been mapped, including the full north–south crossing of Armenia, via the peaks of Azhdahak and Khustup, lakes Arpi and Sevan, the national parks of Dilijan and Arevi, and the canyons of Dzoraget and Debed. A section through Georgia's Upper Svaneti is ready too, where the high-altitude passes aren't snow-free until July.

Trip plan: Trail guides, maps and downloadable GPS data is available for some sections including the Upper Svaneti (allow 10 days) and Armenia's Gegham Mountains (5-7 days), allowing independent hikers to explore without a guide.

Need to know: The security situation in the mountains south of the Russian border can change quickly – check government warnings before travelling.

Other months: Nov-Mar – cold, snow likely; Apr-Jun – warm, spring flowers; Sep-Oct – autumn colours.

Armenia's 9th-century
Tatev Monastery

191

BUENOS AIRES
ARGENTINA

→ **Why now? Learn to tango in the home of the world's sexiest dance.**

Nowhere else are a city and a dance so inextricably linked. Tango is, simply, the heartbeat of Buenos Aires, and the Argentine capital's passion for both the music – exemplified by the songs of Carlos Gardel, which still waft out of many a window – and the dance never seems to diminish. The cool month of August isn't just a wonderful time to visit BA, it also sees the city fling itself into its annual Festival de Tango, with performances and concerts by the finest exponents. At other times you can enjoy more or less touristy (but usually high-calibre) tango shows at various clubs and theatres, or simply watch the weekly Sunday sessions in Plaza Dorrego. But to really feel the spirit of the dance, join a lesson at a San Telmo *milonga* (dancehall) and stay for the late-night free-for-all with expert Porteños afterwards, fuelled by fine Argentine red wine.

Trip plan: The city centre and Recoleta, Palermo and San Telmo districts offer the best accommodation options.

Need to know: The action begins late in Buenos Aires – don't expect dances to get started before midnight.

Other months: Dec-Mar – hot, humid; Apr-May & Sep-Nov – pleasant temperatures, more rain; Jun-Jul – cool but drier.

Watch the pros in action at Plaza Dorrego

© JohnnyGreig / Getty Images

© ThamKC / Shutterstock

SINGAPORE

Laksa – comfort-food, Singapore style

→ Why now? For greenery and gluttony.
Singapore is a hot and tasty prospect year-round. Practically on the equator, it's always warm here, while the food scene – from Michelin-starred to street stalls – is always delicious. August, when local school holidays are over and rain is scarce, can be especially mouthwatering, with the World Gourmet Summit and Singapore Food Festival hitting the city. There's a growing focus on thinking local and sustainable too, with a resurgence in the popularity of the city's hawker market culture and comfort-food faves (*laksa*, *hokkien mee* rice, fried *kway teow* noodles), young 'hawkerpreneur' chefs adding hipness to the traditional scene and attempts to tackle food waste issues. Indeed, Singapore is aiming for a greener future all round, with a pledge to double the size of its nature parks and plant more than a million trees by 2030.

Trip plan: Allow two or three days to visit the Botanic Gardens, the high-tech Gardens by the Bay and the surrounding wildlife-rich rainforests. Also, visit hawker centres – such as Newton and historic Lau Pa Sat – and join a street-food tour to get a taste of different neighbourhoods.

Need to know: Tissue paper may be used to reserve a seat at a hawker market. *Chope* means 'this seat is mine'.

Other months: Nov-Jan – monsoon, wettest; Feb-Jul & Sep-Oct – hot, humid, drier (busiest Jun-Jul).

EAST GREENLAND

 Why now? To gain access to a world-beating wilderness.

It's tough to explore East Greenland. This side of the Arctic island is practically uninhabited outside the Ammassalik region, and its northern reaches – largely encompassed within Northeast Greenland National Park, the biggest national park in the world – are locked in by pack ice for most of the year. But for a few summer months, the ice loosens its grip, the coast opens up just a peep and small expedition ships can make forays into this remotest wilderness. Head for the peak-flanked town of Tasiilaq (August average highs: 10°C/50°F) – it makes a fine base for excursions such as tundra hikes and helicopter flights over the ice cap. Or board a northbound cruise to explore Scoresby Sund (the planet's biggest fjord system), float amid icebergs, zip along glacier faces in inflatable Zodiacs, stop at the isolated community of Ittoqqortoormiit to learn about Inuit culture and trek across the tundra, looking out for musk ox, Arctic fox, seals and seabirds.

Trip plan: Kulusuk Airport is a 2hr flight from Reykjavík; helicopters connect to Tasiilaq. During summer months various expedition cruises are possible – some combine East Greenland with Svalbard or Iceland.

Need to know: Voyage itineraries and landing sites are heavily dependent on weather, sea and ice conditions.

Other months: Nov-Mar – winter, husky-sledding, northern lights; Apr-May & Oct – changeable, cheaper; Jun-Jul & Sep – long days, best weather, travel easiest.

© Adwo / Shutterstock

Kayakers dwarfed by an iceburg in Scoresby Sund

Colourful coral around the *SS Yongala* wreck

© Coral Brunner / Shutterstock

GREAT BARRIER REEF AUSTRALIA

→ **Why now? Explore with care, in clear seas.**

The Great Barrier Reef – 2300km (1429 miles) of coral stretching along the Queensland coast – is in peril, with climate change and pollution threatening this colossal world wonder. Around 85% of visitors experience the reef from Cairns or the Whitsunday Islands, putting added pressure on those areas; to minimise your impact – especially if you're visiting during popular August, when skies are dry and seas are clear – explore from other hubs instead. For instance, head to Townsville to gen up at the Great Barrier Reef Marine Park Authority's national education centre before hopping on a liveaboard boat to dive the lesser-visited central reef (including the SS *Yongala* wreck). Journey to Lizard Island National Park, at the reef's far north, where there's a research station run by the Australian Museum and a lodge dedicated to sustainable practices. Or stay at an eco-resort on Lady Elliot Island, at the reef's southern end, to swim with sea turtles and manta rays, which peak in numbers May-August.

Trip plan: Choose your base. Townsville is 345km (214 miles) south of Cairns. Lady Elliot Island is an 1hr 20min flight from Brisbane. Lizard Island is a 1hr flight from Cairns.

Need to know: When swimming and snorkelling use reef-safe sunscreen free of oxybenzone.

Other months: Dec-Mar – hot, humid; Apr-May – warm, showers; Jun-Jul & Sep – mild, dry, busy; Oct-Nov – hotter, showers.

One of the world's most dangerous roads is also one of the most spectacular

DALTON HIGHWAY, ALASKA USA

→ Why now? To drive across the Arctic Circle.

Unless you're a veteran ice-road trucker, you'll want to drive the Dalton Highway – one of the world's most dangerous roads – in high summer, when temperatures are around 10-20°C (50-68°F) and you're less likely to hit the skids. The gravel highway, which runs for 666km (414 miles) from Livengood (north of Fairbanks) to Deadhorse on Prudhoe Bay, was built as a service road for the Trans-Alaska Pipeline. It is snow-covered for much of the year, services en route are minimal (it passes only three villages) and risks are manifold – everything from crater-size potholes to migrating caribou. But the surrounding scenery is spectacular: you'll pass endless boreal forest and high alpine tundra, cross the Yukon River, the Arctic Circle and one of the highest passes in Alaska, and possibly spot musk ox, Dall sheep, raptors and bears.

Trip plan: The roundtrip from Fairbanks to Deadhorse and back takes at least four days; allow longer to include excursions – maybe backcountry hikes into Arctic National Wildlife Refuge. The old gold rush town of Coldfoot is at the midway point.

Need to know: The speed limit is 80kph (50mph). Not all hire car companies allow travel on gravel roads – check in advance.

Other months: Oct-May – snow, road icy; Jun-Jul – wildflowers, peak mosquitoes; Sep – cool, fewer bugs, autumn colours.

PORTLAND, OREGON
USA

→ **Why now? To eat and drink outside.**
The Pacific Northwest is notorious for its damp, misty weather. However, your best bet for a break with less drizzle is in August: it's one of the region's hottest, driest months, and ideal for soaking up Portland's alfresco summer food scene. At this time of year it's all about exploring the distinct neighbourhoods, hanging out on patios and plazas, grazing from food trucks, browsing farmers' markets, supping at microbreweries (there are around 70) and scootering between award-winning baristas. Indeed, Portland has more roasters and cafes per capita than any other US city – coffee is treated as seriously as wine here. A java-crawl might include rock-star roasters Stumptown, an iced coldbrew at Courier and a cuppa at Bison, the city's only Native American-owned coffee shop.

Trip plan: Portland is an easy city to love. Allow three or more days to soak up the different neighbourhoods (from hippie Hawthorne to upmarket Pearl). If it's too hot, make a break for the beach – the sands of Sauvie Island are a 20min drive from downtown.

Need to know: Portland is linked by train to cities such as LA, Seattle and Vancouver. The city has an extensive network of cycle lanes, as well as bike and e-scooter share schemes.

Other months: Nov-Mar – cold, wet, quietest; Apr-May & Sep-Oct – mild, rainy; Jun-Jul – warmest, driest, most festivals.

© Iulia Shcherbakova / Shutterstock

Boat-shaped roofs on the houses of the Tonakens

SULAWESI INDONESIA

→ **Why now? Blue skies for unique cultures.**
The strange, spidery shaped island of Sulawesi is arguably Indonesia at its most untouched. As well as being home to wild, lush highlands, there are tribes living here much as they have for centuries – not least the Tana Toraja (Tonakens). Although the 21st century is encroaching, the Tonakens still build their distinctive wooden houses with boat-shaped roofs and still perform their elaborate ceremonial funerals, which involve days of feasting and dancing before the deceased are laid in hanging, cliff-side graves. August is a good time to encounter the tribe: it's one of the driest months, and days are largely sunny, with lower humidity and manageable temperatures (27°C/80°F).

Trip plan: Fly in to the southern city of Makassar, home to the Dutch-colonial Fort Rotterdam (now the Museum of Sulawesi Culture). Head north into the mountains for a few days to stay in a traditional ancestral home and trek into the jungle with the Tana Toraja. Fly from Makassar to Manado, in the far north, to finish in Bunaken National Marine Park – the diving is world-class, with pristine coral reefs, wrecks (including WWII planes) and plentiful fish, turtles and sharks.

Need to know: Accommodation can be rustic and road journeys slow, especially in the south.

Other months: Nov-Feb – wettest; Mar-May – mixed weather, humid, damp; Jun-Jul & Sep-Oct – driest, sunny, lower humidity.

197

FAROE ISLANDS

→ **Why now? Get to know the descendants of Vikings.**

The 'Land of Maybe' is famously proud that its sheep population outnumbers its human one. Yet it's the indomitable, independent spirit of the Faroese people that makes a visit so unforgettable – particularly in relatively warm, dry August, when migratory seabirds throng cliffs and daylight seems to last forever. In recent years the inhabitants of these 18 basalt outcrops in the North Atlantic have devised new and playful ways of engaging with visitors: an online 'Faroese Translate' tool, 'Sheepview' webcams and an annual tourism shutdown when volunteers work on eco recovery projects. Take a deep dive into the Faroese psyche (and past) on a road trip visiting sheer cliffs and plunging waterfalls, remote fishing villages, grass-roofed farmsteads and the remains of ancient Viking settlements. Venture to the raucous seabird colonies at Mykines and Vestmanna – home to breeding puffins, gannets, razorbills, fulmars, shags, kittiwakes, guillemots, Arctic terns and great skuas – wander the fishing harbour and medieval old core of tiny capital Tórshavn, and venture to remote settlements such as Saksun, where the farm-museum reveals the rigours of rural life over the centuries. Mostly, savour the slow but lasting smiles of the tough, warm, welcoming people of this extraordinary archipelago.

Trip plan: Fly to the Faroes' only international airport, Vágar, then hire a car.

Need to know: Weather changes rapidly here, so a flexible schedule is best in case ferry or helicopter departures are delayed.

Other months: Oct-Apr – colder, wetter, many facilities closed; Jun-Jul & Sep – warm, drier, long days.

© Yusnizam Yusof / Shutterstock

Keep an eye out for
cuddling proboscis
monkeys

BORNEO MALAYSIA

 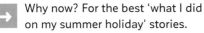

→ **Why now? For the best 'what I did on my summer holiday' stories.**
To add extra awesomeness to the August school vacation, make a break for Borneo, where the best, driest, wildest season handily aligns with when most kids are free – unusual for Southeast Asia (much of which is damp right now). Across the Malaysian states of Sarawak and Sabah there are hot beaches and warm seas for sandcastle-building and snorkelling, while turtles are nesting off Selingan and Lankayan islands. Indeed, wildlife-lovers

of all ages will be spoilt: the rainforests are heavy with fruit, attracting all manner of wildlife – not least charismatic orangutans. See them easily at Sepilok Orangutan Rehabilitation Centre or, for greater adventure, on boat trips along the Kinabatangan River, where you might spot proboscis monkeys and hornbills too.

Trip plan: Families with younger children should focus on the northern state of Sabah; there are flights from Kuala Lumpur to Kota Kinabalu and Sandakan. Include Sepilok (and the adjacent Bornean Sun

Bear Conservation Centre), Kinabatangan boat trips, rainforest lodge stays (for canopy walks and night safaris) and time on the beach, perhaps around Tunku Abdul Rahman National Park. Book well in advance as August is busy.

Need to know: There is a low risk of malaria in inland Borneo – pack insect repellent, cover up and seek advice on prophylaxis.

Other months: Oct-Mar – rainier season, quieter; Apr-Jul & Sep – driest, busiest, turtles (Jun-Jul & Sep).

199

September

WHERE TO GO WHEN

CHALLENGE MYSELF

I WANT TO

TAKE ME OUT FOR...

- FOOD — ● BOHUSLÄN COAST, SWEDEN P213
- DRINK
  - ● NOVA SCOTIA, CANADA P210
  - ● BURGUNDY, FRANCE P222

Crack a claw in Barrington, the lobster capital of Canada

Explore Burgundy's winsome villages

TAKE ME SOMEWHERE...

- BIG — ● DUBLIN, IRELAND P212
- BOUTIQUE — ● VELIKO TÂRNOVO, BULGARIA P219

Tune in to traditional Irish music for a taste of the city on the Liffey in its mellowest season

RELAX/ INDULGE

Catch a coral reef display in the islands of Netherlands Antilles

TAKE ME TO THE BEACH

- REV UP — ● NETHERLANDS ANTILLES P206
- CHILL OUT — ● SOUTHEAST TURKEY P209

Wander around the hillside-stacked houses of Veliko Târnovo

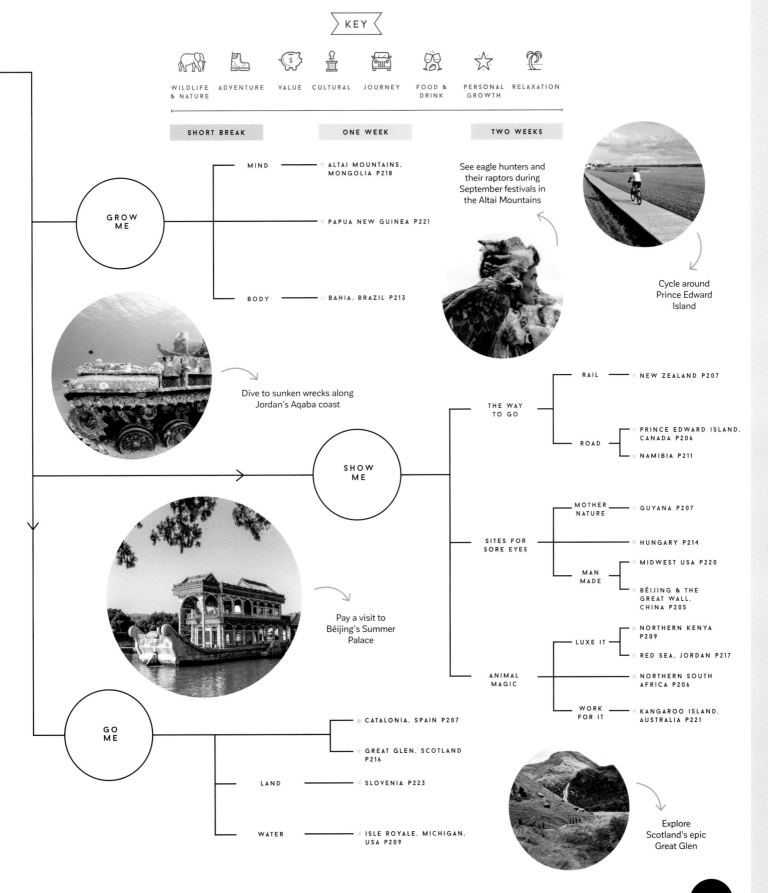

KEY

🐘	🥾	🐷	🏛	🚙	🥂	⭐	🌴
WILDLIFE & NATURE	ADVENTURE	VALUE	CULTURAL	JOURNEY	FOOD & DRINK	PERSONAL GROWTH	RELAXATION

SHORT BREAK	ONE WEEK	TWO WEEKS

GROW ME

MIND ——— ALTAI MOUNTAINS, MONGOLIA P218

PAPUA NEW GUINEA P221

BODY ——— BAHIA, BRAZIL P213

See eagle hunters and their raptors during September festivals in the Altai Mountains

Cycle around Prince Edward Island

Dive to sunken wrecks along Jordan's Aqaba coast

SHOW ME

THE WAY TO GO
- RAIL ——— NEW ZEALAND P207
- ROAD ——— PRINCE EDWARD ISLAND, CANADA P206
  - NAMIBIA P211

SITES FOR SORE EYES
- MOTHER NATURE ——— GUYANA P207
  - HUNGARY P214
- MAN MADE ——— MIDWEST USA P220
  - BĚIJĪNG & THE GREAT WALL, CHINA P205

ANIMAL MAGIC
- LUXE IT ——— NORTHERN KENYA P209
  - RED SEA, JORDAN P217
  - NORTHERN SOUTH AFRICA P206
- WORK FOR IT ——— KANGAROO ISLAND, AUSTRALIA P221

Pay a visit to Běijīng's Summer Palace

GO ME

CATALONIA, SPAIN P207

GREAT GLEN, SCOTLAND P216

LAND ——— SLOVENIA P223

WATER ——— ISLE ROYALE, MICHIGAN, USA P209

Explore Scotland's epic Great Glen

EVENTS
IN SEPTEMBER

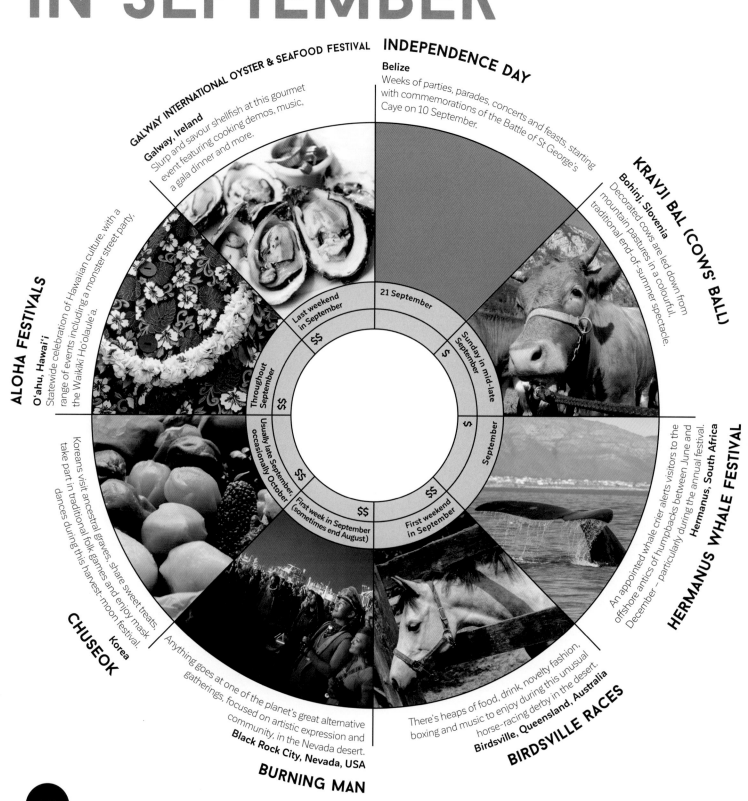

GALWAY INTERNATIONAL OYSTER & SEAFOOD FESTIVAL
Galway, Ireland
Slurp and savour shellfish at this gourmet event featuring cooking demos, music, a gala dinner and more.

INDEPENDENCE DAY
Belize
Weeks of parties, parades, concerts and feasts, starting with commemorations of the Battle of St George's Caye on 10 September.

KRAVJI BAL (COWS' BALL)
Bohinj, Slovenia
Decorated cows are led down from mountain pastures in a colourful, traditional end-of-summer spectacle.

ALOHA FESTIVALS
O'ahu, Hawai'i
Statewide celebration of Hawaiian culture, with a range of events including a monster street party, the Waikīkī Hoʻolauleʻa.

HERMANUS WHALE FESTIVAL
Hermanus, South Africa
An appointed whale crier alerts visitors to the offshore antics of humpbacks between June and December – particularly during the annual festival.

CHUSEOK
Korea
Koreans visit ancestral graves, share sweet treats, take part in traditional folk games and enjoy mask dances during this harvest-moon festival.

BURNING MAN
Black Rock City, Nevada, USA
Anything goes at one of the planet's great alternative gatherings, focused on artistic expression and community, in the Nevada desert.

BIRDSVILLE RACES
Birdsville, Queensland, Australia
There's heaps of food, drink, novelty fashion, boxing and music to enjoy during this unusual horse-racing derby in the desert.

Last weekend in September — $$
21 September
Throughout September — $$
Sunday in mid-late September — $
Usually late September, occasionally October — $$
September — $
First week in September (sometimes end August) — $$
First weekend in September — $$

Explore intricate designs and statues at Běijīng's iconic sites

Paraglide (or just relax) in Ölüdeniz, Turkey

○ SOUTHWEST TURKEY

Join a conservation tour and look for wildlife on Kangaroo Island

○ CATALONIA, SPAIN

○ NETHERLANDS ANTILLES

○ PRINCE EDWARD ISLAND, CANADA

○ NORTHERN SOUTH AFRICA

○ KANGAROO ISLAND, AUSTRALIA

Cycle the volcanic landscapes of La Garrotxa, Catalonia

○ NAMIBIA

Spot white rinos in the Laikipia Plateau, Northern Kenya

Wildlife-watch in game-packed Etosha National Park, Namibia

○ NORTHERN KENYA

○ BĚIJĪNG & THE GREAT WALL, CHINA

○ RED SEA, JORDAN

Ride the TranzAlpine across New Zealand's South Island

○ GREAT GLEN, SCOTLAND

○ VELIKO TĂRNOVO, BULGARIA

○ NOVA SCOTIA, CANADA

○ BOHUSLÄN COAST, SWEDEN

○ DUBLIN, IRELAND

Linger in Hungary's picturesque Esztergom

○ HUNGARY

○ NEW ZEALAND

○ GUYANA

○ SLOVENIA

○ ISLE ROYALE, MICHIGAN, USA

See Guyana's Kaieteur Falls plummet to the depths of the rainforest

Take a capoeira lesson in Bahia

○ MIDWEST USA

○ BAHIA, BRAZIL

○ ALTAI MOUNTAINS, MONGOLIA

Catch the harvest in progress in Burgundy

○ PAPUA NEW GUINEA

Spy a bird of paradise in a courtship display in PNG

○ BURGUNDY, FRANCE

BĚIJĪNG & THE GREAT WALL CHINA

➡️ **Why now? Admire old Běijīng and an even older wall in the autumn.**
The people of Běijīng have an epithet describing this season: '*tian gao qi shuang*' – 'the sky is high and the air is fresh'. After the steamy heat of summer, September brings relief with mellowing temperatures and falling humidity, a window of calm between summer and the national holiday in the first week of October. So get out now to wander its traditional *hútòng* (alleys), perhaps watching elders crouched around a table battling it out with mah-jong or cards, and to explore the city's treasures: the Forbidden City's gates, halls and museums, Tiān'ānmén Sq, the Summer Palace, and the many temples and parks. Autumn is the perfect time to visit the Great Wall, too, when maples are in their fiery fall finery; busy Bādálǐng is picturesque, but other wall sections at Mùtiányù, Sīmǎtái and Huánghuā are quieter and also rewarding.

Trip plan: Běijīng's varied sights – old and startlingly modern – merit several days. Regular departures to various wall sections run from Dōngzhímén Bus Station.

Need to know: To avoid crowds, visit the wall on a week day. Mid-Autumn Festival (late September) is also busy with mooncake-munching holidaymakers.

Other months: Jun-Aug – hot, humid; Oct – cooler, dry; Nov-Feb – very cold; Mar-May – windy, sandstorms.

Take a Great Wall walk in cool autumn climes

NORTHERN SOUTH AFRICA

→ **Why now? For spring in the city and exceptional safaris beyond.**
South Africa in start-of-spring September is a delight – across the country you'll find whales, wildflowers and wildlife aplenty, but peak crowds have gone. It's certainly a good time to explore the colourful maelstrom that is Johannesburg – join a street-art walk, take a community-focused tour of Soweto and look out for early-blooming jacaranda trees. It's ideal for the safari parks of the north too: for instance, Kruger is never better than now, with the bush sparse and animals gathering around rivers and waterholes (making them easier for self-drivers to spot) but the weather warmer than midwinter. Or opt for private reserves such as malaria-free Madikwe, where self-drive isn't permitted but lodges (typically good value at this time) offer 4WD trips, walking safaris and night drives in Big Five country.

Trip plan: Johannesburg is a major transport hub. From here, fly or drive to game parks including Madikwe and Kruger. Allow ten days.

Need to know: On 24 September South Africans mark Heritage Day, which celebrates the nation's multiculturalism and generally involves getting outside for a *braai* (barbecue).

Other months: Nov-Mar – wet, humid, hottest; Apr-May – warm, dry, green; Jun-Aug – cool, dry, good game viewing, busiest; Oct – warm, dry, quieter, great game viewing.

PRINCE EDWARD ISLAND CANADA

→ **Why now? For peaceful pedalling.**
On PEI, the trainspotter's loss has been the cyclist's gain. After the island's rail network was abandoned in 1989, the tracks were repurposed into the Confederation Trail, a 435km (270-mile) network of well-surfaced, car-free, largely level paths (gradients never exceed 2%) that provide a great way to get around Canada's smallest province. And September, when summer crowds have gone and maximum temperatures average 20°C (68°F), is well suited to gentle cycling.

The main branch of the route runs for 273km (170 miles) from northwest Tignish to Elmira in the east; there are also the branches that shoot off to capital Charlottetown and other points on the coast. The scenery is idyllic: expect rolling fields, wildlife-rich woodlands and wetlands, farmers' markets, fishing communities and plenty of railway history – 250 interpretive panels line the way, adding colour and context.

Trip plan: The main transport hub is Charlottetown Airport. Seasonal ferries run between Caribou, Nova Scotia, and PEI's Woods Island (1hr 15min).

Need to know: Whatever the weather, don't leave without sampling PEI-made COWS ice cream. There are outlets in Charlottetown, Borden and Cavendish, all on the Confederation Trail.

Other months: Nov-Apr – coldest, Confederation Trail open to snowmobiles; May-Jun – spring, wildflowers; Jul-Aug – warmest, busiest; Oct – warm, quieter, autumn colours.

NETHERLANDS ANTILLES

→ **Why now? For underwater wonders.**
September is normally a bit of a no-no hereabouts: it's the riskier end of the Caribbean's hurricane season. But the southerly ABC islands – Aruba, Bonaire, Curaçao, part of the Netherlands since the early 17th century – sit outside the hurricane belt, and offer a safe, hot, sunny autumn escape for low-season prices. They also offer awesome diving and snorkelling – especially in Bonaire National Marine Park, the oldest marine reserve in the world, where visibility is excellent year-round and protected reefs attract an array of turtles, rays, squid and fishes. September is also a prime time to try to witness a coral spawning event, where entire coral colonies, prompted by the moon, sun and water temperature, release eggs and sperm simultaneously, engulfing the reef (and lucky divers) in an underwater blizzard of fertility.

Trip plan: Pick an island – each has its own personality: Aruba is the smallest but most touristy; Bonaire is best for diving; cosmopolitan Curaçao is home to Willemstad, one of the most attractive cities in the Caribbean. Flights connect the islands.

Need to know: Coral spawning depends on many factors. The Caribbean Research and Management of Biodiversity releases an annual calendar to predict when spawning events are likely to occur.

Other months: Feb-Aug – consistently warm, dry; Oct-Jan – rainy season.

CATALONIA
SPAIN

→ **Why now? Warm weather for natural adventures.**

While Barcelona is often used as a byword for overtourism, the surrounding area is a beacon of travel done well: Catalonia was the first region to obtain Unesco-backed Biosphere Responsible Tourism certification, in recognition of the symbiotic relationship between humans and nature. That nature is certainly a lot of fun – nestled between the Mediterranean and the Pyrenees, Catalonia is a varied outdoor playground, perfect for exploring in not-too-hot September weather (average highs: 25°C/77°F). Waterbabies will love kayaking between the 500m-high (1640ft) walls of the Mont-rebei gorge, paddling across the bird-flocked Ebro Delta (looking for autumn migrant birds) and rafting the wild Noguera Pallaresa river. Landlubbers can hike amid the 200-odd lakes of Aigüestortes i Estany de Sant Maurici National Park, cycle the volcanic landscapes of La Garrotxa or climb the sheer rock faces of the Val d'Arran.

Trip plan: Launched in 2021, the Grand Tour of Catalonia route combines outdoor activities with cultural highlights including Dalí's egg-topped house in Figueres and the Romanesque churches of the Boi Valley. Allow two weeks.

Need to know: Look out for businesses that have a Catalan Ecolabel, a certificate that recognises products and services that exceed certain environmental quality requirements.

Other months: Nov-Mar – cold, wettest, mountain snowsports; Apr-Jun – warm, wildflowers, uncrowded; Jul-Aug – very hot, very busy; Oct – warm, windy.

GUYANA

→ **Why now? Admire roaring waterfalls and rainforest wildlife.**

Guyana is an extraordinary land, where turtles nest on shell beaches, jaguars stalk the rainforest, giant otters frolic and huge harpy eagles soar over thundering waterfalls. Its climate is also extraordinary, with multiple rainy seasons hitting coast and interior at different times. September is a junction month, when most of the country is dry after the heavy rains, making road travel easier and life more comfortable in general, but with jungles at their lushest. The big-ticket attraction is Kaieteur Falls, which plummets 226m (741ft) in a single drop into the depths of the rainforest. Add to that the canopy walkway and wildlife of Iwokrama, ecolodges offering encounters with Makushi Indigenous peoples, the otters of the Rupununi and the cowboys of vast Dadanawa Ranch, and you have an epic adventure in the making.

Trip plan: Booking an organised tour – with a group or tailor-made – is the way to go. A typical two-week itinerary visits coastal capital Georgetown, Kaieteur Falls, the rainforest at Iwokrama, the Amerindian village at Surama, and includes a chance to meet the giant otters at Karanambu.

Need to know: Malaria is a problem, and mosquitoes are pesky in any case – cover up and use insect repellent.

Other months: Feb-Apr & Oct-Nov – mostly dry, hot; May-Aug & Dec-Jan – wet (Apr-Aug: interior wet).

NEW ZEALAND

→ **Why now? Enjoy ravishing views from the rails.**

With snow still sprinkled on the mountain tops but lambs a-gamboling in the fields, spring-green September can be a month of natural splendour in Aotearoa, with few other tourists around. If you're worried the weather might still be a little cool and unpredictable, opt to explore by Rail New Zealand's scenic lines – that way you'll be insulated from the chill, and free to gaze out the window as the countryside glides by. Start aboard the Northern Explorer, which connects Auckland and Wellington via fertile farmland, Tongariro's volcanoes and the Raurimu Spiral – an impressive feat of rail engineering. Take the ferry to the South Island and then pick up the Coastal Pacific to trace the shoreline from Picton to elegant Christchurch. Then join the TranzAlpine to cross the Canterbury Plains and Southern Alps (via lofty Arthurs Pass) and finish at Greymouth, on the east coast.

Trip plan: While the train journeys aren't epic (5-11hr), allow at least ten days for the trip, adding on excursions – for instance, the Bay of Islands from Auckland, time in Christchurch, visits to Fox and Franz Josef glaciers from Greymouth.

Need to know: New Zealand Travel Scenic Passes are available, covering travel on all three train services and the inter-island ferry. Services do not run every day.

Other months: Dec-Feb – summer, warm, busy; Mar-May & –Oct-Nov – cooler but pleasant; Jun-Aug – winter.

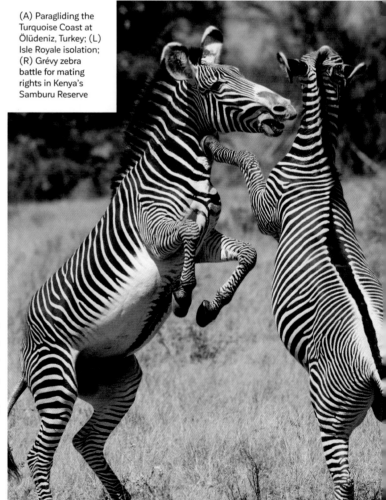

(A) Paragliding the Turquoise Coast at Ölüdeniz, Turkey; (L) Isle Royale isolation; (R) Grévy zebra battle for mating rights in Kenya's Samburu Reserve

SOUTHWEST TURKEY

→ **Why now? For a final summer fling.**
As summer segues into fall, what could be more alluring than a last shot of sunshine on the tantalisingly named Turquoise Coast? Turkey's Mediterranean shore is much quieter now the school holidays have ended but the water is still balmy, the air still warm and the historic sites – of which there are many to lure you off your lounger – still open. Where you head depends on your taste. Lagoon-side Ölüdeniz is top choice for paragliding. At Patara, combine endless-seeming swathes of golden sand with a hint of Christmas – this was the birthplace of St Nicholas (aka Santa). Or head for sleepy Çıralı, a protected area where sea turtles nest – from mid-September you might see the hatchlings emerge. To really get away from it all, opt for the stretch of coast east of Alanya. Once the refuge of pirates, few foreign tourists make it here. The seaside resort of Kızkalesi has an authentically Turkish feel plus fine beaches, caves to explore and an imposing 12th-century castle, floating out at sea.

Trip plan: The region is served by two airports. Dalaman is small, but closer to Ölüdeniz and Patara; bigger Antalya is further east.

Need to know: From Taşucu, west of Kızkalesi, ferries run to Girne (Kyrenia) North Cyprus; the crossing takes about 2hr.

Other months: Nov-Apr – cooler, more rain; May-Jun – warm, water chillier; Jul-Aug – hot, busy; Oct – balmy, warm seas, uncrowded.

ISLE ROYALE, MICHIGAN
USA

→ **Why now? To get well and truly away from everyone.**
Isle Royale is the least-visited national park in the lower 48. It's closed completely for almost half the year and, when it does open, is only accessible via floatplane or non-car ferry, exclusively attracting those keen for a wilderness immersion by boat, kayak or on foot. It's well worth the effort though. The park is a wetland wonderland, comprising one large, forest-swathed island and some 450 smaller ones, jutting into Lake Superior; an International Biosphere Reserve, it's the realm of otters, moose and wolves, herons, hawks and loons. September is less busy and less buggy than peak summer, but still warm enough to paddle, trek and wild camp. There are 272km (169 miles) of trails to explore – experienced hikers will lust after the tough 150km (93-mile) Wonderland Trail. Kayakers can explore the eastern shore's inland lakes and fjord-like bays – Malone Bay to McCargoe Cove makes a good multi-day adventure.

Trip plan: Ferries to Isle Royale run from Houghton, Copper Harbor and Grand Portage; floatplanes leave from Houghton.

Need to know: There is a daily fee (currently $7pp) to enter the national park. There are 36 campsites – camping permits are mandatory but free for groups of up to six people.

Other months: Nov-Apr – very cold, Isle Royale closed to visitors; May-Jun – spring, quiet; Jul-Aug – warmest, busiest, good fishing; Oct – warm to cool, quieter, fall colours.

NORTHERN KENYA

→ **Why now? Spot rare wildlife in dramatic, less-visited reserves.**
North of Mt Kenya stretches the Laikipia Plateau and eventually the Samburu National Reserve. Never heard of them? Exactly – that's why this area of kopje-studded plains and acacia-clad hills is a dream. Whereas in the Masai Mara at peak times each lion might be ringed by a dozen minibuses, in the reserves and community run conservancies of northern Kenya you'll probably be alone with the wildlife (and local Maasai and Samburu peoples). That's especially true in September, after the height of the season when safari-goers flock to Kenya to see the Great Migration, but before the rains. Prices fall with tourist numbers, which is good for the wallet as well as for wildlife-watching. But this is no second-rate experience: as well as the biggies – lions, cheetahs, elephants, rhinos black and white – you might spot endangered species such as wild dog and Grévy zebra.

Trip plan: Domestic airlines fly to Lewa Downs and Samburu from Wilson Airport, Nairobi. Rates at safari lodges usually include most wildlife-watching activities, meals and drinks, but not airstrip transfers.

Need to know: Daily conservation fees are payable at most reserves and community conservancies – when booking, check whether these are included in accommodation rates.

Other months: Jun-Aug & Oct – warm, dry; Nov- Dec – 'short rains'; Jan-Mar – hot, fairly dry; Apr-May – 'long rains'.

Sossusvlei silhouette
in the red-duned
Namib Desert

Fresh Bay of Fundy
scallops await your
plate in Digby

NOVA SCOTIA CANADA

→ **Why now? To fill up in fall.**
The start of the season of mellow fruitfulness is ideal for taking a foodie tour around Nova Scotia, the most delicious of the Maritimes. First, seek out succulent seafood: try scallops from the Bay of Fundy (where over-summering whales may still be spotted), eat a lobster roll by the beach (head to Barrington, 'Lobster Capital of Canada') and slurp an oyster or two, perhaps at the Halifax Oyster Festival (held late September). Then, as the harvest gets underway, sample local wines. Boutique vineyards pepper the province, from the Annapolis Valley's Domaine de Grand Pré, the granddaddy of Nova Scotian wine (open daily June-September), to Benjamin Bridge, which produces acclaimed fizz in the Gaspereau Valley. And don't forget the fruit: this month brings gluts of blueberries and apples, which find their way into delicious pies, province-wide.

Trip plan: Graze from Halifax along the South Shore (via Lunenberg) to the west coast (Barrington). Continue north to Digby (scallop capital) on the Bay of Fundy and east along the Annapolis Valley towards Cape Breton (look for Glenora, makers of North America's first single-malt whisky). Allow two weeks.

Need to know: Look out for fresh, young white wines labelled Tidal Bay, Nova Scotia's first appellation, designed to reflect the maritime *terroir*.

Other months: Nov-Apr – cold, snowy; May-Jun – warm; Jul-Aug – hottest, busiest, whales; Sep-Oct – warm, quieter, fall colour, whales.

© Mark Read / Lonely Planet

NAMIBIA

→ **Why now? For great game.**
Desert-dominated Namibia is a pretty arid place at the best of times. And September *is* the best of times – at least, if you've come looking for the country's big game. Temperatures are on the up this month (making early safari wake-up calls less chilly) but there likely hasn't been a drop of rain for months, meaning thin vegetation and wildlife congregating at an ever-decreasing number of water sources. Spotting everything from elephant to the long-nosed elephant shrew, from cheetah to rare black rhino becomes a doddle in these conditions – especially in game-packed areas such as Etosha National Park. You don't even need a guide: Etosha's excellent road network makes a self-drive safari simple; just park next to a waterhole and wait for the wildlife to arrive.

Trip plan: Allow two weeks to make a northern circuit. Drive west from capital Windhoek into the Namib Desert to see the dunes at Sossusvlei. Head north to Swakopmund/Walvis Bay (to see seals, and possibly whales), then northeast to Etosha. Return to Windhoek via the Central Highlands.

Need to know: Most of Namibia's roads can be tackled with a 2WD, though moderate your speed when driving on gravel, fill up with fuel regularly and don't drive at night.

Other months: Dec-Mar – rainiest, hottest; Apr-May – dry, green; Jun-Aug & Oct – dry, warm/hot; Nov – unpredictable.

The Long Room
at Trinity College
Library, Dublin

DUBLIN IRELAND

→ **Why now? Get a taste of the city on the Liffey in the mellowest season.**
Dublin in September, often the sunniest month, sees a diminishing numbers of tourists, after the crowds of July and August have dispersed. This city is many things to many people. Yes, you'll find lively pubs (and they deserve detailed examination), historic marvels, humour and national pride, but Dublin is also a cultural powerhouse, boasting magnificent galleries and museums, notably the Chester Beatty Library in Dublin Castle, one of Europe's finest. During September, too, the Irish capital welcomes hundreds of arts performances during the fortnight-long Dublin Fringe festival.

Trip plan: Wander the genteel streets of the Georgian Southside, admiring the ancient illuminated Book of Kells (and the spectacular library in which it's displayed) in Trinity College, mighty Dublin Castle and the arts-and-bars hub of Temple Bar, then sample the Guinness in one (or more) of the famed music-filled bars to experience a night of legendary Irish bonhomie. Repeat till you're out of time, money or stamina...

Need to know: For a break from city action, take the 75-min bus ride to Glendalough, a dramatically sited medieval monastic settlement in a lovely glacial valley.

Other months: Jun-Aug – warmest, dry; Oct – cooler, fairly dry; Nov-Feb – cold; Mar-May – rainy.

BAHIA BRAZIL

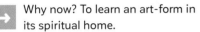

→ **Why now?** To learn an art-form in its spiritual home.

Brazil's northeastern Bahia province dances to the beat of its own drum, quite literally. This is the hub of Black Brazilian culture; more than 90% of locals can trace their roots to Africa and the trade in enslaved people. And it's the birthplace of capoeira, a unique martial art meets acrobatic dance said to originate from Angolan tribes. It's mesmerising to watch, and fun to try. The best place to take lessons is in the thrumming metropolis of Salvador. The Portuguese established Brazil's first colonial capital here in the 16th century, leaving a legacy of pastel-hued mansions and cobbled squares, once the site of markets where the enslaved were sold. In the early 20th century, it's where Mestre Bimba founded the modern form of capoeira. You can take classes at his school, making the most of tropical Bahia's dry, warm September weather (22-28°C/72-82°F) to practice your moves, from the *ginga* (the

© golero / Getty Images

Catch a coastal capoeira session in Salvador

basic step) to the *gato* (hand-spring).

Trip plan: Spend two or three days in Salvador. Then head inland for hikes amid the table-top mountains of Chapada Diamantina National Park. Also consider Praia do Forte, 90km (56 miles) north of Salvador, which attracts nesting turtles between September and March.

Need to know: Bahia's Afro-Brazilian cuisine is characterised by the generous use of *malagueta* chilli peppers. The signature dish is *moqueca*, a seafood stew.

Other months: Dec-Mar – hot, humid, Carnaval (Feb/Mar); Apr-Jul – wettest, cooler; Aug & Oct-Nov – driest, warm.

BOHUSLÄN COAST SWEDEN

→ **Why now?** Think pink along Sweden's seafood-crazy shore.

Love shellfish? The world's your oyster on west Sweden's Bohuslän coast north of Göteborg (Gothenburg). This tessellated shoreline, noted for its pink granite rocks, produces Sweden's finest seafood. September marks the start of lobster season, the perfect time to explore the 8000 or so islands and rocky islets along the coast, sampling

the local langoustines, prawns, mussels, oysters and, of course, those bigclawed crustaceans. Join a 'seafood safari' with fishermen from Smögen to catch and cook your own, or – even better – hire a canoe and paddle among colourful fishing villages such as Gullholmen, Käringön and Fiskebäckskil, stopping off to taste test the area's welcoming eateries: try Salt & Sill in charming Klädesholmen.

Trip plan: Göteborg, Sweden's second city,

is the gateway to the Bohuslän coast and has international flights. Travel is easiest with a vehicle, though cycling around local centres is a great idea. Islands are linked to the mainland by bridges or short ferry rides.

Need to know: Don't be alarmed if someone proposes *fika* – Swedes are partial to these regular pauses for coffee and cake.

Other months: Jun-Aug – sunny, busy; May & Oct – pleasant, quiet; Nov-Apr – cold.

HUNGARY

→ **Why now? For a bit of everything, after the summer crowds.**

Big-hitting Budapest can steal the limelight in otherwise overlooked Hungary. But there's much more to discover here, with mild, autumnal-glowing September a good time for a grand tour without the peak-season masses. Start in the capital, with its grand architecture, magnificent opera house and Art Nouveau spas, then veer northwest along the Danube Bend, pausing in pretty Szentendre, holy Esztergom and medieval Sopron. Lake Balaton lies south (it'll still be warm enough to swim in); further south is Pécs, with its laidback vibe and sunny microclimate. Next, head east to lively Szeged, then across the Great Plain to the offbeat Bereg region, rich in folk traditions. Then take in the grape-heavy vineyards of Tokaj, before turning southwest to elegant Eger, to admire its hilltop castle and raise a glass of local Bull's Blood wine before returning to Budapest.

Trip plan: Allow two weeks for an all-corners adventure. Hiring a car offers the greatest flexibility; many highlights can be accessed by (cheap) trains, including Sopron, Pécs and Eger.

Need to know: Consider arriving in Hungary by train – Budapest is well connected to other European cities including Vienna (2hr 40min), Bratislava (2hr 20min) and Bucharest (16hr).

Other months: Nov-Mar – cold, Christmas markets (Nov-Dec); Apr-Jun – warmer, wetter, blossoms; Jul-Aug – very hot; Oct – mild, uncrowded, autumn colours.

(L) The neo-Renaissance Hungarian State Opera House (R) Pretty Szentendre has dozens of art museums, galleries and churches

GREAT GLEN
SCOTLAND

→ **Why now? To cross a less-crowded country.**

The Great Glen, a dramatic diagonal fissure slicing from coast to coast, is classic Scotland. It's flanked by lofty mountains (including the UK's highest), filled with vast lochs (including Nessie's home), inhabited by a range of wildlife (ospreys, deer, golden eagles) and resounds with centuries of Highlands heritage. It is, of course, a big draw. But by the mild days of September, the masses – and the maddening midges – are on the wane, making it a perfect time to explore. One way to avoid any lingering tourists is to trace the Great Glen by canoe, paddling along the lochs and Caledonian Canal to link Fort William and Inverness, wild camping on the banks each night. Walkers may prefer to hike the Great Glen Way, perhaps detouring to bag Munros en route. Cyclists can use the canal towpath, forest roads and quiet lanes to make the trip too.

Trip plan: The Great Glen is 125km (78 miles) long. Allow around six days to canoe, five or six to hike and one or two to cycle.

Need to know: Canoeing the Great Glen doesn't require previous paddling experience, but good fitness is necessary – the water is mostly flat but wind can stir up waves on larger lochs.

Other months: Nov-Mar – cold, wet, short days; Apr-May – warming, uncrowded, good birding; Jun-Aug – warmest, very busy, peak midge season; Oct – mild, quieter, autumn colours.

Canoeing the Caledonian Canal near Fort William

© Matthew Williams-Ellis / Getty Images

© Ehab Othman / Shutterstock

Exploring the coral-encrusted wreck of the *Cedar Pride*

RED SEA JORDAN

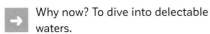

→ **Why now? To dive into delectable waters.**

As the stifling heat of the Jordanian summer begins to drop, things really heat up along the Red Sea coast. September and October are among the best months to dive here, with the air temperature hot but bearable, and the oh-so-clear water around a balmy 26°C (79°F) and jam-packed with activity: look out for eagle rays, moray eels, seahorses, turtles, lionfish and an array of other colourful fishes – over 510 species

have been recorded. There are 30-plus dive sites along the Aqaba coast, most close to shore and many good for snorkelling too. These range from shallow coral gardens and gaping canyons to shipwrecks, including that of the *Cedar Pride*, which sits at a depth of just 7-25m (23-82ft). Good value learn-to-dive courses are available in Aqaba and resorts along the coast.

Trip plan: Amman to Aqaba direct is 330km/205 miles (a 3hr 30min drive). It would be rude not to add on a trip to the

ancient rock-hewn city of Petra, a 2hr drive from Aqaba.

Need to know: A 3mm wetsuit should suffice for September diving. Choose a reputable dive centre that is equipped with safety gear and promotes sustainable diving practices.

Other months: Nov-Mar – coolest, water temperature falls; Apr-May – warm, plankton blooms can hinder visibility; Jun-Aug – very hot, uncomfortable for sightseeing; Oct – hot, water warm.

ALTAI MOUNTAINS
MONGOLIA

→ **Why now?** Learn about the skills and lifestyles of traditional eagle hunters.

In the breathless Altai Mountains at the very centre of the Asian landmass, four borders converge – this is where Russia, China, Kazakhstan and Mongolia lean in towards one another. And among those peaks in western Mongolia, Kazakh nomads maintain the ancient tradition of hunting with golden eagles – a legacy celebrated during festivals in Altai, Ülgii and Sagsai in September and October each year, when eagle hunters don customary garb and display their prowess with the majestic raptors. This pleasantly cool, dry season is also ideal for exploring the mountains of Altai Tavan Bogd National Park, hiking between waterfalls, ancient petroglyphs and glistening lakes – trek with Bactrian camels or ride Mongolian horses for extra authenticity, bedding down in *gers* (yurts) as local peoples have for millennia. During the festivals, dozens of hunters clad in animal skins, with huge fur-lined hats and colourfully embroidered clothes, demonstrate their skills between bouts of wrestling, archery contests, camel races and boisterous horseback goatskin tug-o-war.

Trip plan: Fly west from Ulaanbaatar to Üglii and trek among the 'Holy Five' peaks of Tavan Bogd, admiring Lakes Khurgan and Khoton, visiting a golden eagle hunter at Sagsai and enjoying the festival.

Need to know: The largest and most popular eagle festival is held in Ülgii in October – book accommodation well in advance.

Other months: Nov-Mar – bitterly cold; Apr-May & Oct – cooler, drier; Jun-Aug – hot, rainy.

Hunting with golden eagles remains a living tradition in Mongolia's Altai

© Kertu / Shutterstock

Cobblestoned
Veliko Târnovo from
Tsarevets Fortress

© S-F / Shutterstock

VELIKO TÂRNOVO BULGARIA

→ Why now? Soak up student life in a super little city.

Veliko Târnovo used to be a big deal. During Bulgaria's medieval heyday, it was the country's capital, and second only to Constantinople in terms of grandeur. These days things are a little more low-key but, with its hillside-stacked houses tumbling around and about the River Yantra, it remains one of Bulgaria's most attractive cities. Autumn climes are good for exploring; also, the streets are lively with returning students (it's home to Bulgaria's second-largest university). Highlights are hilltop Tsarevets Fortress, former seat of the medieval tsars, and the old fortified quarter of Trapezitsa; the city's cobbled streets, lined with antique shops, bakeries,

cafes and craft workshops, are also good for a wander. Then explore beyond: head to the small village of Arbanasi to see artisan producers at work, or the town of Tryana, renowned for its woodcarving.

Trip plan: Veliko Târnovo is around 3hr by bus from Sofia and Varna. There are direct trains from Plovdiv; trains from Sofia and Varna arrive in Gorna Oryahovitsa, 7km (4 miles) from Veliko Târnovo and connected by public transport/taxis.

Need to know: Numerous eco-trails wriggle over the surrounding hills, including routes from the city to Lyaskovets monastery and Kartala waterfalls.

Other months: Nov-Mar – cold, quiet; Apr-May – warm, wetter; Jun-Aug – hot; Oct – warm, uncrowded.

219

The interior of Unity Temple in Oak Park - the epicentre of FLW architecture

MIDWEST USA

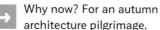

→ Why now? For an autumn architecture pilgrimage.

Frank Lloyd Wright (1867-1959) is an American icon. Pioneer of 'organic architecture' – the idea that buildings should exist in harmony with their surrounds – he designed more than 1000 structures, many of which can be visited on an inspiring fall road-trip across the Midwest. Start in Chicago, where the Frank Lloyd Wright Trust offers bus trips, exclusive interiors tours and bike rides around Oak Park (home to more FLW buildings than anywhere in the world, including his own Home and Studio). Then head north to pick up the Frank Lloyd Wright Trail in southern Wisconsin, driving across the rural Driftless Region where he grew up to see his masterpieces in Racine, Burnham and Madison. The highlight is Taliesin, the architect's own 800-acre estate overlooking the Wisconsin River, only open for tours May-October.

Trip plan: Allow around four days for the Wisconsin Frank Lloyd Wright Trail. Add time in Chicago and possibly other FLW sites in Illinois, such as a downstate loop via his early Prairie-style B Harley Bradley House and the vast Dana-Thomas House (open for guided tours).

Need to know: Advance booking for Taliesin is recommended. Some Frank Lloyd Wright properties are not open to the public or are only open on set days – check before visiting.

Other months: Nov-Apr – cold, some attractions closed; May-Jun – spring, lush; Jul-Aug – hottest, busiest; Oct – warm, autumn colours.

KANGAROO ISLAND AUSTRALIA

→ **Why now? Lend a hand to local species.**

As is suggested by its name, Kangaroo Island – 13km (8 miles) off the South Australian mainland – is all about wildlife. Wildfires in 2019/2020 had a devastating effect here. But the regeneration efforts in the aftermath have been robust. The Australian Wildlife Conservancy's Western River Refuge has been created, providing a safe haven for threatened species. Also, conservation tours that include citizen science elements have been launched: as well as exploring the island to look for its koalas, echidnas, little penguins and endangered residents (such as the dunnart, a mouse-sized, carnivorous marsupial), visitors can head out with experts to monitor camera traps and fence lines, and help collect data. September is an excellent time to lend a hand, with dry, mild climes (average highs of 18°C/64°F) and plenty of springtime wildlife activity: the birdwatching is superb, with many migratory species present; baby marsupials begin to emerge from their pouches; and southern right whales might be spotted off the coast.

Trip plan: Day-trips are possible but multi-day trips are better. Combine guided wildlife tours, hiking, biking and kayaking; must-sees include the lighthouse at Cape Willoughby and the Remarkable Rocks.

Need to know: Ferries between Cape Jervis (mainland) and Penneshaw (KI) take 45min.

Other months: Jun-Aug – cheaper, cooler, whales; Oct-Nov – spring, flowers; Dec-Feb – hottest, animals retreat into bush; Mar-May – warm, calm.

Early morning on the Kokoda Trail

© Andrew Peacock / Getty Images

PAPUA NEW GUINEA

→ **Why now? To see the greatest show.**

In truth, PNG is hot, wet and humid most of the time. But the slightly drier, fractionally cooler season (May-October) makes exploring this out-there Pacific nation a little less sticky. And September comes with an extra bonus: the Goroka Show when, for one weekend (usually the middle the month), around 100 tribes descend on this sleepy highlands outpost and compete – in full, resplendent regalia – in a carnival of dance and song. Combine the sing-sing revelry with some equally flamboyant birdwatching – male birds of paradise might be seen making their courtship displays August to February. It's also a good time to take on the 100km (62-mile) Kokoda Track, a tough hike through history-filled rainforest.

Trip plan: Infrastructure in PNG is poor – travelling on a guided trip is best. Tribal encounters are a highlight, but question your tour operator beforehand to ascertain the authenticity and community impact. Allow at least ten days for a cultural trip, and an additional eight days to hike the Kokoda Track.

Need to know: Capital Port Moresby is served by flights from several Asian and Australian cities (flight time from Singapore is 6hr 30min, from Cairns 7hr 30min). Domestic flights are the easiest way to get around.

Other months: May-Oct – driest, busiest, most festivals; Apr & Nov – shoulder months, humid and hot; Dec-Mar – wet.

BURGUNDY
FRANCE

→ **Why now? For a delicious drop.**
The Route des Grands Crus (the 'road of great wines') cuts through Burgundy's most acclaimed grape-growing country. Running 60km (38 miles) from Dijon and Beaune to Santenay, it's a most intoxicating byway, flanked by 38 winsome villages and almost 1250 *climats* – the region's precisely demarcated vineyard plots, each with a unique *terroir*. Tiny domain Romanée-Conti, from where the world's most expensive reds hail, is here. In September you might catch the harvest in progress. And, with average highs of 20°C (68°F), it will be warm enough to use the hiking and biking trails that weave between wineries or to happily sit outside a pavement cafe sipping a Côte de Nuits Pinot Noir or buttery Chardonnay. Consider basing yourself in beautiful Beaune, home to the spectacular Hôtel-Dieu (venue of the annual, all-important Burgundy wine auction), numerous wine merchants' houses and cellar doors, and many Michelin-starred restaurants.

Trip plan: Dijon is well-connected by rail (Dijon-Paris, 1hr 40min). Allow two days to explore by car/bus, longer if walking or cycling.

Need to know: The cheapest way to explore is via bus 113, which runs year-round between Dijon and Beaune (1hr 30min), passing through many wine villages en route.

Other months: Nov-Mar – cold, wettest; Apr-May & Oct – cool, quiet; Jun-Aug – reliably warm, grape harvest (Aug-Sep).

Meursault, a handsome staging post along Burgundy's Route des Grands Crus

© Marco Arduino / 4Corners Images

A two-wheeled traverse of
Slovenia's Soča River

SLOVENIA

→ **Why now? To bike through green landscapes.**

Slovenia knows a thing or two about greenness – 62% of the country is covered in trees. It also knows a bit about cycling: it's produced a disproportionate number of world-class riders and boasts an excellent network of trails. So no surprise, then, that one of the newer trails combines these things: Bike Slovenia Green is a 250km (155-mile) route from Kranjska Gora to Koper, connecting

destinations awarded a Global Sustainable Tourism Council-recognised Slovenia Green certificate for developing sustainable tourism and committing to a green future. But the route isn't just worthy – it's a beaut, too. Using largely quiet country roads and bike paths, it runs beneath the Julian Alps, across the forested Pokljuka plateau, between magical lakes Bled and Bohinj, along the emerald-hued Soča River, through wine country and the stone villages of the Karst and finishes by the

Adriatic Sea where, in September, you can finish with a balmy dip.

Trip plan: The nearest airport to Kranjska Gora is Ljubljana (50min). Venice, Treviso, Trieste, Klagenfurt and Graz airports are a 2-3hr drive. The route finishes near Trieste. Allow eight days for the ride.

Need to know: The route is graded easy, with a low level of technical difficulty.

Other months: Nov-Apr – coldest, snow possible; May-Aug & Oct – best cycling season, warm/hot, all businesses open.

223

October

WHERE TO GO WHEN

I WANT TO

CHALLENGE MYSELF

TAKE ME OUT FOR...

FOOD ● TOHOKU, JAPAN P235

LE MARCHE, ITALY P230

DRINK ● OKANAGAN VALLEY, BRITISH COLUMBIA, CANADA P236

Taste Tohoku's seasonal delights

Have a glass of Le Marche's Verdicchio wine

TAKE ME SOMEWHERE...

ANCIENT ● FEZ, MOROCCO P228

MODERN ● MARSEILLE, FRANCE P247

Soak up still-warm autumn sun in Marseille

RELAX/ INDULGE

Admire the intricate tilework and ornately carved doors of Fez

TAKE ME TO THE BEACH

REV UP ● MENORCA, SPAIN P231

CHILL OUT ● SEYCHELLES P231

Swim in the Seychelles' pristine beaches

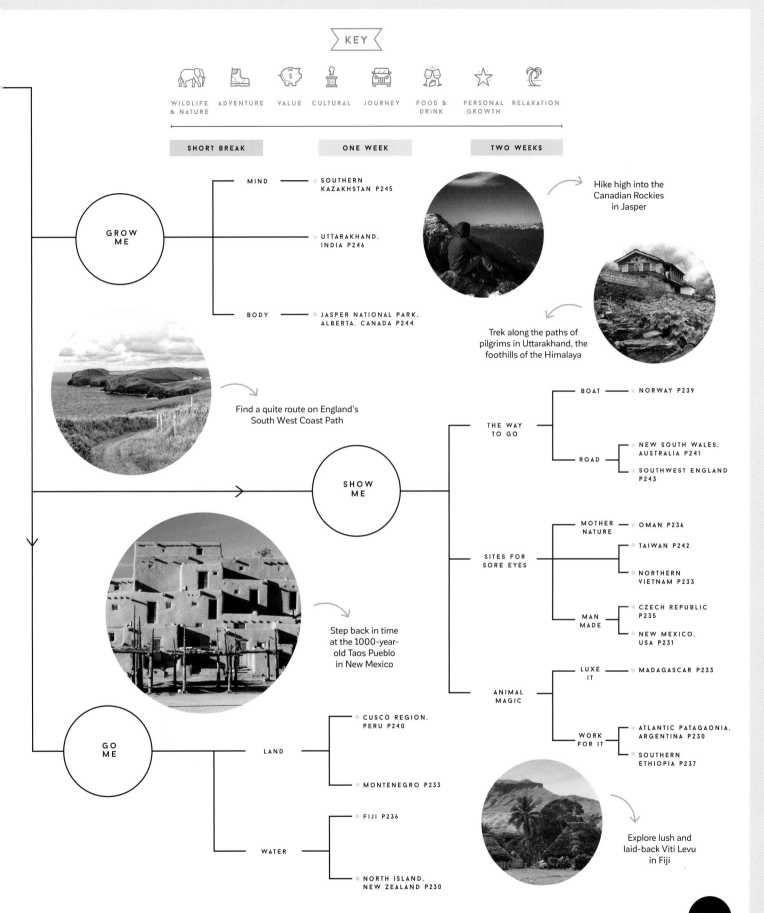

KEY

🐘	🥾	🐷	⚱	🚙	🍷	⭐	🌴
WILDLIFE & NATURE	ADVENTURE	VALUE	CULTURAL	JOURNEY	FOOD & DRINK	PERSONAL GROWTH	RELAXATION

SHORT BREAK   **ONE WEEK**   **TWO WEEKS**

GROW ME

MIND — SOUTHERN KAZAKHSTAN P245

UTTARAKHAND, INDIA P246

BODY — JASPER NATIONAL PARK, ALBERTA, CANADA P244

Hike high into the Canadian Rockies in Jasper

Trek along the paths of pilgrims in Uttarakhand, the foothills of the Himalaya

Find a quite route on England's South West Coast Path

SHOW ME

THE WAY TO GO — BOAT — NORWAY P239

ROAD — NEW SOUTH WALES, AUSTRALIA P241

SOUTHWEST ENGLAND P243

SITES FOR SORE EYES — MOTHER NATURE — OMAN P236

TAIWAN P242

NORTHERN VIETNAM P233

MAN MADE — CZECH REPUBLIC P235

NEW MEXICO, USA P231

ANIMAL MAGIC — LUXE IT — MADAGASCAR P233

WORK FOR IT — ATLANTIC PATAGAONIA, ARGENTINA P230

SOUTHERN ETHIOPIA P237

Step back in time at the 1000-year-old Taos Pueblo in New Mexico

GO ME

LAND — CUSCO REGION, PERU P240

MONTENEGRO P233

WATER — FIJI P236

NORTH ISLAND, NEW ZEALAND P230

Explore lush and laid-back Viti Levu in Fiji

EVENTS
IN OCTOBER

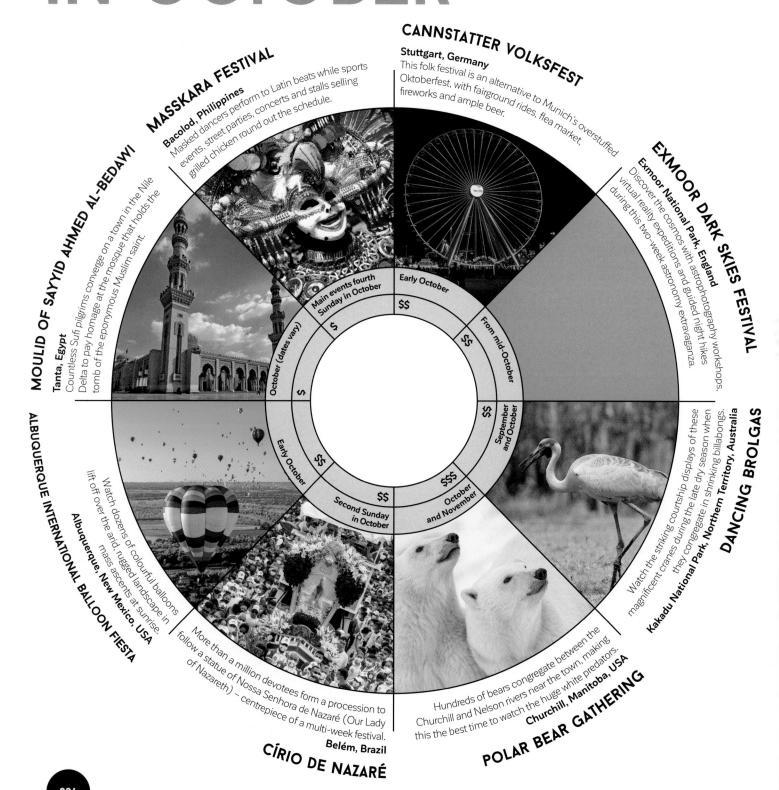

CANNSTATTER VOLKSFEST
Stuttgart, Germany
This folk festival is an alternative to Munich's overstuffed Oktoberfest, with fairground rides, flea market, fireworks and ample beer.

MASSKARA FESTIVAL
Bacolod, Philippines
Masked dancers perform to Latin beats while sports events, street parties, concerts and stalls selling grilled chicken round out the schedule.

MOULID OF SAYYID AHMED AL-BEDAWI
Tanta, Egypt
Countless Sufi pilgrims converge on a town in the Nile Delta to pay homage at the mosque that holds the tomb of the eponymous Muslim saint.

EXMOOR DARK SKIES FESTIVAL
Exmoor National Park, England
Discover the cosmos with astrophotography workshops, virtual reality expeditions and guided night hikes during this two-week astronomy extravaganza.

DANCING BROLGAS
Kakadu National Park, Northern Territory, Australia
Watch the striking courtship displays of these magnificent cranes during the late dry season when they congregate in shrinking billabongs.

POLAR BEAR GATHERING
Churchill, Manitoba, USA
Hundreds of bears congregate between the Churchill and Nelson rivers near the town, making this the best time to watch the huge white predators.

CÍRIO DE NAZARÉ
Belém, Brazil
More than a million devotees form a procession to follow a statue of Nossa Senhora de Nazaré (Our Lady of Nazareth) – centrepiece of a multi-week festival.

ALBUQUERQUE INTERNATIONAL BALLOON FIESTA
Albuquerque, New Mexico, USA
Watch dozens of colourful balloons lift off over the arid, rugged landscape in mass ascents at sunrise.

Inner wheel labels
- Main events fourth Sunday in October — $
- Early October — $$
- From mid-October — $$
- September and October — $$
- October and November — $$$
- Second Sunday in October — $$
- Early October — $$
- October (dates vary) — $

Commune with ancestors among Avebury's standing stones

○ SOUTHWEST ENGLAND

Road trip around New South Wales and stop at thundering waterfalls along the way

○ NEW SOUTH WALES, AUSTRALIA

○ FIJI

Raft the Kaituna River in New Zealand's north

○ JASPER NATIONAL PARK, ALBERTA, CANADA

Relax like a local in the piazza at Ciutadella, Menorca

○ MENORCA, SPAIN

○ NORTH ISLAND, NEW ZEALAND

Get a taste of old Arabia in Oman

○ OMAN

○ MONTENEGRO

○ NEW MEXICO, USA

Hike the serrated summits of Montenegro's Durmitor National Park

○ SEYCHELLES

○ LE MARCHE, ITALY

○ TAIWAN

○ CUSCO REGION, PERU

○ FEZ, MOROCCO

Hunt for truffles in Le Marche

See an unmatched repository of Chinese art at the National Palace Museum in Taipei, Taiwan

○ NORTHERN VIETNAM

○ TOHOKU, JAPAN

○ CZECH REPUBLIC

Prepare for a wildlife overdose in Madagascar

○ ATLANTIC PATAGONIA, ARGENTINA

Fill up at farm-to-fork eateries in Canada's fruit-filled Okanagan Valley

○ MARSEILLE

○ UTTARAKHAND, INDIA

○ SOUTHERN ETHIOPIA

○ NORWAY

○ OKANAGAN VALLEY, BRITISH COLUMBIA CANADA

Visit Turkestan, the spiritual capital of the Turkic world, in Kazakhstan

○ MADAGASCAR

Take a ride on the Norwegian Coastal Express

○ SOUTHERN KAZAKHSTAN

FEZ MOROCCO

→ **Why now? Lose yourself in a medieval medina.**

Stepping through blue-tiled Bab Bou Jeloud is as close as most of us will get to time travel – a journey back 1200 years to a city without motorised traffic, the most mesmerising and extensive medieval city in the Islamic world. Visit in October, between sweltering summer and chilly, damp winter, to explore (or, more likely, get hopelessly lost in) the tangled skein of 9400 alleys in Fes el-Bali. This oldest section of the walled medina is romantic and relentless in equal measure. You can admire glorious Moorish *zellij* tilework and ornately carved wood and alabaster adorning *medersas* (Islamic colleges), feast on *pastilla* (pigeon pie), tagines and a traditional glass of mint tea, and bed down in an Arabian Nights-worthy palace, *riad* or *dar* (courtyard mansion). But you'll also be deafened by the hubbub of

the *souks* (bazaars) and hit by the stench of the colourful but pungent tanneries.

Trip plan: Stay in Fes el-Bali for maximum atmosphere; consider hiring a licensed guide to get a feel for the medina's warren before tackling it alone. Don't miss the Chouara Tannery, the beautiful decorations of Bou Inania and El Attarine *medersas*, and the ornate crafts displayed in Dar Batha Museum.

Need to know: Many facilities, including modern hotels and the train station, are in the Ville Nouvelle (New Town) southwest of the medina.

Other months: Nov-Mar – mild, more rain; Apr-May – pleasantly warm, quieter; Jun-Sep – very hot.

(L) Get lost in Fez's buzzing *souks*; (R) Fez's ornate doorways are sights in their own right

LE MARCHE
ITALY

→ **Why now?** Hunt truffles, wines and other tasty treats.

'It's the next Tuscany!' declare cognoscenti, vaunting their new favourite 'hidden' corner of Italy with culinary and cultural cachet. Well, Le Marche, sandwiched between the Adriatic and the Apennines, has no pretensions to be the next anywhere. As yet largely uncrowded, its low-key historic gems, Verdicchio and Conero wines, fungi and other local flavours speak for themselves – and do so most persuasively in harvest season. Autumn brings pleasant temperatures for hopping between medieval hilltop towns and hiking in Monti Sibillini National Park, watching for chamois, wolves and bears. True, some aspects evoke a whiff of Tuscany: the walled historic centres of Urbino and Áscoli Piceno, packed with medieval and Renaissance architecture, and the vine-striped hillsides. But Le Marche has flavours all its own, evident in beautiful villages such as Gradara and Offida, renowned for its wines, and Acqualagna and Apecchio, both hosting white-truffle fairs in autumn – toast your trip with fine Apecchio beers.

Trip plan: Coastal trains run between Pésaro, Fano, Ascona and San Benedotto del Tronto, with branch lines to Áscoli Piceno and Macerata; buses connect to Urbino. You'll want your own wheels to roam the hinterland, Monti Sibillini's hiking trails and the karst caves of Grotte di Frasassi.

Need to know: Late heatwave? Cool off on the beaches beneath the spectacular white cliffs of Monte Conero.

Other months: Nov-Mar – chilly; Apr-Jun & Sep – pleasant weather, quieter; Jul-Aug – hot, seaside resorts and historic sites busier.

NORTH ISLAND
NEW ZEALAND

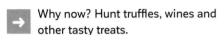

→ **Why now?** Ride the wildest waters.

New Zealand ticks all the boxes for a thrilling whitewater rafting adventure: ice- and snow-clad peaks on which rain falls, feeding rivers that surge wildly through forests and rocky gorges. In spring, winter downpours have fully charged those snaking torrents just as the mercury's creeping up, boosting river levels further with mountain meltwaters. On the North Island, tempting waterways for rafting flow north – the Tongariro into Lake Taupo, and the Rangitaiki, Motu and Kaituna to the Bay of Plenty – south along the Rangitikei, and east into Hawke Bay – the Ngaruroro and Mohaka. When water levels are high, typically around October, the Ngaruroro offers opportunities for family-friendly multi-day wilderness expeditions, drifting through gorges, fishing for trout and traversing Kaweka Forest Park. The Mohaka, though gentler along its upper course with a few Grade II and III sections, rages ever wilder through Grade IV and V rapids as it descends – turbulence reflected in its Māori name, translating roughly as 'a place for dancing'.

Trip plan: Various operators are based in central and eastern North Island, departing from Rotorua (for the Bay of Plenty), Turangi (for the Tongariro) and Napier (for the Mohaka and Ngaruroro). Trips range from half-day whitewater epics to gentle five-day drifts downstream.

Need to know: Rafting on some stretches, particularly on the Ngaruroro, is dependent on rain upstream; itineraries may be diverted according to conditions.

Other months: Nov-Apr – most commercial rafting trips operate; May-Sep – colder, few rafting tours run.

ATLANTIC PATAGONIA
ARGENTINA

→ **Why now?** Meet friendly whales, penguins and elephant seals.

When spring arrives, there's only one thing on the minds of the feathered, furred and finned denizens of Peninsula Valdés: making babies. Or, in some cases, eating them – the beaches at Caleta Valdés and Punta Delgada are famed for the unique hunting strategy of killer whales that hurl themselves up onto the strand to grab sea-lion pups. As well as the sea lions – best encountered on a thrilling (and carefully regulated) snorkel safari in Punta Loma Provincial Nature Reserve – you'll witness gargantuan male elephant seals vying for mating rights; wander among hundreds of thousands of Magellanic penguins pairing up and laying eggs in burrows at Estancia San Lorenzo and Punta Tombo; and meet hundreds of extraordinarily friendly southern right whales that calve in the protected waters of Golfo Nuevo and Golfo San José.

Trip plan: Puerto Madryn, which has an airport linked to Buenos Aires and other Argentine cities, is a handy base for the various wildlife-watching experiences, though it's also possible to stay on the peninsula. Buses run from Puerto Madryn onto the peninsula and south to the Welsh towns; otherwise, book tours from operators in the town.

Need to know: The Chubut Valley south of Puerto Madryn hosts a cluster of 19th-century Welsh settlements. Visit the tea room in Gaiman and attend the annual October Eisteddfod in Trelew for insights into traditional culture and language.

Other months: Oct-Dec – spring, warming, wildlife active; Jan-Mar – summer, warm; Apr-Sep – cooler (whales arrive Jun).

MENORCA SPAIN

→ **Why now? Swim, cycle and stroll in 'winter's spring'.**

After the heat of high summer abates, hardcore beach-loungers depart but the sun hasn't quite finished with the easternmost Balearic. In the first weeks of autumn – sometimes dubbed *primavera l'hivern*, describing the bright, warm days of 'winter's spring' – tourist facilities are yet to close up shop and the Mediterranean lapping Menorca's glorious beaches remains delightfully balmy, yet you'll have many places to yourself. Despite the odd shower as October wears on, conditions are fine for discovering the Anglo-Spanish heritage of charismatic capital Maó (Mahón) and former chief settlement, Ciutadella, marvelling at four-millennia-old megalithic monuments, and hiking or biking the undulating 185km (115 mile) Camí de Cavalls coastal circuit. Menorca as a whole is a Unesco Biosphere Reserve, centred on the bird-bustling wetlands of Parc Natural S'Albufera des Grau – pack binoculars, load up with famed Menorcan pastries and explore in glorious peace.

Trip plan: The ferry from Barcelona takes 7hr 30min to sail to Maó, which also receives domestic and international flights; services from Valencia, docking at Ciutadella, take about twice as long. Regular ferries also link Ciutadella with Alcúdia in northern Mallorca, enabling a twin-island break. Hire a car or, better still, a bike to get around.

Need to know: To see the islands bedecked with white and pink almond blossoms, visit in February instead.

Other months: Dec-Mar – cool, wet; Apr-May – warming, drier; Jun-Aug – very hot, dry; Sep & Nov – warm, getting wetter.

NEW MEXICO USA

→ **Why now? For cool weather and hot air.**

New Mexico, officially the 'Land of Enchantment', is especially enchanting in sunny, mild October – the 20°C (68°F) days are ideal for discovering the historical riches and extraordinary outdoors of this foreign-feeling United State. Sites such as 1000-year-old Taos Pueblo nod to the region's Native American roots, while capital Santa Fe (founded by Spanish missionaries in 1610) combines old adobe houses, Romanesque architecture and a slew of modern-art galleries. Then there's the plentiful wilderness, from the Sangre de Cristos mountains of the north to the blinding-white dunes of the south. Scenic drives cut through these badlands, while there are opportunities for activities and ranch stays aplenty.

Trip plan: With one week, loop the north. From Albuquerque, drive the Turquoise Trail to Santa Fe; browse the galleries of Canyon Rd and bird-watch at the Audubon Center. Trek among ancient ruins at Bandelier National Monument then head to boho Taos for margaritas and hikes or horserides around Taos Pueblo. Climb Wheeler Peak, New Mexico's highest, then return to Albuquerque on the High Rd, via the arty villages of Cordova and Chimayó.

Need to know: Albuquerque International Balloon Fiesta is held in early October.

Other months: Mar-May – mild, windy; Jun-Aug – hot, wettest; Sep & Nov – warm; Dec-Feb – mild (cold at altitude).

SEYCHELLES

→ **Why now? Calm seas in paradise.**

The Seychelles is probably how Pixar would draw paradise: swaying palms, supernaturally blue seas, bling-white sand, artfully smoothed and scattered boulders, plus a few cute turtles wriggling ashore. Fantasy made real. Given these high levels of loveliness, and the balmy 25-30°C (77-86°F) year-round temperatures, there's no awful time to visit this Indian Ocean archipelago. However, October, the period between the brisker southeasterly trade winds switching to the lighter northwesterlies, brings especially calm conditions, so is excellent for swimming, snorkelling and diving. The water can be 29°C (84°F), visibility is around 30m (100ft) and migrating whale sharks have arrived. It's also cheaper than the peak of June to August.

Trip plan: The Seychelles has over 100 islands. Use ferries to hop between mountainous, arty Mahé (the main island), car-free La Digue and Praslin, home to the Vallée de Mai's raunchy coco de mer palms. Elsewhere, Bird Island is brilliant for, er, birds. North Island is the world's most exclusive resort. The remote Aldabra Group, 1150km (715 miles) from Mahé and only accessible by boat, is the Indian Ocean's Galápagos, home to over 100,000 giant tortoises.

Need to know: Festival Kreol, the Seychelles' biggest cultural event, is held across Mahé in late October.

Other months: Nov-Mar – rainier season; Apr – between trade winds, calm, warm, cheaper; May-Sep – dry, warm, windy.

(A) Madagascar's baby ring-tailed lemurs are at their cutest in October; (L) Women working in a field in Vietnam; (R) Hiking in Unesco-listed Durmitor National Park

MADAGASCAR

Why now? Coo at lemur babies.
Isolated from Africa for some 160 million years, Madagascar became a hothouse of evolution – today around 90% of its plant and animal species are endemic, found nowhere else on Earth. Spot swivel-eyed chameleons, diverse orchids, giraffe-necked beetles, dog-cat-mongoose-cross fossa and of course those perennial pin-ups, lemurs: more than 100 species scamper, climb and hop across Madagascar, including the elusive, bat-eared nocturnal aye-aye, dancing sifakas and adorable ring-tailed lemurs, whose babies are at peak cuteness in October. In fact, this is an all-round great month to explore – largely dry and pleasantly warm, with eye-popping purple jacaranda blossoms lining roads.

Trip plan: Clue's in the name: the 'Great Red Island' is huge – don't try to see it all in one hit. In the north, take in cacao plantations, the *tsingy* (limestone pinnacles) and lemurs of Ankarana Special Reserve, and the beaches, chameleons and turtles of Nosy Be. A good southerly itinerary starting in Tana encounters the rainforest birdlife of Andasibe-Mantadia National Park before heading south along the main RN7 road to Ranomafana (for aye-ayes), then to Anja Reserve and Isalo National Park (for baby ring-tails and rare lemur species), and the beaches of Ifaty, backed by weird spiny forest.

Need to know: Humpback whales migrate through the waters around Île Sainte-Marie July-September.

Other months: Dec-Mar – hotter, wetter (east-coast cyclones most common Feb-Mar); Apr-Sep – largely cooler, drier; Nov – pleasant.

NORTHERN VIETNAM

Why now? Meet hill tribes and hike the heights.
In the lush, mountainous northwest, bordering Yunnan in China and northeast Laos, live Vietnam's diverse hill tribes. Each group has its own distinctive cultures, clothing, crafts, architecture, music and languages. Many of the more remote communities (poorly served by transport infrastructure and often trickiest to explore) are in prime settings for hiking – surrounded by waterfalls, lakes, terraced hillsides and forested peaks. October, after the heaviest rains have eased but before temperatures fall too low, is a fine month to hike the mountains – and, since it's still wet in much of the country, offers good value, too. October, after the heaviest rains have eased but before temperatures fall too low, is a fine month to explore the mountains – and, since it's still wet in much of the country, offers good value, too.

Trip plan: From Hanoi, head north and trace an anticlockwise circuit. Meet Tay people among the lakes and limestone peaks of Ba Be National Park; be dazzled by the bright costumes of the Black Lolo of Cao Bang province; trek between Hmong and Red Dao communities around Hà Giang and Sapa, beneath Vietnam's highest peak, Fansipan; and enjoy Thai music around Lai Châu. Hire a guide and driver or join a tour to reach more remote villages.

Need to know: Overnight trains run from Hanoi to Lào Cai, for transfers to Sapa; sleeper berths cost around $15, more for private carriages.

Other months: Nov-Apr – dry, chilly in the mountains; May-Sep – warm, wet.

MONTENEGRO

Why now? Hit the heights.
Don't pack away the hiking boots just yet – thanks to their southerly latitude, the mountains of Montenegro remain open and awesome for ambling until November. And what mountains: the highest are within Unesco-listed Durmitor National Park, a cluster of dark, serrated summits (of which 48 soar to over 2000m/6065ft) scattered with pine forest, lush meadows and glittering glacial lakes, and home to all manner of wildlife, from birds to bears; there's also good walking amid the peaks and primeval forests of Biogradska Gora National Park. Coastal high-points such as mounts Orjen and Lovćen offer sweeping views of the Adriatic – mix hikes here with dips in the azure sea, which remains beautifully inviting throughout October, and is wonderfully crowd-free. A week's walking could include an ascent of Rumija, on the south coast; hiking in the Kučka Krajina range near capital Podgorica; admiring the autumn colours around Mt Bjelasica in Biogradska Gora; and varied trekking in Durmitor, with the chance to stand atop Bobotov Kuk (2523m/8277ft), the country's highest peak.

Trip plan: The most convenient airports are at Podgorica and Dubrovnik (Croatia). Ferries sail from Bari in Italy to Bar in Montenegro once-weekly in October (more frequently in summer).

Need to know: Bobotov Kuk is a strenuous but not technical climb, though the final step to the peak requires you to use fixed cables.

Other months: Nov-Mar – cold, skiing possible; Apr-Jun & Sep – warm, less crowded; Jul-Aug – hot, busy.

233

Autumn in Tohoku: (clockwise from top left) Hirosaki-jō; in-season apples; autumn scenery; and steaming onsen

TOHOKU JAPAN

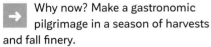

→ **Why now? Make a gastronomic pilgrimage in a season of harvests and fall finery.**

Most visitors to Japan head west from Toyko towards Kyoto and Fuji, or bypass northern Honshu to reach Hokkaidō. More fool them: the six prefectures comprising Tohoku encompass steaming onsens (try Nyuto), gleaming castles (Hirosaki), golden-halled temples (Chuson-ji in Hiraizumi), peaceful farming valleys and forest-clad mountains, now flaming red and gold. The clear days of harvest season are perfect for exploring the region's culinary highlights: fabulous seafood and fish, of course – squid and mackerel are particular specialities – plus local takes on ramen, soba and udon noodles, apples and excellent sake. Fuel up for hikes among the cedars on Mount Haguro, through the virgin beech forests of mountainous Shirakami-Sanchi or along the 1000km-plus (621 miles) Michinoku Coastal Trail.

Trip plan: From Tokyo, head north through Nikko, Sendai (for the islands of Matsushima Bay), Hiraizumi – peeling off to forage the Tono Valley's villages for river fish, dumplings and noodles – Moriota (for Nyuto Onsen), Hachinhohe (for fresh seafood) and Aomori (for more seafood and apples). Return via Akita and Niigata, hopping across to Sado Island. Allow at least two weeks, more for hikes in the Shirakami Sanchi mountains or to the shrines of Dewa Sanzen.

Need to know: The JR East Tohoku Area Pass, valid for five consecutive days, covers travel on JR trains and buses.

Other months: Dec-Feb – very cold, snowy; Mar-Apr – cool, dry; May – warm, busier – Jun-Sep – hot, wet, increasingly humid; Nov – fall colours, pleasant temperatures.

© Veronika Galkina / Shutterstock

Come in *podzim* (autumn) for quieter cobbled streets

CZECH REPUBLIC

→ **Why now? Embrace eats, arts and autumn hues.**

Did you hear? Prague has a mesmerising medieval centre, all cobbles, castles, churches and Charles Bridge flanked by saint statues. Oh, you did? Of course – and in summer it seems the entire planet is in on the secret. Visit in *podzim* (autumn) instead, when crowds and costs have eased a little in Prague and elsewhere. Conditions are ideal for hiking among the sandstone rock pillars, arches and gorges of Český ráj (Bohemian Paradise) and České Švýcarsko (Bohemian Switzerland) National Parks, their trees ablaze with reds and fiery yellows. Fresh from the grape harvest, Moravian wine bars serve sweet, low-alcohol *burčák* (young wine). Pumpkins ripen and festivals bring cheer to cities, towns and villages. Museums, castles and other cultural marvels, many of which close in November, are delightfully quiet, too.

Trip plan: Prague is well connected to European and other Czech cities by bus and train. Short on time? Mighty rock-perched Gothic Karlštejn Castle and atmospheric Kutná Hora are near Prague; just a little farther away are medieval Český Krumlov and Jindřichův Hradec, and brewery towns Plzeň and České Budějovice. With extra days, continue east to Moravia's vineyards, caves and wooden churches, best explored from Olomouc.

Need to know: The country celebrates the anniversary of Czechoslovak independence on 28 October with events, exhibitions and chances to explore state buildings and monuments usually closed to the public.

Other months: Nov-Mar – cold; Apr-Jun & Sep – warm, quieter; Jul-Aug – hot, busy.

OMAN

➜ **Why now? Mellow fruitfulness, mellow weather.**

Wonderfully warm climes (30°C/86°F); markets overflowing with fresh-harvested walnuts and pomegranates; 20,000 turtles laying their eggs... October is an amazing time to visit Oman, the spectacular Gulf state that offers a taste of old Arabia. There is modern development, but mainly it's a land of raw canyons and rippled desert, date plantations, palm-fringed sands, adobe villages and spicy souks. Most trips begin in capital Muscat, where the old port area of Muttrah mixes urban sprawl with glitzy beach resorts. Southeast lies Ras al Jinz where thousands of green turtles haul ashore to nest; take a guided night tour. Inland is Sharqiya Sands, a perfect sea of dunes where camel rides, sandboarding and 4WD dune-bashing can be arranged from desert camps. Further west still, the Hajar Mountains rise in craggy splendour, cut by caves and canyons, and speckled with sites such as ancient Nizwa – the spot to explore a fort, buy a goat and strike out into the hills.

Trip plan: Allow nine days to loop northern Oman. Add extra to sail around the inlet-notched Musandam Peninsula.

Need to know: Muscat's massive Sultan Qaboos Grand Mosque is Oman's only mosque open to non-Muslims.

Other months: Dec-Feb – coolest; Mar-Apr – warming, quiet; May-Sep – very hot, humid (monsoon in south); Nov – hot, harvest.

FIJI

➜ **Why now? For a quieter Pacific paradise.**

Fiji is paradise made easy. The most accessible and tourism-attuned outpost of the South Pacific, Fiji has an idyll to suit everyone across its 333 islands. That makes it popular, which is why October is perfect: it's after peak season but still pleasantly cool and dry; you may find cheaper deals, and you will find fewer people. There's white-sand-blue-sea magnificence across the archipelago – the dreamy Yasawa and Mamanuca groups are the most 'developed', but even here no buildings are taller than a coconut palm. You could happily swim, surf, snorkel and loll about at a lively or low-key resort here for weeks. Viti Levu, Fiji's largest island, offers the greatest variety. Make a circuit: drive the coastal Queens Rd and highlands Kings Rd, hike at the Sigatoka sand dunes and gaze at colonial architecture while tasting Fijian-Indian cuisine in capital Suva.

Trip plan: Fly to Nadi (Viti Levu). Boats run from here to various ports on the Yasawas and Mamanucas – pick a base or hop between spots. Allow a week to explore Viti Levu. Divers should head for Astrolabe Reef or Taveuni's waters.

Need to know: English is the official language; *bula* means hello in Fijian.

Other months: Jul-Sep – dry, busy; May-Jun – dry, shoulder seasons, quieter; Nov-Apr – wet, cyclones possible.

OKANAGAN VALLEY, BRITISH COLUMBIA
CANADA

➜ **Why now? Savour a grape escape.**

The leaves are turning, the sun's blaze has mellowed to a bath-warm glow, and the last peaches and pears have gone from the Okanagan's orchards. So too, have most of the tourists and highest accommodation prices. After peak season ebbs away, October's the sweet spot for touring Canada's premier wine-producing region, a 180km-long (112 miles) valley meandering north from the US border. Unsurprisingly, given the plentiful soft-fruit farms and orchards yielding plump peaches, pears, apricots and apples, sustainable food is a focus here, too, with many delightful farm-to-fork eateries – it's a fabulous destination for an oenological expedition fuelled by great cuisine. En route, connect with the cultures of Indigenous peoples such as the Nlaka'pamux, Syilx and Secwepemc Nations – blend interests at Nk'Mip Cellars, claimed to be North America's first Indigenous winery.

Trip plan: Hwy 97 links Osoyoos to Vernon via Oliver, Okanagan Falls, Penticton and Kelowna, passing plenty of vineyards and cellar doors. For a mellower experience, take quieter back roads or, better still, cycle – the region is laced with excellent bike paths including the scenic Kettle Valley Rail Trail, with a spur running south from Penticton to Osoyoos via Oliver. Just don't drink and pedal!

Need to know: The Fall Okanagan Wine Festival is on in October. Some attractions, accommodations and activities shut up shop in late September or October.

Other months: Nov-Mar – chilly but relatively mild; Apr-May – spring, pleasant; Jun-Aug – warm, busy; Sep – warm, quieter.

SOUTHERN ETHIOPIA

 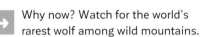

→ **Why now? Watch for the world's rarest wolf among wild mountains.**

Ethiopia is a land unlike any other, with unique customs, languages, food, religious traditions – and wildlife, hosting dozens of endemic (and, in many cases, endangered) species. October, when the rains have eased but the land is lush and fertile, is the time to explore its forests and highlands, binoculars in hand. In the Simien Mountains, often visited on a northern loop along with the royal sites of Gonder and the sunken rock churches of Lalibela, you'll meet huge troops of grass-eating, golden-maned gelada (sometimes called baboons) and, if you're lucky, catch sight of the magnificent curved horns of the Walia ibex. But perhaps the richest pickings lie in the south, particularly in Bale Mountains National Park, where more than 300 bird species and 70-plus mammals have been recorded. Hike or horse-ride to the Sanetti Plateau to spot hefty mountain nyala, Menelik's bushbuck, giant molerat and the largest-surviving population of the world's rarest canid, the Ethiopian wolf.

Trip plan: Head south from Addis Ababa, pausing to enjoy some fine birdwatching around the Rift Valley lakes and to trek the Bale Mountains – allow five or six days for a satisfying hike with an expert local guide providing cultural as well as natural insights. Consider continuing to Nechisar National Park for savannah species.

Need to know: Check the current security situation before booking a trip in light of periodic unrest, particularly in border regions.

Other months: Nov-Feb – sunny, mostly dry; Mar-Sep – rainy.

© Santiago Urquijo / Getty Images

A gelada snacking on grass in the Simien Mountains

237

NORWAY

→ Why now? Be dazzled by a celestial light show amid dramatic fjords.

Norway's coast is a geological wonderland of sheer-sided fjords and islands etched by glaciers and studded with colourful fishing harbours and historic towns: Art Nouveau Ålesund; Bergen, with its pretty old Bryggen district; and Trondheim, crowned by Nidaros Cathedral. Discover the panoply of experiences on year-round Norwegian Coastal Express ships sailing the 2400km (1494 miles) between Bergen and Kirkenes, in the Arctic north, via some 34 ports. Most leisure passengers book for the long, bright days of high summer – yet autumn, when forests spark into fall finery and crowds have thinned, is in many ways the ideal season to undertake this epic voyage. In September and October only, northbound vessels sail into the Hjørundfjord, a less-visited but spectacular inlet hemmed in by the steep slopes of the Sunnmøre Alps. Aurora Borealis activity tends to be particularly powerful now, around the autumn equinox – so your Arctic expedition could be enchanted by a shimmering performance of the Northern Lights.

Trip plan: The full Bergen-Kirkenes route takes seven days in either direction. The 12-day itinerary offers the chance to experience stops at different times – potentially seeing in daylight a port visited at night in the other direction.

Need to know: Hurtigruten Coastal Express vessels are comfortable but not luxurious – don't expect the casinos and lavish entertainment found on expensive cruise ships.

Other months: Nov-Apr – cold (Arctic below freezing and very dark Dec-Feb), May-Sep – warmest, sunniest (Jul-Aug – most expensive).

Preserved wooden buildings of Bryggen in Bergen

CUSCO REGION PERU

See the mesmerising
Lake Humantay on the
Salkantay Trek

→ **Why now? Traverse alternative Inca trails.**

'The' Inca Trail winds for around 42km (26 miles) over breath-snatching passes and past ancient remains to end with the big reveal framed by the Sun Gate: Machu Picchu. But it's far from the only Inca trail. Those ingenious ancient Peruvians constructed a vast network of highways – the Qhapaq Ñan, spidering some 30,000km (18,641 miles) throughout the Andes – much of which remains more or less intact today, beckoning hikers keen to explore past glories and meet modern

Quechua people. Visit in October, after peak season but before the rains set in, to roam these historic paths in peace. The Salkantay Trek traverses thrilling Andean wilderness: snow-clad peaks, glaciers and mesmerising lakes. The Lares Trek, north of the Sacred Valley, boasts fewer Incan sites but ample interaction with local communities. And Choquequirao rewards with another ridge-top citadel – a mini-Machu Picchu, with tiny crowds to match.

Trip plan: Various tour operators in Cusco offer guided, supported treks along several of the surviving Inca Trails around the

Sacred Valley and Machu Picchu – choose from Choquequirao, Lares, Salkantay or alternatives. Allow at least 10 days to explore Cusco's monuments and to visit to Pisac, Ollantaytambo, Chinchero and other historic sites.

Need to know: If you plan to hike the 'classic' Inca Trail to Machu Picchu, book far ahead – only 500 permits are available for each day, including guides and porters, so it sells out months in advance.

Other months: Dec-Apr – rainy; May-Sep – dry, busy; Nov – fairly dry, quieter.

Natural and cultural
wonders abound on the
Pacific Highway

NEW SOUTH WALES AUSTRALIA

→ **Why now? Drive between quiet national parks.**

Sun, sand, surf, scuba, schooners – standard-issue fun awaits along the Pacific Highway, the justifiably well-trodden trail between Sydney and Brisbane. But a world of natural and cultural wonders awaits just a little inland, some well known – the cliffs, cascades, caves and trails of the Blue Mountains – others much less visited. Spring shoulder season brings warm sunshine, wildflowers and a flurry of animal activity, but without the crowds and costs of high summer – even the trails around

Katoomba are quieter. Take the road less travelled to discover canyons and caves, historic mines and glow-worm tunnels, Aboriginal rock art and dizzying rainforest biodiversity.

Trip plan: Allow at least a week to drive between Sydney and Coffs Harbour. Hike to waterfalls in Blue Mountains National Park; admire ancient rock art in Yengo NP; kayak beneath soaring rocks at Ganguddy in Wollemi NP; swim in Goulburn River NP's creeks; roam among the Gondwana rainforest and strangler figs of Barrington Tops NP; and hike to thundering waterfalls

along the dramatic gorges of Oxley Wild Rivers NP. Find heaps of ideas and practical info at the NSW National Parks and Wildlife Service site (nationalparks.nsw.gov.au).

Need to know: For immersive insights into Indigenous culture, join an Aboriginal-led tour – perhaps through Wiradjuri Country in Goulburn River NP.

Other months: Dec-Feb – hot, busy, fairly rainy; Mar-May – pleasant, still quite wet; Jun-Aug – cool, drier; Sep & Nov – spring, warm, wildflowers.

241

TAIWAN

 Why now? The best weather for exploring an offbeat isle.

Taiwan surprises people. Dubbed Ilha Formosa ('Beautiful Isle') by 16th-century sailors, this East Asian stunner has more latterly become famed for manufacturing high-quality products. But while its economy has developed apace, the country has also managed both to preserve more Chinese traditions than mainland China and to forge a cosmopolitan culture that's distinctly Taiwanese. The food – Chinese and Japanese dishes, Hakka specialities, sizzling street food – is sensational too. Autumn is the best time to visit. It's cooler and less humid (meaning locals start leaping into the hot springs), and maple leaves are starting to turn. Start in capital Taipei, to visit the National Palace Museum (a matchless repository of Chinese art); add on Sun Moon Lake, Taroko Gorge, old Lugang and Foguangshan (a huge Buddhist monastery where you can stay overnight). The water is still warm enough for snorkelling in coastal Kenting National Park, while the mountains of Alishan offer good hiking.

Trip plan: Allow two weeks and explore Taiwan by train – the rail network connects cities and national parks; include the Forest Train, which rumbles into Alishan.

Need to know: Ferries run between mainland China and Taiwan.

Other months: Jan-Feb – coldest, drier; Apr-May – unpredictable, rainy; Jun-Aug – hot, humid, typhoons; Sep-Nov – cooler, dry (typhoon season ends in Oct).

© Sumeth anu / Shutterstock

The imposing Buddhist monastery, Foguangshan

SOUTHWEST ENGLAND

→ **Why now?** Roam historic marvels and glorious countryside in serene autumn.

England's shapely left leg is crowded with grand mansions and stately homes, castles and abbeys, megalithic henges and barrows. In summer they're jammed with tourists; many then close, at least partly, from the end of October. This month's ideal, then, for a road trip immersing yourself in centuries of history: playing lord or lady of the manor at Montacute or Cotehele, communing with ancestors among Avebury's standing stones, or jousting with King Arthur at Tintagel. Now, too, the hiking routes – not least England's longest, the South West Coast Path – are wonderfully quiet, and cosy country pubs more enticing than ever.

Trip plan: Explore one patch in depth: Cornwall's quoits, tin mines and Tintagel; South Devon for Agatha Christie's Greenway, 1920s chic Coleton Fishacre and Castle Drogo on Dartmoor; or Elizabethan Montacute, the poet Coleridge's cottage and magical Dunster Castle in Somerset. Or plan a best-of anticlockwise circuit from Bath through Somerset, North Devon, Cornwall, South Devon, Dorset and Wiltshire.

Need to know: Most historic houses and monuments are managed by the National Trust (nationaltrust.org.uk) or English Heritage (english-heritage.org.uk); consider annual membership of one or both. Access to many outdoor sites – stone circles and the like – is often free of charge; Stonehenge is a notable exception.

Other months: Dec-Feb – cold, dark, many historic properties closed; Mar-May – spring, pleasant, fairly quiet; Jun-Aug – summer, coast busy; Sep & Nov – autumn colours, getting cooler and damper.

243

The Jasper Dark Sky Preserve is one of the best spots for seeing the Northern Lights

JASPER NATIONAL PARK, ALBERTA
CANADA

Why now? Enjoy celestial fireworks under the darkest skies.

Not all skies are equal: when you're searching for constellations and galaxies, the darker the better. With minimal light pollution, Jasper Dark Sky Preserve – the world's second-largest, spanning some 11,000 sq km (4247 sq miles) of forests, glacial lakes and Rocky Mountain peaks – is among the finest destinations for surveying the cosmos. October, with its mild temperatures, blazing fall colours and clear skies, is designated Dark Sky Month in Jasper National Park, optimal time for both enthusiasts and expert astronomers – many of whom gather here for the annual Dark Sky Festival in mid-October, offering talks and guided stargazing excursions. Even if clouds gather, the town's well-equipped Planetarium offers a virtual tour of the heavens. Bonus: October often experiences high Aurora Borealis (Northern Lights) activity.

Trip plan: Base yourself in Jasper, a 4hr drive or bus ride west from Edmonton, the nearest airport. Within the national park, recommended spots for stargazing include Pyramid Island, Maligne Lake, Old Fort Point and the toe of the Athabasca Glacier. During the day, hike Maligne Canyon, kayak or SUP on Lac Beauvert, or watch for elk, moose and (if you're lucky) wolves around the Athabasca Valley. More time? Drive the Icefields Parkway to Lake Louise, Moraine Lake and Banff (3hr 30min).

Need to know: The best time for Northern Lights displays is between midnight and 2am.

Other months: Nov-Mar – cold, snowy; Apr-May – cool, quieter; Jun-Sep – warm, wildlife active.

SOUTHERN KAZAKHSTAN

Why now? To get lost in space.
Offbeat Kazakhstan is a mystery to most. Any trip here is likely to expand your horizons – particularly a visit to the country's Baikonur Cosmodrome. This is the planet's first and largest space-launch centre – Sputnik 1 (the first artificial satellite) and Yuri Gagarin (the first man in space) took off from here in 1957 and 1961, respectively. It's possible to tour the Test Facility complex, visit the Space and Spaceport History Museums and see houses once inhabited by famous cosmonauts. Combine this out-of-this-world destination with some rather older southern Kazakh sites. Head to the historic city of Turkestan, known as the 'Spiritual Capital of the Turkic World'; visit the great Silk Road settlement of Sauran; explore the 11th- and 12th-century monuments of Aisha-Bibi Mausoleum, Babaja Hatum and Karakhan Mausoleum near Taraz; and admire the snow-capped peaks around former capital Almaty.

Trip plan: Kazakhstan is huge: allow at least 10-12 days to sample even the south. The nearest airport to Baikonur is Kyzylorda, a 3hr 30min drive across the steppe. The slow trains of the Trans Aral Railway link Baikonur, Kyzylorda and Turkestan, with branches to Taraz and Almaty.

Need to know: Baikonur Cosmodrome is leased by the Russians and is technically Russian territory – bring roubles to buy souvenirs.

Other months: Nov-Mar – freezing, snowy; Apr-Jun – green, mild, potentially rainy; Jul-Aug – very hot; Sep – pleasant, good rafting.

UTTARAKHAND
INDIA

➜ **Why now?** Hike between traditional Himalayan villages with local guides.

Sandwiched between lush lowlands and gleaming peaks in northwest India lies a region little touched by international tourism: the old kingdom of Kumaon in Uttarakhand, dubbed Devbhumi – 'Land of Gods' – for its many pilgrimage destinations. Here, among the wooded foothills of the Himalaya, community trekking organisations have supported the creation of simple guesthouses and set up hiking routes between hamlets in the Binsar Forest Sanctuary and the loftier Saryu and Pindar Valleys, encouraging visitors to meet local people who benefit from new ecotourism opportunities. On forest ambles you might spot pine marten, chital deer or, if you're lucky, leopard; you'll certainly enjoy endless cups of milky chai, and absorb rich insights into lives little changed in centuries.

Trip plan: Trains from Delhi to Kathgodam, railhead for Kumaon, take six or seven hours; the overnight Ranikhet Special sleeper service, which originates in Jaisalmer and passes throughwh Jodhpur, is a good option. It's a 3hr drive to Binsar, and another four or so to the higher Himalayan Valleys – arrange transfers in advance. A 10-day itinerary might visit the Binsar villages of Kaththdhara, Gonap, Risal and Satri plus the guesthouses in the Saryu and Pindar Valleys.

Need to know: Food at guesthouses is vegetarian, based almost entirely on locally grown produce.

Other months: Dec-Jan – dry, very cold in higher regions; Feb-Mar & Nov – pleasant, clear skies; Apr-Sep – hot, rainy (wettest Jun-Aug).

(A) Lofty Pindar Valley; (B) Lush Binsar Forest Sanctuary

© Pawan Tamta / Shutterstock

© Amit kg / Shutterstock

© Architects Rudy Ricciotti & Roland Carta / Mucem, Philippe Paternolli / 500px

Museum of European and Mediterranean Civilisations

MARSEILLE FRANCE

→ **Why now? Party in a pepped-up port.**

History-soaked Marseille – first founded by the Greeks in around 600 BCE – has long had a somewhat unsavoury reputation. But since the instigation of the largest regeneration project in southern Europe, not to mention its 2013 tenure as European Capital of Culture, the multicultural Provençal port has cleaned up its image. The once dilapidated Docks des Suds area is now home to the flagship Museum of European and Mediterranean Civilisations,

designer shops and buzzing concert venues, while abandoned tobacco factories have become culture and craft-beer hubs. Soak up the old-new ambience in still-balmy October (average highs 21°C/70°F). Take the ferry to fortress island Château d'If (immortalised in Alexandre Dumas' novel *Count of Monte Cristo*). Wander the bohemian quarter, with its cool bars, street art, galleries and restaurants, and seek out the nightspots around the Vieux Port and Rue Sainte or Rue d'Endoume. Or time your visit for the four-day Fiesta des Suds (early

or mid-October), when an eclectic mix of world music blasts from the docks.
Trip plan: Allow two days in the city, then visit the ravishing cliffs and bays of the Parc National des Calanques (sometimes off-limits in high summer due to fire risks); excursions by boat and kayak are possible.
Need to know: Most Marseille museums close on Mondays.
Other months: Dec-Mar – mild, quiet; Apr-Jun – warm; Jul-Aug – hottest, busiest; Sep-Nov – still warm, cooler evenings.

247

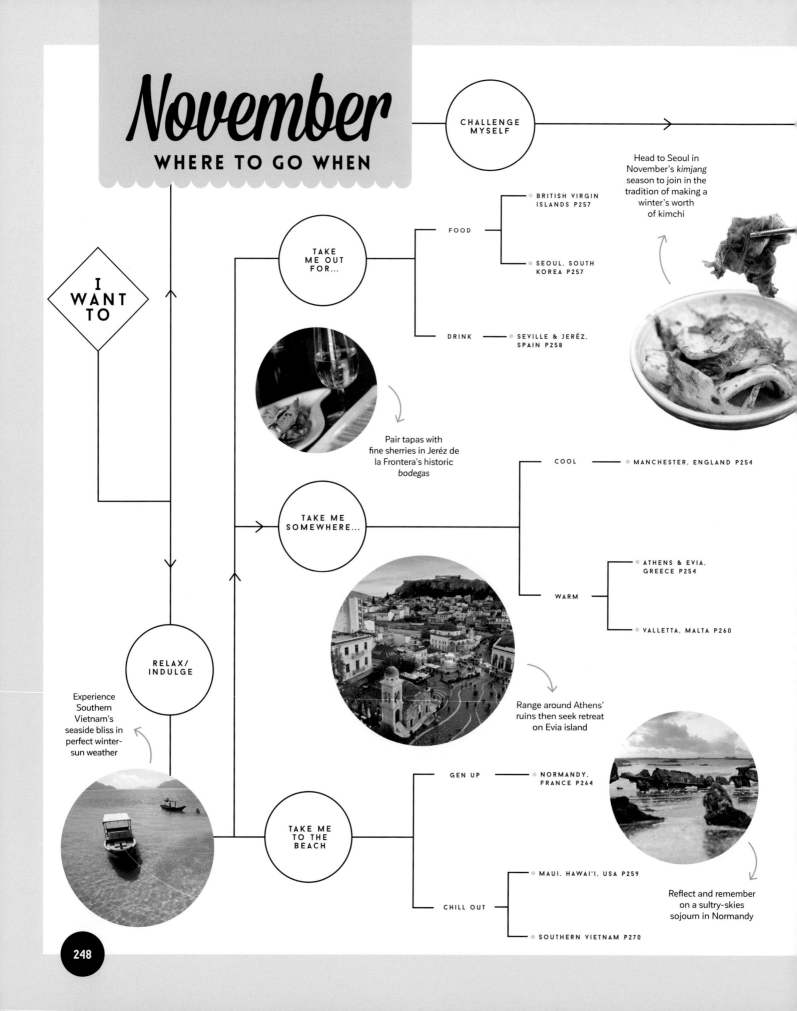

November

WHERE TO GO WHEN

CHALLENGE MYSELF

Head to Seoul in November's *kimjang* season to join in the tradition of making a winter's worth of kimchi

I WANT TO

TAKE ME OUT FOR...

FOOD
- BRITISH VIRGIN ISLANDS P257
- SEOUL, SOUTH KOREA P257

DRINK
- SEVILLE & JERÉZ, SPAIN P258

Pair tapas with fine sherries in Jeréz de la Frontera's historic *bodegas*

TAKE ME SOMEWHERE...

COOL
- MANCHESTER, ENGLAND P254

WARM
- ATHENS & EVIA, GREECE P254
- VALLETTA, MALTA P260

Range around Athens' ruins then seek retreat on Evia island

RELAX/ INDULGE

Experience Southern Vietnam's seaside bliss in perfect winter-sun weather

TAKE ME TO THE BEACH

GEN UP
- NORMANDY, FRANCE P264

CHILL OUT
- MAUI, HAWAI'I, USA P259
- SOUTHERN VIETNAM P270

Reflect and remember on a sultry-skies sojourn in Normandy

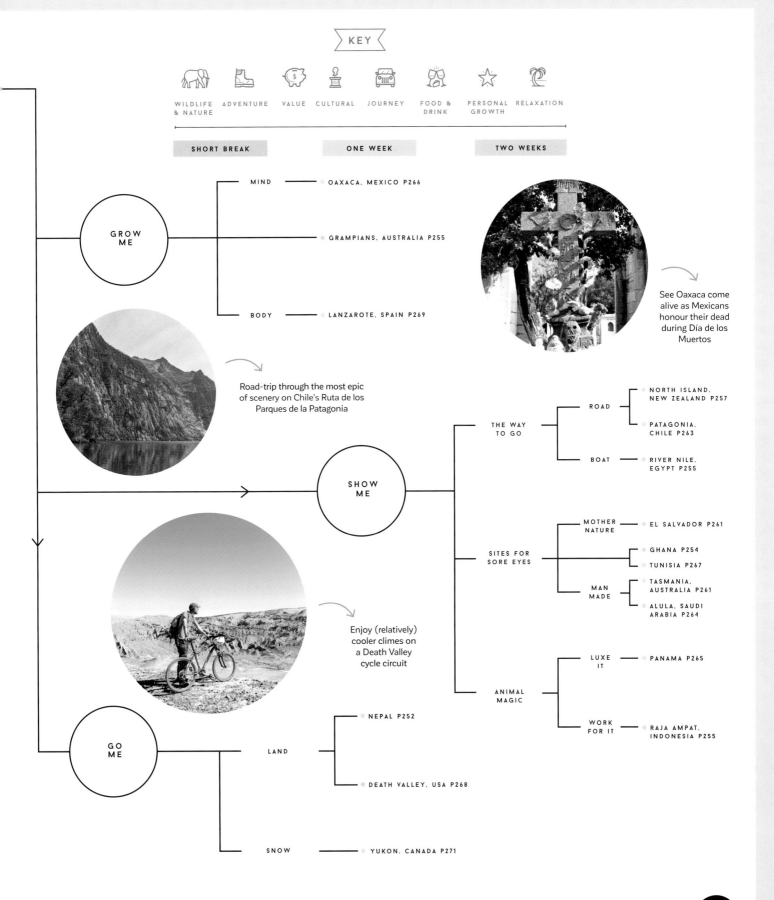

KEY

WILDLIFE & NATURE | ADVENTURE | VALUE | CULTURAL | JOURNEY | FOOD & DRINK | PERSONAL GROWTH | RELAXATION

SHORT BREAK   ONE WEEK   TWO WEEKS

GROW ME

MIND — OAXACA, MEXICO P266

GRAMPIANS, AUSTRALIA P255

BODY — LANZAROTE, SPAIN P269

See Oaxaca come alive as Mexicans honour their dead during Día de los Muertos

Road-trip through the most epic of scenery on Chile's Ruta de los Parques de la Patagonia

SHOW ME

THE WAY TO GO

ROAD — NORTH ISLAND, NEW ZEALAND P257
PATAGONIA, CHILE P263

BOAT — RIVER NILE, EGYPT P255

SITES FOR SORE EYES

MOTHER NATURE — EL SALVADOR P261

GHANA P254
TUNISIA P267

MAN MADE — TASMANIA, AUSTRALIA P261
ALULA, SAUDI ARABIA P264

ANIMAL MAGIC

LUXE IT — PANAMA P265

WORK FOR IT — RAJA AMPAT, INDONESIA P255

Enjoy (relatively) cooler climes on a Death Valley cycle circuit

GO ME

LAND — NEPAL P252
DEATH VALLEY, USA P268

SNOW — YUKON, CANADA P271

EVENTS
IN NOVEMBER

PIRATES WEEK FESTIVAL

Cayman Islands

A-haaaarrr!! Indulge in some swashbuckling fantasies by playing Pirates in the Caribbean – with added fireworks, food festivals, parades and costume competitions.

BON OM TUK

Cambodia

Communities along the Tonlé Sap Lake and river celebrate the reversal of the water's flow with fireworks and feasting.

BLACK-NECKED CRANE FESTIVAL

Phobjikha Valley, Bhutan

Stately black-necked cranes return to the lofty Phobjikha Valley, welcomed with traditional folk songs and dances at Gangtey Gompa (monastery).

MELBOURNE CUP

Melbourne, Victoria, Australia

The biggest horse racing fixture Down Under is preceded by a raft of events and entertainment.

ICELAND AIRWAVES

Reykjavik, Iceland

Catch a diverse array of cutting-edge Icelandic and international music at this now-famous four-day festival.

BAT MIGRATION

Kasanka National Park, Zambia

Some 10 million bats arrive in Kasanka, arguably the world's biggest mammal migration – and when they emerge en masse at dusk it's a jaw-dropping spectacle.

LA DIABLADA

Puno, Peru

The devil – a colourful character – leads a parade to the tune of traditional Andean music at this festival on the shores of Lake Titicaca.

RÄBECHILBI TURNIP FESTIVAL

Richterswil, Switzerland

Yes, you read right – expect a spectacular parade of carved root vegetables and candlelit floats.

Consecutive weekends from early November — $$

Usually early Nov — $

11 November — $$

Early November — $$$

First week in November — $$

Second Saturday in November — $$

October to December — $$$

Early Nov — $$

Follow in the footsteps of Marx and Engels to browse the shelves at Manchester's Chetham's Library

○ NORTH ISLAND, NEW ZEALAND

Plunge into a Rotorua thermal spring on New Zealand's North Island

○ LANZAROTE, SPAIN

○ MAUI, HAWAI'I, USA

○ MANCHESTER, ENGLAND

Take advantage of sub-zero temperatures to dogsled through the Yukon snows

Gorge on gorgeous Caribbean beaches and gourmet meals in the British Virgin Islands

○ SOUTHERN VIETNAM

○ YUKON, CANADA

○ BRITISH VIRGIN ISLANDS

○ ATHENS & EVIA, GREECE

Explore off-season Tunisia for uncrowded sights like Matmata troglodyte village

○ TUNISIA

○ VALLETTA, MALTA

Wander medieval alleys built by knights in still-warm Valetta

○ EL SALVADOR

○ TASMANIA, AUSTRALIA

Spot birdlife like the New Holland honeyeater on Australia's Grampians Peaks Trail

○ RIVER NILE, EGYPT

○ SEOUL, SOUTH KOREA

Cruise down the Nile to see iconic Egyptian relics in Luxor's Valley of the Kings

○ GRAMPIANS, AUSTRALIA

○ PANAMA

○ NEPAL

○ ALULA, SAUDI ARABIA

○ PATAGONIA, CHILE

○ DEATH VALLEY, USA

○ RAJA AMPAT, INDONESIA

○ SEVILLE & JERÉZ, SPAIN

○ OAXACA, MEXICO

○ GHANA

Find street-food Shangri-la in Seoul markets like historic Namdaemun

○ NORMANDY, FRANCE

Stroll among abundant wildlife in Ghana's Mole National Park

NEPAL

→ **Why now? The clearest skies over the highest Himalaya.**

Crisp, cloud-free, warm, dry – a delight. November is perfect for exploring all of Nepal, from its mountain highs to its jungly lows and the culture-rich ripples in between. In the Kathmandu Valley, 22°C (72°F) days are comfortable for temple touring in Patan and Bhaktapur. Down on the steamy *terai* (plain), it's 27°C (81°F) and mud-free, so it's easier to search for rhinos, tigers and other creatures that lurk therein. Rivers are full countrywide, and offer great rafting for all levels – from the serene Seti to the raging Kali Gandaki. And then there are the mountains: 8000m (26,000ft) peaks soaring into clear blue skies; myriad hiking trails open for business. The main routes, such as the Annapurna Sanctuary, will be busy – good for trekker camaraderie. But choose one of Nepal's more offbeat routes (perhaps Kanchenjunga Base Camp in the Upper Dolpo) if you'd prefer to hike away from the crowds.

Trip plan: In two weeks, link the Kathmandu Valley, Chitwan and lakeside Pokhara, incorporating short walks. Multi-day treks, which can be remote, may require longer stays.

Need to know: Practise the traditional Nepali greeting: hold your palms together, and say 'namaste' (I salute the divine within you).

Other months: Oct – clear, dry; Dec-Feb – dry, colder; Mar-May – warm, flowers; Jun-Sep – hot, monsoon (Jul-Aug: wettest).

Annapurna Base Camp, highest point on the Annapurna Sanctuary trek

ATHENS & EVIA
GREECE

Why now? To run or rest amid ancient ruins.

Ever wanted to run a marathon? Then do it here, in its spiritual home. In 490 BCE, Pheidippides dashed from Marathonas to Athens to announce the Greek army's victory over the Persians (then promptly died). Today's Athens Marathon, held along the same route in early November, is a great way to combine a personal challenge with a warm city-and-beach break. However, you don't have to run 26.2 miles to enjoy Athens in autumn. The temperatures (10-18°C/50-64°F) are ideal for wandering the sites, from the Acropolis to panoramic Lykavitós Hill. Most fun is exploring Athens' neighbourhoods – Pláka, Monastiráki, Psyrrí – and hopping between bars and tavernas until the small hours. Then, do as the Athenians do and escape to Evia, Greece's second-largest island, but one largely overlooked by foreign tourists. It has glittering Aegean beaches, a mountainous interior, ancient sites and great food – perfect for recovering from a marathon, or modern life in general.

Trip plan: Allow three days in Athens before decamping to Evia. Chalkida, Evia's ancient capital, is halfway down the west coast; explore from here.

Need to know: Evia is linked to the mainland by two bridges plus ferry services.

Other months: Mar-May & Oct – warm, cheaper; Jun-Sep – sweltering; Dec-Feb – cool, wet.

MANCHESTER
ENGLAND

Why now? For indefatigable and festive spirit.

OK, it's not that hot here right now but, then, Manchester is always cool. This northern British city has a swagger and self-assurance entirely unrelated to the season, born of its past industrial prowess, history of radical thinking and cultural heft. It may be grey, but that shouldn't stop you visiting. Clock-in at the People's History Museum, which charts Britain's 200-year pathway to democracy. Browse Chetham's Library, the oldest public library in the English-speaking world, where Marx and Engels once studied. Worship the beautiful game at the National Football Museum, even if you're not a fan of local mega-clubs, United and City. And join a music pilgrimage to the places that brought forth The Smiths, Oasis and Joy Division. Plus, from the middle of the month to late December, Christmas Markets add extra sparkle, should you need it.

Trip plan: Manchester has rail connections to various UK cities including London (2hr), Edinburgh (3hr 15min) and Birmingham (1hr 30min). Within the centre, a bus provides a free hop-on, hop-off service.

Need to know: The only way to guarantee seats for a Manchester United home game is via a Matchday VIP Experience. Alternatively, take a look behind the scenes on a Manchester United Museum & Stadium Tour.

Other months: Jan-Feb – cold, grey; Mar-May – warming; Jun-Aug – warmest, festivals; Sep-Oct – cool, football-season fervour; Dec – cold, festive.

GHANA

Why now? It's excellent weather for everything.

Ghana's got a great mix. In this diverse wedge of West Africa you'll find lush rainforests, soft-sand beaches, rich history, vibrant villages and parks a-scutter with life. Loitering just above the equator, the temperature here changes little year-round (expect 27-30°C/80-86°F) but November marks the start of the drier months, when travel is easier and the countryside abundantly green, but the harsh harmattan wind hasn't yet started blowing from the Sahara. It's a good time to visit the Unesco-listed shrines of the great Ashanti civilisation, safari in spots such as Mole National Park (where you can walk amid elephants and vervet monkeys) and retrace the coast's haunting past – 40 fortresses were built here, where enslaved people were held before facing the horrors of the Middle Passage; Cape Coast and Elmina castles are especially moving. November is also a good time to meet Ghana's people: head to the fishing settlements in the south, the animist Lobi villages of the north and the many communities in between.

Trip plan: Allow two weeks, to include capital Accra, the coast, Kumasi (for Ashanti culture), Mole and the far north. Be prepared for some long and bumpy drives.

Need to know: Remain open to cultural encounters – serendipitous opportunities to browse markets, meet tribal chiefs and attend funerals can be trip highlights.

Other months: Dec-Mar – dry, warm, wildlife gathers at waterholes (harmattan winds Dec-Mar); Apr-Sep – wet (worst Apr-Jun, Sep-Oct), flooding possible.

GRAMPIANS
AUSTRALIA

→ **Why now?** Hit the highs on a cultural wilderness trail.

As far as the traditional owners of the Gariwerd (Grampians) are concerned, November is when Petyan, season of regrowth and wildflowers, turns into butterfly-filled Ballambar, the onset of summer. It's a lovely time to get out amid the escarpments, outcrops and stringybark forests of these sandstone ranges – waterfalls are full, bushfire risk is low and temperatures ideal (23°C/73.4°F). One of the finest ways of exploring is via the Grampians Peaks Trail, a 160km-long (100-mile), 13-day hiking route completed in 2021. Stretching from the township of Dunkeld to the flanks of Mount Zero, it passes rugged peaks, panoramic lookouts and cool cascades, and offers a deep immersion in the landscapes that the Jardwadjali and Djab Wurrung people have called home for millennia.

Trip plan: Melbourne-Dunkeld is a 3hr drive or 4hr 30min by bus. You can hike independently or join a supported tour. Accommodation is in campsites en route. A three-day, 36km (22-mile) return loop to/from Halls Gap via park icons such as Venus Baths, the Grand Canyon and the Pinnacle Lookout provides a taster.

Need to know: The Grampians are home to 80% of Victoria's rock art sites. Learn more about Aboriginal culture at the Brambuk Cultural Centre in Halls Gap.

Other months: Dec-Feb – hottest, highest bushfire risk; Mar-May – mild; Jun-Aug – cold; Sep-Oct – wildflowers, warming.

RAJA AMPAT
INDONESIA

→ **Why now?** To dive in calm, captivating seas.

Indonesia, the largest archipelagic country in the world, is made up of some 17,000 islands. Raja Ampat comprises around 600 of them – perhaps the most striking sprinkle of the lot. Here, in Indonesia's far east, at the edge of the Coral Triangle, deep currents channel nutrients into the reefs and seagrass beds, creating an unspoilt, bedazzling underwater world where over 1000 species of fish sparkle in every hue, wobbegong sharks lurk in camouflage, giant clams pulsate and majestic manta rays fly through the blue. It's the most biodiverse marine region on earth and, in short, diving heaven. Temperatures here on the equator are always hot (30°C/85°F) but in November the water is calm, visibility is at its best and there's a greater chance of seeing manta rays at cleaning stations. Book a resort-based diving trip or explore by liveaboard boat – seek out *pinisi*, the region's traditional sailing vessels.

Trip plan: Raja Ampat liveaboard trips range from seven to 14 nights, with itineraries depending on local conditions. Most sail from Sorong, a 4hr flight from Jakarta. Conservation-focused expeditions, incorporating marine surveys, are also possible.

Need to know: Take eco-friendly sun screens, soaps and shampoos to minimise harm to the reefs.

Other months: Dec-Apr – drier, best diving, calm waters; May-Aug – wettest, seas roughest; Sep-Oct – windy.

RIVER NILE
EGYPT

→ **Why now?** For delightful days on the river.

The Nile is the lifeblood of Egypt. Along this river, ancient civilisations have thrived and modern Egyptians still live in traditional ways. A cruise, dropping anchor at temples, tombs and palm-lined villages, provides a window into what makes the country tick. And November, when summer's intense heat finally dips (expect 25-30°C/77-86°F), means warm days on deck but manageable temperatures for wandering sites that span millennia of history. Must-stops include Luxor, for the colossal columns of Karnak, Luxor Temple and the Valley of the Kings; Elephantine Island and the Tombs of the Nobles; the crocodile mummies at Kom Ombo; the relocated temple of Abu Simbel; and Aswan's grand Old Cataract Hotel, to sip cocktails on the veranda.

Trip plan: Most cruises ply the temple-lined section of the Nile between Aswan and Luxor, taking from three to five days; sailing northwards, with the current, is quicker, especially if travelling by wind-powered felucca (basic sailing boat). It's possible to cruise from Cairo to Aswan – allow two weeks. Factor in time in Cairo, for the Pyramids and the new Grand Egyptian Museum.

Need to know: Feluccas can moor anywhere. Cruise boats are less flexible. Make enquiries before travelling – vessels may moor several abreast, meaning a 'river view' cabin ends up staring into another boat.

Other months: Dec-Feb – cool, busy (more expensive Christmas/New Year); Mar-May & Oct – warm, good exploring weather; Jun-Sep – very hot, uncomfortable for sightseeing.

255

(A) Rotorua thermal waters, NZ; (L) Cheonggyecheon Stream, Seoul; (R) Anegada lobster, BVI

NORTH ISLAND
NEW ZEALAND

Why now? Hit the road for less.
Quiet, scenic roads; sleeping in out-of-the-way places; the chance to go wherever the mood takes you... There are few better ways to explore New Zealand than by campervan. High summer seems best for a road trip, but it's also more expensive, whereas hiring a camper outside peak season can be up to 50% cheaper. End-of-spring November is a smart choice: lower prices and fewer tourists, but warming up nicely and rampant with wildflowers. The North Island will be a bit warmer than the South – Auckland highs average 20°C (68°F) this month. It's also bubbling with geothermal activity, so if it does get a little chilly you can warm up at Rotorua and Lake Taupo's hot-spring complexes, or find wild-and-free thermal pools such as Kerosene Creek (near Rotorua), which has a hot waterfall. There's also plenty of warmer-weather fun: blackwater raft through Waitomo's glowworm caves, shelter amid the Hobbiton film set or walk beneath Waipoua Forest's towering kauri trees.

Trip plan: From Auckland, spend a week or two looping south to Wellington and back. With more time, add on Northland, north of Auckland.

Need to know: Distances can be deceptive due to the North Island's hilly, twisty roads – allow plenty of time.

Other months: Dec-Feb – warmest, priciest; Mar-May & Sep-Oct – mild/cool, cheaper; Jun-Aug – winter, more challenging driving.

SEOUL
SOUTH KOREA

Why now? For bright lights and communal cookery.
November is peak leaf-peep time in South Korea, when the country's trees reach full flaming glory and provide a beautiful natural back-drop to even Seoul's high-tech-ery. Take a walk along the city's Cheonggyecheon Stream at this time and you'll find it bright with both autumn colour and the illuminations of the Seoul Lantern Festival. But maybe even more important than autumn, it's *kimjang* season, when friends and family gather to make massive batches of kimchi to last through the winter. Seoul holds a Kimchi Festival (usually the first week of November): you might get to make the famed fermented cabbage with hundreds of locals. Still peckish? Go to Gwangjang Market, a great place to try Korean street food such as *mayak gimbap* (rice rolls), *sundae* (blood sausage) and *bindaetteok* (mung-bean pancakes). Then graze the stalls of Namdaemun Market, which dates to the 15th century, and visit Noryangjin Fish Market to sample fresh seafood 24/7.

Trip plan: Incheon International Airport is 1hr by train from the city centre. Seoul has an extensive Metro. The Hongdae neighbourhood, known for its university, makes a good base, with varied restaurants, street food and nightlife.

Need to know: When eating in a restaurant, don't leave a tip – it's not expected and may be considered an insult.

Other months: Dec-Mar – very cold; Apr-May – warm, cherry blossom; Jun-Aug – hot, humid, wettest; Sep-Oct – cool, autumn colours.

BRITISH
VIRGIN ISLANDS

Why now? To eat well for less.
The best thing about the British Virgin Islands? If anything can challenge the turquoise waters, powder-soft beaches, superb sailing and fine fishing, it's the food scene. The headline act is the Anegada lobster, the finest in the Caribbean. But there are so many more tastes to tempt here, from *rotis* (curry-filled flatbreads) and *fungi* (okra-laced polenta) to rum cocktails and conch fritters. And the annual BVI Food Fête – held throughout November – is the perfect way to eat and drink your way around this awesome archipelago, accompanied by music and other entertainment. Past events have included celeb chef cook-offs, pork parties, bar crawls and rum cocktails a-plenty. All accompanied with blue skies and sunshine: November (averaging 25-30°C/77-86°F) is officially still hurricane season but is rarely stormy, and offers a luxe-Caribbean vibe at slightly cheaper prices.

Trip plan: Decide which island suits you. Main isle Tortola has powdery beaches, lush mountains and sheltered harbours; Virgin Gorda has trails leading into national parks; Jost Van Dyke has a chilled-out party vibe; flat coral-fringed Anegada is where you'll find the namesake lobsters. Or combine them all, and other BVI outcrops, on an island-hopping adventure.

Need to know: Frequent and fast ferry services run between the larger islands of the BVI and to the neighbouring US Virgin Islands. Water taxis are also available.

Other months: Dec-Mar – dry, busy; Apr-May – hotter; Jun-Oct – wetter, hurricanes possible.

Jungle-swathed Ohe'o Gulch in Maui's Haleakalā National Park

© leonov.o / Shutterstock

SEVILLE & JERÉZ SPAIN

Flamenco in full flow, Seville

 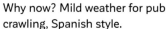

➜ Why now? Mild weather for pub crawling, Spanish style.

Let's all raise a glass to November in southern Andalucía. While most of Europe begins to chill, it's still T-shirt weather here (expect highs of 20°C/68°F), perfect for sightseeing without the crowds and for enjoying a tipple or two... The top choice hereabouts is sherry, particularly in and around the fine city of Jeréz de la Frontera. Many historic *bodegas* – such as vast González–Byass and the cathedral-like cellars of Bodega Lustau – offer tours and tastings, while characterful drinking holes pack the old centre, serving dry and smoky-sweet sherries accompanied by authentic flamenco (the passionate music is said to originate here). Combine Jeréz with Seville,

also jam-packed with tapas bars as well as world-class sights: visit the magnificent Mudéjar-style Real Alcázar palace, enter the world's largest Gothic cathedral, stroll along the Guadalquivir River and wander the atmospheric Triana district, home of flamenco, bullfighting and exquisite ceramic tiles.

Trip plan: Start with three days in Seville, staying in the hip Alameda de Hércules neighbourhood. Then spend two in Jeréz de la Frontera, to crawl between its handsome *bodegas* and visit the city's own smaller Moorish Alcázar and cathedral.

Need to know: Jeréz is a 1hr 15min train journey from Seville.

Other months: Dec-Feb – mild, cheaper; Mar-May – warm, pleasant; Jun-Aug – very hot; Sep-Oct – hot, harvest festivals.

MAUI
HAWAI'I, USA

→ **Why now? For fewer people in paradise.**

The jaw-dropping looks and adventure potential of Maui have not gone unnoticed. The second-biggest Hawai'ian island is packed with tourists year-round. Except, that is, in November, when honeymooners and school vacationers and have gone but winter-sun seekers are yet to arrive. Temperatures still average 28°C (82.4°F); you might get some showers but they're a small inconvenience when the pay-off is experiencing Maui's golden sands, emerald valleys and volcanic theatrics without the crowds (and at lower prices). Take the opportunity to explore the ancient culture and otherworldly landscapes of Haleakalā National Park, to hike through the 'Iao Valley, to snorkel with black-tip sharks in Molokini Crater, to visit the historic whaling village of Lahaina and to simply kick back on the exquisite beaches – try gorgeous Keawakapu, black-sand Pa'iloa, Honolua Bay (for winter swells) and Launiupoko (for beginner surfers).

Trip plan: Maui's Kahului Airport is a 30min flight from Honolulu on O'ahu. The best way to get around is by car (reserve a vehicle in advance). Most hotels are in the west and south; the west coast is drier than the east.

Need to know: Ferries connect Maui to the neighbouring island of Lana'i.

Other months: Dec-Mar – rainy season, busy, good surf, whales; Apr-May – dry, uncrowded; Jun-Sep – dry, busiest; Oct – some rain, quieter.

VALLETTA
MALTA

➜ **Why now? Combine city sites with late Med sun.**

Little Malta is a big draw this month. The mild, Mediterranean climate means it stays almost summery through November, with temperatures around 21°C (70°F) and the sea still warm enough for a dip. Even if not, there's plenty of interest away from the beach. Valletta, the harbour-hugging capital, makes for a super off-season city break. European Capital of Culture in 2018, and Unesco-listed in its entirety, it was founded by the Knights of Malta in the 16th century and hasn't changed a lot since. Wander its maze of medieval alleyways and piazzas, nose into the baroque palaces and fine churches, trace the well-preserved fortifications and dip into the National Museum of Archaeology and modern MUŻA art museum. To appreciate Valletta from water-level, sail across the Grand Harbour in a traditional *dghajsa* (open boat). Then disembark at Vittoriosa, one of the three cities facing Valletta, and get lost in its sinuous backstreets.

Trip plan: Allow two or three days to explore Valetta; stay in the centre and explore on foot – the main attractions are all within walking distance. With a week, venture further afield, including to the walled former capital of Mdina.

Need to know: For the best views of Valletta, head to the colonnaded Upper Barrakka Gardens – walk up or take the Upper Barrakka Lift.

Other months: Dec-Mar – mild, quiet; Apr-Jun & Oct – warm, uncrowded; Jul-Sep – hot, dry, busiest.

Valletta view over to Vittoriosa's medieval Fort St Angelo

© Matt Munro / Lonely Planet

TASMANIA
AUSTRALIA

→ **Why now? Enjoy a quieter contemplation of convict history.**

Rural, rumpled and wild, with 19 national parks and 300-plus offshore isles, Tasmania is renowned as an outdoor playground. But its colonial history is as fascinating as its topography: some 72,000 criminals were sent to 'Van Diemen's Land' – 42% of all convicts sent to Australia – and the state has been shaped by this legacy. Plot a road trip combining key convict sites and spectacular scenery in late-spring November, when days are long and warming, attractions are open and roads are quiet. Port Arthur, on the Tasman Peninsula, is a highlight: visit the eerie penitentiary ruins, perhaps on a nighttime ghost tour, and take a boat trip (look out for migrating whales). Other possible stops include handsome Richmond (home to Tassie's oldest gaol), the convict-built edifices of Campbell Town, Maria Island (a prison isle turned wildlife haven) and Hobart's Cascades Female Factory, where transported women were interred in grim fashion.

Trip plan: Allow four days for a 200km (124-mile) loop from Hobart to Port Arthur via Richmond; allow a week or more to include Maria Island, Campbell Town and Woolmers (one of Tasmania's best-preserved heritage homes, constructed by convicts).

Need to know: The old penitentiary on car-free Maria Island is now a hostel; the island is reached by passenger ferry from Triabunna (45min).

Other months: Dec-Feb – warmest, busiest; Mar-Apr – changeable, whales; May-Aug – cold, snow possible; Sep-Oct – mild, wildflowers, whales.

A dip in Chorros de la Calera, on the Ruta de las Flores

EL SALVADOR

→ **Why now? Drier days for offbeat exploring.**

Compact, welcoming, diverse and often misunderstood, El Salvador is the sliver of Central America that few visit but more should. There's a bit of everything here, in one bijou package. You'll find handsome towns of bright Spanish colonial architecture – Suchitoto is a particular gem. There's dramatic countryside, pocked with volcanoes and hiking trails – not least around rugged Cerro El Pericón and El Imposible National Park. There are Maya relics, notably the ceremonial site of El Tazumal. There are coffee *fincas* and chocolate plantations, where you can taste the spoils. There's the chance to gen up on recent history – Perquín's moving Peace Museum remembers the bloody 1980-92 Civil War, while former guerrillas lead walks through

Cinquera Forest. And there's some of the best surf in the world – try the beaches around Punta Roca. November, at the start of the dry season and before the Christmas peak, is a good choice; you might even spot nesting leatherback turtles.

Trip plan: Allow 10-14 days to combine capital San Salvador with the Ruta de las Flores (home of artisan communities and coffee plantations), national parks, towns such as Suchitoto and the undeveloped Pacific coast.

Need to know: El Salvador is quite conservative. Polite formalities are appreciated: on meeting someone, it's a good idea to shake hands and say 'mucho gusto' (nice to meet you).

Other months: Dec-Apr – driest, warm, busy (busiest Christmas/Easter); May-Aug – wet; Sep-Oct – wettest, most storms.

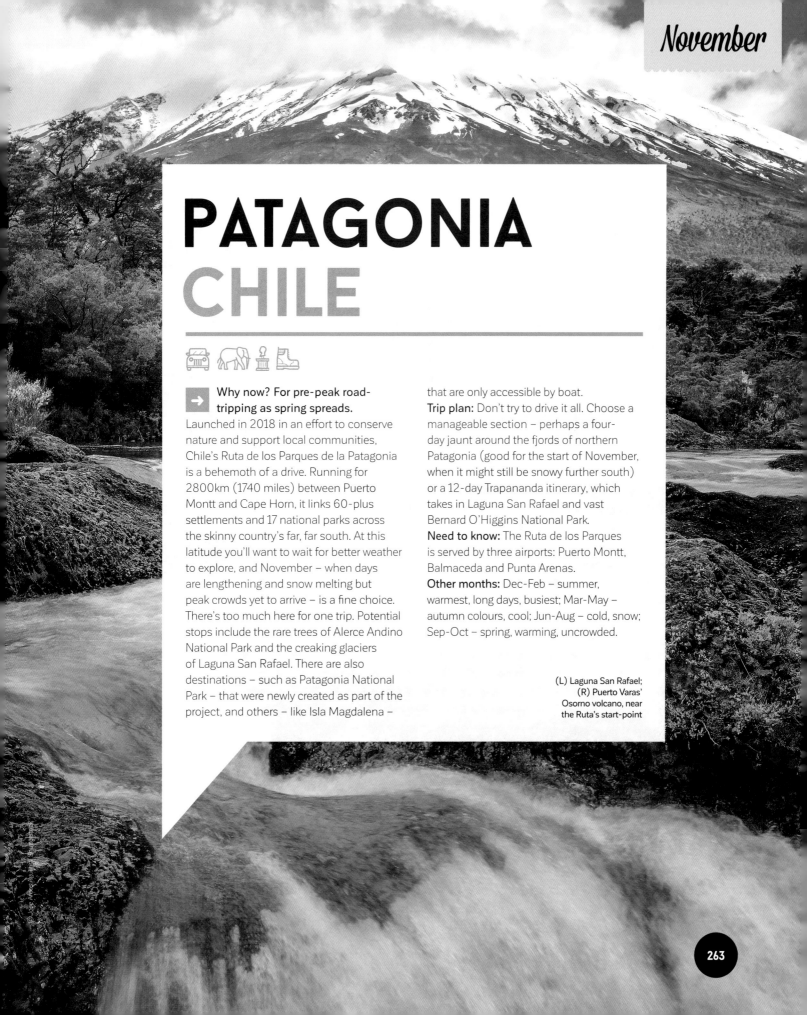

PATAGONIA
CHILE

Why now? For pre-peak road-tripping as spring spreads.
Launched in 2018 in an effort to conserve nature and support local communities, Chile's Ruta de los Parques de la Patagonia is a behemoth of a drive. Running for 2800km (1740 miles) between Puerto Montt and Cape Horn, it links 60-plus settlements and 17 national parks across the skinny country's far, far south. At this latitude you'll want to wait for better weather to explore, and November – when days are lengthening and snow melting but peak crowds yet to arrive – is a fine choice. There's too much here for one trip. Potential stops include the rare trees of Alerce Andino National Park and the creaking glaciers of Laguna San Rafael. There are also destinations – such as Patagonia National Park – that were newly created as part of the project, and others – like Isla Magdalena – that are only accessible by boat.

Trip plan: Don't try to drive it all. Choose a manageable section – perhaps a four-day jaunt around the fjords of northern Patagonia (good for the start of November, when it might still be snowy further south) or a 12-day Trapananda itinerary, which takes in Laguna San Rafael and vast Bernard O'Higgins National Park.

Need to know: The Ruta de los Parques is served by three airports: Puerto Montt, Balmaceda and Punta Arenas.

Other months: Dec-Feb – summer, warmest, long days, busiest; Mar-May – autumn colours, cool; Jun-Aug – cold, snow; Sep-Oct – spring, warming, uncrowded.

(L) Laguna San Rafael;
(R) Puerto Varas' Osorno volcano, near the Ruta's start-point

AlUla, enclosed in a dramatic cradle of sandstone cliffs

ALULA SAUDI ARABIA

Why now? Bearable heat for history.

The raw, desert region of AlUla, in northwest Saudi Arabia, has 200,000 years of human history – yet has only just revealed itself to the outside world. Recent investments, aiming to create 38,000 new jobs and bring in 2 million tourists a year by 2035, have developed this open-air museum. Sites such as the Unesco-listed Nabataean tombs of Hegra (Saudi's Petra), ancient Dadan and the old walled city of AlUla itself have opened up; hiking and horseback trails through the canyons and oases have been created; and new arts and culture experiences are available, from excursions with *rawi* (storytellers) and chances to watch stone carvers at work, to catching a concert at Maraya, the largest

mirrored building on Earth. It's a whole new world, and best explored November-February, when the merciless heat dips to manageable levels.

Trip plan: AlUla is an 8hr drive/1hr 10min flight from Jeddah, an 11hr drive/1hr 45min flight from Riyadh. With 10-12 days, travel overland from Jeddah to Riyadh, via the holy city of Medina, AlUla and Jubbah's Unesco-listed rock art.

Need to know: During Ramadan, the month of fasting, shops don't serve food before sunset and eating in public during the day isn't permitted. Upcoming Ramadan starting dates are: 23 March 2023, 11 March 2024, 1 March 2025, 18 February 2026.

Other months: Dec-Feb – coolest; Mar & Oct – shoulder months, hot; Apr-Sep – sweltering.

NORMANDY
FRANCE

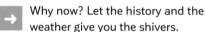

Why now? Let the history and the weather give you the shivers.

If you're seeking sand-n-sun fun, this isn't the time to hit Normandy's beaches. November conditions are unpredictable, and temperatures average a brisk 5-12°C (41-54°F). But if you're coming to learn more about one of the bleakest periods of recent history, this potentially dreary weather helps set the tone. Nearly 130,000 soldiers – Allied and German – died in Normandy in 1944; many were killed on the D-Day beaches of Utah, Omaha, Gold, Juno and Sword. Their lives can be remembered at spots such as the bunkers and bomb craters at Pointe du Hoc, the artificial harbour in Arromanches, the Caen Memorial Museum and the 27 war cemeteries that dot the region. Time your visit for Armistice Day (11 November) and you'll find remembrance ceremonies in progress. Also, take some cheer from the fact that accommodation will be cheaper and sites less busy – especially useful if you also want to take in over-touristed but magnificent Mont St-Michel.

Trip plan: Allow four or five days to visit the Normandy beaches, cemeteries and war memorials. Consider an organised tour – a knowledgeable guide will add to the experience.

Need to know: Caen is served by train from Paris (2hr). Ferries run from Portsmouth (UK) to Caen/Ouistreham (6hr).

Other months: Dec-Mar – cold, damp; Apr-Jun & Sep-Oct – mild, uncrowded (busy 6 Jun, D-Day anniversary); Jul-Aug – warm, busy.

© Ondrej Prosicky / Shutterstock

Keel-billed toucan in
Panama's Soberíana
National Park

PANAMA

→ **Why now? For an abundance of avian action.**

Panama boasts some of the best birding in Central America. Almost 1000 species have been recorded on this narrow isthmus – from big-billed toucans and bright-plumed trogons to motmots, manakins, puffbirds and jacamars. And in October/ November, numbers swell, as almost 2 million broad-winged hawks, Swainson's hawks and turkey vultures migrate south via Panama's jungle, joining an assemblage of sloths, howler monkeys and colourful

frogs too. Soberíana National Park is a superb place to try to spot them. Easily accessible from Panama City, and sitting astride the Panama Canal, the park has a range of self-guided walking routes (the 17km/10.5 miles Pipeline trail is renowned for its brilliant bird-sightings). It's also possible to arrange guided strolls, night excursions and boat trips, and to stay in a lodge perched up in the canopy.

Trip plan: Combine Soberíana with the Panama Canal and Panama City. Add beach time on the wild Azuero Peninsula

– this area is drier than the rest of the country, so a good choice for end-of-wet November.

Need to know: Head to the Miraflores Visitors Center to learn more about the Panama Canal and watch ships transiting the locks (transits are most frequent 9am-11am and 3pm-5pm).

Other months: Dec-Apr – driest, warm, busiest (spring bird migration Apr); May-Aug – sporadically wet; Sep-Oct – wettest, most storms.

265

OAXACA
MEXICO

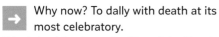

→ **Why now? To dally with death at its most celebratory.**

Día de los Muertos – the Day of the Dead – is celebrated over three nights, from 31 October to 2 November. According to Mexican tradition, it's when the deceased may briefly cross into the world of the living. Families construct grave-side altars, adorned with photos, candles, marigolds and sweets; skull masks are worn, marching bands play, everyone feasts. While celebrations might be experienced countrywide, the state of Oaxaca – known for its strong indigenous culture, unique cuisine and flourishing arts and crafts – is an excellent choice. Oaxaca city is a riot of artisan workshops, baroque plazas and busy markets (where you can buy sugar skulls and *pan de muerto*, bread of the dead); the Museum of Oaxacan Cultures is also worth a look. Then explore further afield: visit the weaving town of Teotitlan, historic Tlacolula market and Soledad Etla's flamboyant Comparsa Parade. By night, head to the region's many cemeteries for the festivities.

Trip plan: Oaxaca city is 6-7hr by bus from Mexico City. Explore the city and surrounding area, head into the Sierra Norte for community-run hiking and cycling, and finish on the surf beaches of the Pacific coast. Allow 10 days.

Need to know: The Day of Dead is a religious festival – remain respectful and don't take photos without asking permission.

Other months: Dec-Apr – driest, warm; May-Oct – rainy season (wettest Aug-Sep), humid.

Día de los Muertos decorations in Oaxaca's Sierra Norte

© Norma Cordova / Getty Images

TUNISIA

→ **Why now? For a date with cool climes.**

In high summer the resorts along Tunisia's Mediterranean coast become very busy. Much better is to come in autumn and avoid both: that is, both the sweltering heat and the hermetic tourist enclaves that do little to benefit local people. With highs of around 22°C (71.6°F), November is excellent for exploring historic sites such as vast Ancient Carthage, El Djem's amphitheatre, the subterranean Roman ruins of Bulla Regia and the troglodyte village of Matmata (cinematic stand-in for *Star Wars'* Tatooine). And it's ideal for wandering around laidback Djerba Island, where Muslim, Berber and Jewish communities have coexisted for centuries; and the whitewashed, hill-tumbling streets of Sidi Bou Saïd, where local restaurants and cafes will give you an authentic flavour of Tunisia. Also be sure to visit leafy Saharan oases to see the date harvest in full flow.

Trip plan: Tunisia is compact. With a week you could combine coastal and desert sites. Tunis-Carthage International is the main airport. Ferries run from various ports in Italy and France year-round; for example, Palermo-Tunis (roughly 10hr) and Marseilles-Tunis (20hr).

Need to know: Arabic and French are the main languages. English isn't widely spoken outside tourist resorts.

Other months: Dec-Mar – cool, changeable; Apr-Jun – warm; Jul-Sep – dry, sweltering, beaches busy; Oct – pleasantly mild, harvest.

A needle-straight
route into Death
Valley National Park
near Beatty, Nevada

DEATH VALLEY
USA

→ Why now? Hot(ish) riding.

It's not unknown for the mercury to top 50°C (122°F) in Death Valley during July. That is emphatically *not* the time to visit. Better to wait until November, when the average high in this lowest, hottest, driest of national parks is a pleasant 25°C (77°F), all the campgrounds are open (camping season runs mid-October to April) and it's quieter than spring. Indeed, these conditions are ideal for cycling. While winter grips many a road across the country, Death Valley's tarmac and dirt track (of which there is over 1200km/745 miles) is ice-free and traffic-light, and offers a great way of getting in amid the peaks, escarpments, dunes, faults, saltflats and weird rock formations. Top rides include the descent from Daylight Pass into the valley, the flat push from broiling Furnace Creek to Stovepipe Wells, and the climb to Dante's View for a panorama over the Black Mountains and Badwater Basin. Or plot a 400km-plus (249 miles) through-ride from Las Vegas to Lone Pine via Death Valley.

Trip plan: There are entrance points to the national park on highways to the east (via Las Vegas), west (Lone Pine) and south (Shoshone); Furnace Creek is 230km (143 miles) from Las Vegas.

Need to know: Plan rides around water – carry more than you think you'll need and check availablity en route.

Other months: Dec-Feb – winter, snow on peaks; Mar-Apr – wildflowers, mild, busy; May-Sep – very hot; Oct – warm, camping season begins, uncrowded.

© travelview / Shutterstock

LANZAROTE SPAIN

Placid waters at Charco
de San Gines, Arrecife

Why now? To master warm winter waves.

The northernmost, easternmost Canary Isle laughs at the idea of hibernating for winter. With November temperatures still reaching 23°C (73.4°F) on land and 22°C (71.6°F) in the ocean, Lanzarote continues to be brilliant for water-based fun. Sailors, surfers, kite-surfers and kayakers can keep practicing all year long; it's a good place to learn new skills too, as conditions are reliable and many operators offer lessons. The cooler months (November-March) are especially good for surfing – pros can tackle the legendary left-hand reef break of El Quemao while beginners should head to the beach breaks and surf schools of Caleta de Famara and Orzola. Lanzarote also has many calm, sheltered lagoons, ideal for paddleboarding – Charco de San Gines in Arrecife, Playa Blanca and Playa Mujeres are all popular. No matter what you do, the island – a Unesco Geopark of volcanic cones, lava fields and lunar-like weirdness – makes a dramatic backdrop.

Trip plan: Lanzarote's Arrecife Airport is on the east coast. It's a 30min drive from the airport to Famara, or 2hr 30min by bus. Surf lessons are available, ranging from half a day to a full week.

Need to know: Ferries connect Lanzarote to other Canary Islands; for instance, regular services link Playa Blanca on Lanzarote and Corralejo on Fuerteventura (the closest island), taking 30min.

Other months: Dec-Feb – mild, busy; Apr-Jun – warm, dry; Jul-Aug – hottest; Sep-Oct – pleasant, quieter.

269

SOUTHERN VIETNAM

→ **Why now? Swim, snorkel, sunbathe and explore the Mekong Delta.**

Indochina's southern tip is a lucky dip of the region's best bits: the heady rush of Saigon, moving relics of war, the Mekong Delta's paddies and villages, and beautiful, beach-lined Phu Quoc and Con Dao Islands. Both hosted colonial French prisons – you can visit the haunting remains – but are now better known as chill-out getaways, perfect in November after rain and humidity have eased.

Phu Quoc, closer to Cambodia than Vietnam, has varied accommodation, great snorkelling and some lovely, quiet beaches. Con Dao is more remote and rugged, hosting nesting turtles (June to September) and dugongs as well as peaceful resorts on breathtaking beaches.

Trip plan: Both Phu Quoc and Con Dao are accessible by air from Ho Chi Minh City, so it's easy to combine a relaxing stay on an island idyll with an exploration of the compact south. Be sure to visit the Cu Chi Tunnels, a subterranean Viet Cong lair during the war, as well as exploring the Mekong Delta and indulging in fine seafood in Ho Chi Minh City.

Need to know: On Phu Quoc, seek out *bún kèn* – a seafood noodle salad with sweet-and-sour fish broth. Note that prices and visitor numbers rise towards Christmas.

Other months: Dec-May – warm, dry; Jun-Oct – humid, wet (rainy season longer on Con Dao).

(T) Paddling Mekong Delta backwaters; (B) The serene beach scene at Phu Quoc

© DEDDEDA / Alamy Stock Photo

Huskies leading the
way on a dog-sled
Yukon traverse

YUKON CANADA

Why now? For a dog's life.
The onset of winter isn't seen as a hardship in the Yukon, it's an opportunity. As the mercury falls in November (between -1°C/ 30°F and -15°C/5°F, warmer than the following few months!), the snow fun begins: downhill skiing, cross-country skiing, snowshoeing, snowmobiling, ice fishing, fat biking... But perhaps no activity is more 'Yukon' than dogsledding. Experiences are available from hubs such as Carcross, Dawson City and Whitehorse. Head out for half a day with a guide,

or – for a real taste of Yukon life – plan a multi-day mushing adventure: learn how to care for your own team of huskies and drive them over frozen lakes and glistening tundra, sleep out in rustic cabins, wilderness ranches or cosy tents, warm up in hot springs and saunas, and keep an eye on those dark night skies for the magical Northern Lights.

Trip plan: Yukon's Whitehorse airport is served by flights from several Canadian cities. Join an organised husky-sledding tour; some companies have First Nations

guides and include storytelling and insights into local Indigenous culture.

Need to know: The number-one rule of husky sledding: even when stopped, keep hold of the handlebar and keep your foot on the brake – the dogs might make a dash for it at any time.

Other months: Dec-Mar – very cold, snow sports, best for aurora; Apr-May – thawing, migratory birds; Jun-Aug – warmest, long days; Sep-Oct – cool, autumn colours.

December

WHERE TO GO WHEN

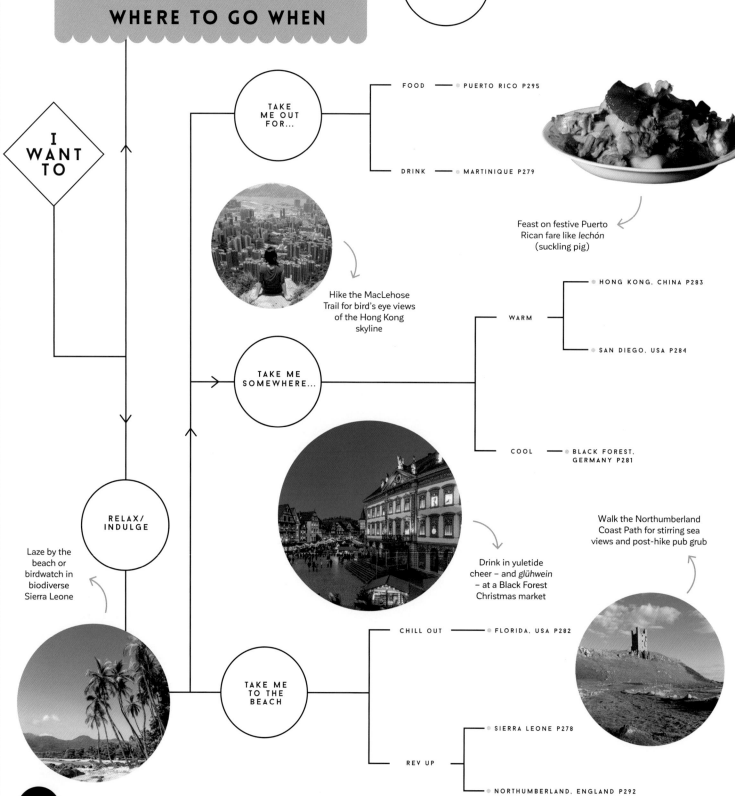

CHALLENGE MYSELF

I WANT TO

TAKE ME OUT FOR...

FOOD ——— ● PUERTO RICO P295

DRINK ——— ● MARTINIQUE P279

Feast on festive Puerto Rican fare like *lechón* (suckling pig)

Hike the MacLehose Trail for bird's eye views of the Hong Kong skyline

TAKE ME SOMEWHERE...

WARM

● HONG KONG, CHINA P283

● SAN DIEGO, USA P284

COOL ——— ● BLACK FOREST, GERMANY P281

Walk the Northumberland Coast Path for stirring sea views and post-hike pub grub

Drink in yuletide cheer – and *glühwein* – at a Black Forest Christmas market

RELAX/ INDULGE

Laze by the beach or birdwatch in biodiverse Sierra Leone

TAKE ME TO THE BEACH

CHILL OUT ——— ● FLORIDA, USA P282

● SIERRA LEONE P278

REV UP

● NORTHUMBERLAND, ENGLAND P292

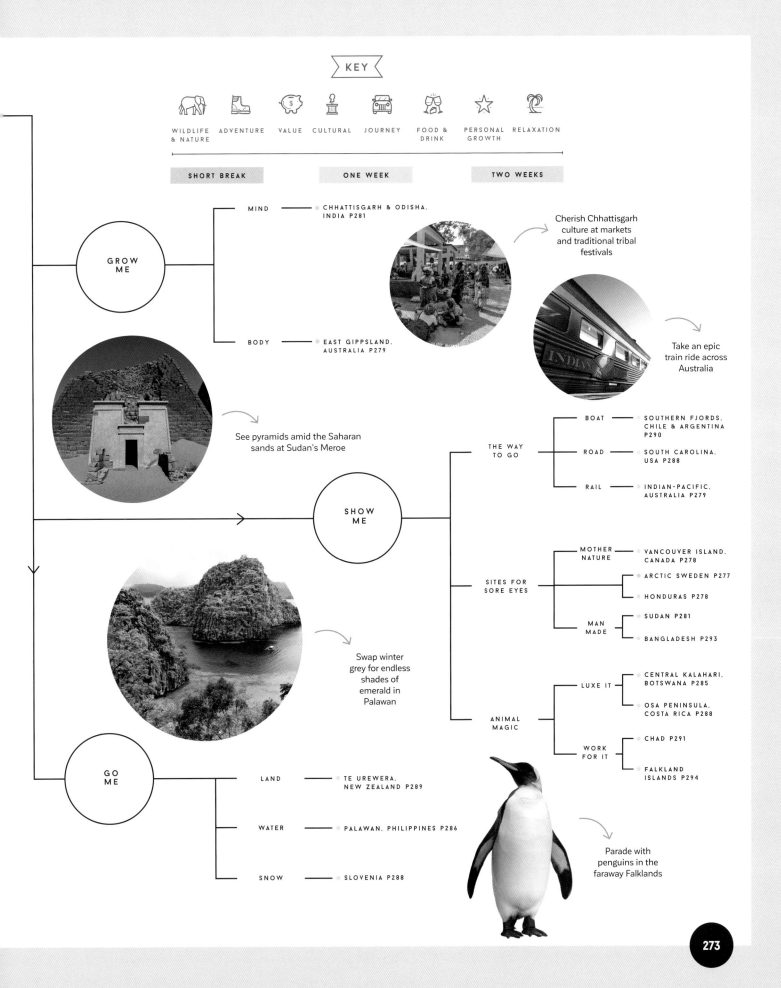

WILDLIFE & NATURE   ADVENTURE   VALUE   CULTURAL   JOURNEY   FOOD & DRINK   PERSONAL GROWTH   RELAXATION

SHORT BREAK   ONE WEEK   TWO WEEKS

GROW ME

MIND —— CHHATTISGARH & ODISHA, INDIA P281

Cherish Chhattisgarh culture at markets and traditional tribal festivals

BODY —— EAST GIPPSLAND, AUSTRALIA P279

Take an epic train ride across Australia

See pyramids amid the Saharan sands at Sudan's Meroe

SHOW ME

THE WAY TO GO
- BOAT —— SOUTHERN FJORDS, CHILE & ARGENTINA P290
- ROAD —— SOUTH CAROLINA, USA P288
- RAIL —— INDIAN-PACIFIC, AUSTRALIA P279

SITES FOR SORE EYES
MOTHER NATURE
- VANCOUVER ISLAND, CANADA P278
- ARCTIC SWEDEN P277
- HONDURAS P278

MAN MADE
- SUDAN P281
- BANGLADESH P293

ANIMAL MAGIC
LUXE IT
- CENTRAL KALAHARI, BOTSWANA P285
- OSA PENINSULA, COSTA RICA P288

WORK FOR IT
- CHAD P291
- FALKLAND ISLANDS P294

Swap winter grey for endless shades of emerald in Palawan

GO ME

LAND —— TE UREWERA, NEW ZEALAND P289

WATER —— PALAWAN, PHILIPPINES P286

SNOW —— SLOVENIA P288

Parade with penguins in the faraway Falklands

EVENTS
IN DECEMBER

INTERNATIONAL FESTIVAL OF THE SAHARA
Douz, Tunisia
Desert peoples gather at the 'gateway to the Sahara' to celebrate their heritage through traditional music, dance and sports like horse racing and camel wrestling.

FIESTA DE SANTO TOMÁS
Chichicastenango, Guatemala
Exuberant celebrations honouring St Thomas the Apostle climax as pairs of roped dancers leap from the 30m palo volador (flying pole).

SAINT SPYRIDON'S DAY
Corfu, Greece
Corfu Town is strewn with lights, churches ring with carols, and tavernas serve tsitsibira (ginger beer), ouzo and kumquat liqueur.

WOODFORD FOLK FESTIVAL
Woodford, Queensland, Australia
More than 2000 performers bring music, dance, comedy, theatre, Indigenous traditions and much more to dozens of venues over six days at the turn of the year.

KRAMPUSNACHT & FEAST OF ST NICHOLAS
Innsbruck, Austria
Demonic creatures parade through the streets of Tyrol's capital on the night before genial Saint Nick takes charge.

MONARCH BUTTERFLIES
Michoacán, Mexico
The oyamel fir trees of central Mexico are cloaked in orange as millions of monarch butterflies roost over winter – an extraordinary natural spectacle.

JUNKANOO
Bahamas
Thousands of brightly clad performers gyrate to the music of horns, whistles, cowbells and goatskin drums in a joyous, raucous celebration of local culture.

CHICHIBU YOMATSURI
Chichibu, Japan
Enormous floats, festooned with lanterns and decorated with mythical beasts and figures are hauled through the streets to a soundtrack of drums and flutes.

Inner wheel labels

- Four days in late December — $$
- 21 December — $
- 12 December — $
- 2 and 3 December — $$$
- 26 December and 1 January — $$
- November to February or mid-March — $
- 5 & 6 December — $$
- 27 December to 1 January — $$

VERY FAMILY FRIENDLY

● ARCTIC SWEDEN

Find Northern Lights, dark days and beds of ice in Arctic Sweden

● FLORIDA, USA

● SAN DIEGO, USA

Saunter San Diego's diverse 'hoods and the myriad museums of Balboa Park

● NORTHUMBERLAND, ENGLAND

● BLACK FOREST, GERMANY

● PUERTO RICO

● MARTINIQUE

Have a Caribbean Christmas in Martinique, with beachtime and Chanté-Nwel festivities

Seek out snow-sports in Slovenia, from ice-climbing to skiing

● SLOVENIA

● SOUTH CAROLINA, USA

Gift-shop till you drop and see NYE fireworks from the Hong Kong waterfront

Discover little-visited wildlife hotspots in Costa Rica's Osa

● OSA PENINSULA, COSTA RICA

● HONG KONG, CHINA

● HONDURAS

EXPENSIVE BUT WORTH IT

GOOD VALUE

● EAST GIPPSLAND, AUSTRALIA

Help conserve koalas by volunteering at an East Gippsland research station

Spy Magellan penguins and cruise Glacier Alley in the Southern Fjords

● SOUTHERN FJORDS, CHILE & ARGENTINA

● FALKLAND ISLANDS

Strike out on the road less travelled with a Zakouma safari in Chad

● INDIAN-PACIFIC, AUSTRALIA

● CHAD

● SUDAN

● TE UREWERA, NEW ZEALAND

● PALAWAN, PHILIPPINES

Tackle a lakeside Great Walk without the crowds in Te Urewera

● CHHATTISGARH & ODISHA, INDIA

Walk through wild Vancouver weather and keep eyes peeled for some wildlife, too

● CENTRAL KALAHARI, BOTSWANA

● SIERRA LEONE

Boat-trip through Bangladesh's steamy Sunderbans to seek tigers and Ganges dolphins

● VANCOUVER ISLAND, CANADA

● BANGLADESH

LEAVE THE KIDS AT HOME

ARCTIC SWEDEN

→ **Why now? Sleep on ice beneath the Northern Lights.**

At the Swedish village of Jukkasjärvi, one degree of latitude north of the Arctic Circle, the sun never rises in the last three weeks of the year. In December, darkness is the dominant state – perfect for watching the swirling light show of the Aurora Borealis in inky skies. Jukkasjärvi is the home of the original Icehotel, carved anew each year from the pristine waters of the Torne River, where you can spend a night in a bed made of ice. It's also a base for cross-country skiing, husky sledding, snowmobiling, sleigh rides, meeting reindeer and learning about traditional Sámi culture – magical for kids and grown-ups alike. Some 100km (62 miles) to the northwest, Abisko National Park is even further removed from the light, an otherworldly landscape offering arguably the world's best aurora-watching – head to the top of 900m (2953ft) Mt Nuolja for spectacular views of light and land.

Trip plan: Kiruna, 16km (10 miles) west of Jukkasjärvi and 20min away by car, has an airport, served by flights from Stockholm and international cities. Trains from Kiruna to Abisko take 1hr.

Need to know: The Northern Lights are sparked when charged particles from the sun hit the earth's atmosphere. Various websites offer reasonable forecasts based on solar activity.

Other months: Jan-Apr – winter, Icehotel open; May-Jul – warmer, Midnight Sun; Aug-Sep – autumn; Oct-Nov – cool, dark, good aurora-watching.

Husky-sledding through Jukkasjärvi

SIERRA LEONE

➜ **Why now? Lounge on palm-fringed beaches and spot rare wildlife.**

Like its diamonds, so bitterly contested in the 1990s, Sierra Leone's sparkle is bright: the beautiful white-sand beaches that lured international holidaymakers in the 1970s are still as lovely, the pockets of biodiversity are as captivating as ever, and the slavery-era heritage is both compelling and challenging. The warm, dry days of December are ideal for both beach-lounging and exploring, and are an excellent time for spotting the country's dazzling birdlife – David Attenborough came here to film his first-ever nature documentary, about his quest for a rare rockfowl.

Trip plan: Wander the colourful streets of capital Freetown, taking in the bat-hung, 500-year-old Cotton Tree where enslaved people were once sold, and visiting the white-sand beach at River No 2, nearby Tacugama Chimp Sanctuary and the remains of the fort on Bunce Island. Then head east to Tiwai Island in the Moa River, where you might spot chimps, red colobus and Diana monkeys, and – if you're lucky – pygmy hippos. Further east, Gola Rainforest National Park harbours rare bird and mammal species.

Need to know: Though Sierra Leone is a friendly, largely safe destination, check your government's travel advice before booking a visit.

Other months: May-Oct – rainy (Jul-Aug: wettest); Nov & Jan-Apr – very hot, dry, windy.

VANCOUVER ISLAND CANADA

➜ **Why now? For really wild times.**

Things are a-brewing off western Canada right now. As winter arrives, the restive region where Arctic and subtropical air collides shifts south, and low-pressure systems build in the Gulf of Alaska. This equals stupendous storms, which thwack the Pacific coast of Vancouver Island, stirring up gigantic swells, roaring winds and epic skies. It's Mother Nature at her most marvellously unhinged and cinematic – and it's worth braving a bit of weather for front-row seats. On the edge of Pacific Rim National Park, the little town of Ucluelet (meaning 'people of the safe harbour') is a great place to watch the action unfold. Take a walk – the Wild Pacific Trail skirts the rocky, rainforested shores close enough to feel the sea spray – then, after the hoolie has passed, head out to beachcomb, to see what's been dredged up. Or retreat to a cosy hotel with a spa, a bar and big sea-facing windows to watch while warmly tucked indoors.

Trip plan: Ucluelet is a 4hr drive from Victoria and 2hr 30min from Nanaimo. Several accommodation providers in Ucluelet offer discounted storm-watching packages that include the use of raincoats and wellies.

Need to know: From October to March winter tyres are required when driving Hwy 4 to Ucluelet.

Other months: Nov & Jan-Mar – dramatically stormy; Apr-May – mild; Jun-Aug – peak season, busy, warmest; Sep-Oct – quiet, storms building.

HONDURAS

➜ **Why now? To mix it up without the masses.**

The second-largest country in Central America but one of the least-visited, Honduras offers an authentic, crowd-free, good-value mix of regional highlights, from top-draw Mayan ruins to wildlife-profuse highlands and idyllic beaches. In less-sticky December there are fewer people than the following peak months – all the better for exploring Unesco-listed Cópan, the southernmost Maya city, with its enormous glyph-carved stelae. For something wilder, delve into Pico Bonito National Park, the most biodiverse in Honduras, dominated by its pointy namesake mountain. Birding is brilliant this month – hawks, eagles, parrots, hummingbirds and loons might be spotted; there are opportunities for canopy tours, rafting and night hiking too. Finish in the Bay Islands (Utila and Roatán in particular), where the sand is sugary-white and the snorkelling and diving spectacular. Make time to meet members of the Garifuna community, descendants of enslaved Africans and indigenous peoples.

Trip plan: Most flights land at San Pedro Sula. From here, head west for Cópan and coffee plantations, east for Pico Bonito National Park and the Bay Islands (accessible by flight or ferry). Allow 10 days. Or combine Honduras with neighbouring Guatemala.

Need to know: Don't linger in cities such as capital Tegucigalpa or San Pedro Sula. Crime rates are high and time is better spent elsewhere.

Other months: Jan-Apr – dry season, lower humidity; May-Nov – rainy (hurricanes most likely Aug-Oct).

INDIAN-PACIFIC,
AUSTRALIA

→ **Why now? For sunny views from a spectacular train.**

Hop aboard Australia's longest rail ride. The Indian-Pacific connects its titular oceans, taking four days to cover 4343km (2699 miles) of Aussie epic-ness. December is classed as shoulder season, when train tickets are a smidgen cheaper, but it's definitely summer outside: sunny and, yes, hot, but perfect for jumping into the waves at either end. Plus air-conditioned carriages will keep you cool as the parched plains pass by. The journey, in vintage but plush 1970s carriages, reveals a whole heap of Oz, running from Sydney to the Blue Mountains, across the Outback, into genteel Adelaide, across the majestic emptiness of the Nullarbor Plain, past the gold mines of Kalgoorlie, finishing in laidback Perth.

Trip plan: The Indian Pacific runs once a week in each direction, year-round.

Need to know: Fares are all-inclusive and cover off-train experiences such as the ghost town of Cook and Broken Hill sculpture park. Available experiences vary depending on the direction of travel and weather.

Other months: Nov-May – train shoulder season, warm (very hot Jan-Mar); Jun-Jul – coolest, low season; Aug – shoulder season; Sep-Oct – pleasantly mild, peak season.

MARTINIQUE

→ **Why now? To sing carols with a Creole twist.**

December doesn't just mean Christmas in the French Caribbean. It means Chanté-Nwel. One of Martinique's biggest annual festivities, held across the island from November to Christmas Day, it sees people gather to sing carols to Creole rhythms (a practice dating back to the days of slavery) and feast on local favourites including yams, pâtés, *boudin créole* (blood sausage), yule logs and potent *shrubb* – a Christmas cocktail crafted from dried orange peel, sugarcane syrup and white rum. Very festive. All that's missing is the snow: with sunny skies and average highs of 28°C (82.4°F), this is perfect beach weather; chill out on the vast sweep of white sand at Les Salines or the black sand of Anse Noire. Also make time to breathe in the heady scents of the Jardin de Balata botanical gardens, visit La Savane des Esclaves outdoor museum (for a deeper understanding of the slavery era) and hit La Route du Rhum, a tour of the island's traditional distilleries.

Trip plan: Book well in advance to visit Martinique at this time. While there, keep an eye out for Chanté-Nwel signs or ask around about local parties.

Need to know: Chanté-Nwel gatherings are usually potluck style, with every guest bringing a homemade dish or bottle of rum punch.

Other months: Jan-Apr – dry season, warm, busiest; May-Nov – rainy season, hurricanes possible (storms worst Aug-Oct).

EAST GIPPSLAND
AUSTRALIA

→ **Why now? To help nature.**

East Gippsland, in Victoria's far southeast, is something of a wildlife wonderland; here, diverse ecosystems meet, and native flora and fauna thrive. It was also hit badly by Australia's devastating 2019 bushfires. But there is still much to see, and heading out on a safari amid the verdant rainforests, Ramsar-protected lakelands, golden beaches, coastal heath, crystal-clear rivers and lofty eucalypts will provide close encounters with a wide range of creatures, from huge eastern grey kangaroos to snuffling echidnas, swamp wallabies, greater gliders and superb lyrebirds. There's also a chance to lend a hand: get involved in koala research, help clear beach flotsam or collect data for bushfire-recovery surveys. December is hot, but not as fierce as the later summer months, and the hospitality is just as warm. East Gippsland is known as the food bowl of Australia, flush with fresh produce and boutique vineyards; December-February sees farm gates open for pick-your-own sales.

Trip plan: Bairnsdale, in East Gippsland, is a 3hr 30min drive from Melbourne, or 4hr by train. The easiest way to explore is by car, or join a wildlife tour. Allow four or five days.

Need to know: Bushfires are most prevalent between November and February. Check the Fire Danger Rating of your destination and always adhere to rules regarding campfires.

Other months: Jan-Feb – hot, lively; Mar-May – warm, quieter; Jun-Aug – coolest; Sep-Nov – mild, wildflowers.

(A) Chitrakote Falls, the 'Indian Niagara'; (L) Snow-dusted Freiburg, Black Forest; (R) Meroe pyramid, Sudan

CHHATTISGARH & ODISHA INDIA

→ **Why now? For cultural encounters in milder weather.**

The neighbouring states of Odisha (Orissa) and Chhattisgarh (a breakaway chunk of Madhya Pradesh) offer perhaps the most authentic insight into rural India. These regions are largely neglected by tourists, perhaps due to their lack of 'big' sights. But the appeal here is in getting away from the cities and meeting the people, such as the majority Gond (famed for their vibrant art), the tattooed Kutia Kondh, the indigenous groups of the jungles around Jeypore, the bead-wearing Bonda or the cultural melee of a *haat bazaar* (weekly market), where many tribal groups gather to haggle over everything from butter and salt to clothes and jewellery. The Bastar region of Chhattisgarh is a good place to start – visit markets, hike between village homestays and witness tribal festivals: the Madai Festival, which moves around the communities of Bastar, Kanker and Dantewada, is celebrated from December to March (when temperatures are mild, too).

Trip plan: Raipur is the capital of Chhattisgarh; flights from Kolkata take 1hr 30min. Allow 10 days to tour from Raipur to Jagdalpur, including visits to tribal villages, the Maikal Hills, Chitrakote Falls and Kanger Valley National Park.

Need to know: Use local guides – they are essential for better understanding tribal cultures and visiting in a sensitive fashion.

Other months: Oct-Nov & Jan-Mar – coolest, dry, green, many festivals (Madai festival Dec-Mar); Apr-Jun – hot, humid; Jul-Sep – monsoon, very hot.

BLACK FOREST GERMANY

→ **Why now? For a touch of Teutonic magic.**

The Black Forest is Germany's most romantic, fairytale-laced region. And never more so than in December, when its rolling hills and dense-packed evergreens might be sprinkled with snow and when everywhere is sprinkled with Christmas. The lively university town of Freiburg is a fine festive choice. Its medieval centre of cobbled lanes and gabled houses is lovely to wander at any time, but now smells of *glühwein* and gingerbread; browse the Christmas market, where you can make your own candles and cookies, ride the Ferris wheel and feast on raclette and wurst. Further afield, take the train or bus to nearby Hinterzarten for the striking Ravennaschlucht market, where traditional stalls cluster in a gorge beneath the Devil's Valley Railway viaduct. Then hike or cablecar up 1284m (4212ft) Schauinsland, Freiburg's local mountain, for winter hiking, snowshoeing or cross-country skiing and to take in the views from the lookout tower at the top.

Trip plan: The closest major airports to Freiburg are Basel (1hr by bus), Frankfurt (2hr by train) and Zürich (2hr by train).

Need to know: Free shuttlebuses run from Freiburg and Hinterzarten to the Ravennaschlucht market. Alternatively, trains connect Freiburg and Hinterzarten (35min). The market is a scenic 3km (2-mile) hike from Hinterzarten.

Other months: Nov & Jan-Mar – cold, snow possible, markets (Dec); Apr-May – spring flowers; Jun-Aug – hottest, busiest, festivals; Sep-Oct – warm.

SUDAN

→ **Why now? It's just about mild enough to explore.**

A fractious recent past has deterred many from visiting Sudan. But, now things are more peaceful, the country's rich ancient history should change your mind. Sudan is where Saharan sands sweep, two Nile rivers combine, the Red Sea laps and millennia-old civilisations have left marvellous marks. It's always incredibly hot here, but bone-dry December, with maximums of 'only' 32°C (89.6°F), is significantly more pleasant than most months. In Khartoum, Sudan's compelling capital, you can cruise on the Nile and watch traditional Nuba wrestling. To the north lie Old Dongola (with its Muslim shrines and ruined Coptic churches), Atrun Crater (where nomads gather salt) and the Pyramids of Nuri. The highlight is Meroe, heartland of the powerful Kingdom of Kush from the 8th century BCE, where 200-plus Nubian pyramids slump in the desert sands.

Trip plan: Join a guided tour – infrastructure is limited, journeys long and guides essential for cultural engagement and understanding. Allow eight to 10 days to loop north from Khartoum, taking in the main archaeological sites as well as wild camping in the desert and encounters with local tribes.

Need to know: All visitors must obtain a permit to take photos or videos. Don't take pictures in public places.

Other months: Jan-Feb – coolest, dry; Mar-Apr & Oct-Nov – very hot; May-Sep – very, very hot, rainy season.

FLORIDA USA

Look, but don't touch – manatees swimming in the Florida shallows

➜ **Why now? To swim with cuddly sea cows.**

It's not just sun-seeking retirees that congregate in subtropical Florida come winter – West Indian manatees do too. From mid-November to March, these so-called 'sea cows' migrate to the warm, clear, shallow creeks and pools of Crystal River National Wildlife Reserve, where natural springs keep water temperatures constant at around 22°C (71.6°F). Watch them from boardwalks or viewing platforms or join an ethically-run tour to snorkel with them – these huge, peaceful, adorable creatures, which can weigh up to half a tonne, are naturally curious and often approach swimmers.

Trip plan: Crystal River, in Citrus County, is a 1hr 30min drive northwest of Orlando.

It's the only place in Florida where it's legal to swim with manatees. Tour companies will provide wetsuits, masks and snorkels. The area has some good hiking routes, too – try the Withlacoochee State Trail, a bike/hike rail trail that spans the county.

Need to know: There are strict guidelines for swimming with manatees. Enter the water slowly to limit splashing; never approach or follow a manatee – wait for the manatee to come to you; do not touch them; never swim between a mother and calf. Before booking a tour, ask questions about the company's practices.

Other months: Nov & Jan-Mar – dry, warm, manatees (from Dec); Apr-Aug – hot, humid, busy; Sep-Oct – quieter, hurricanes most likely.

HONG KONG
CHINA

→ **Why now? For cool Christmas shopping.**

White Christmas? Maybe not. But you're guaranteed a bright Christmas in Hong Kong: dry, mild December brings sunny skies and a truckload of extra sparkle, from the festivities and fairylights of WinterFest to Hong Kong Disneyland's Christmas celebrations. It's also when many stores have their winter sales, so it's a great place to do your gift shopping – head to Queen's Road Central for big-name stores, Hollywood Road and Cat Street for antiques, revitalised Sham Shui Po for fashion finds and electrical bargains, and shop-packed Tsim Sha Tsui for everything. The mild weather (15-20°C/59-68°F) is ideal for hitting the city's hiking trails too: wander across quiet Lantau Island or tackle sections of the 100km (62-mile) MacLehose Trail, walking via fishing villages and taking in indigenous Hakka heritage, with views of the glittering skyscrapers in the distance.

Trip plan: Express trains connect Hong Kong Airport to the centre in 25min. Allow two/three days for the main sites, longer to include the surrounding countryside.

Need to know: If you're still here on 31 December, head to Tsim Sha Tsui promenade, West Kowloon Waterfront or the Central Ferry Pier for the best views of New Year's Eve fireworks.

Other months: Oct-Nov – warm, dry, sunny; Jan-Mar – cool, dry, cloudy; Apr-May – hotter, wetter; Jun-Sep – wettest, typhoons possible.

Neon nights in the shoppers' paradise of Hong Kong

283

(L) San Elijo State Beach, a short hop from central San Diego; (R) Gaslamp Quarter

SAN DIEGO USA

Why now? For city life, winter sun, Santa and cetaceans.

Winter is relative in southern California. In San Diego (aka 'America's Finest City') rain is more likely but days remain mild (average highs: 19°C/66°F). It's certainly still warm enough to wander the city's village-like neighbourhoods – fancy La Jolla, surfy Encinitas, alternative Ocean Beach, foodie Little Italy, the lively, bar-packed Gaslamp Quarter – and to lose yourself in enormous Balboa Park, with its museums (Air & Space, Art,

Natural History) and world-famous zoo. For further wildlife encounters, book a boat tour or head to the cliff-top trails of Torrey Pines State Natural Reserve in the hope of spotting dolphins and migrating grey whales, which pass along the coast here between December and March. It's a city that likes to get festive too, from San Diego Bay's Parade of Lights (when a festooned flotilla of 80-odd boats floats by) to Balboa Park's December Nights, a festive feast of food trucks, music and decorations.

Trip plan: San Diego International Airport is close to downtown. Use public transport to explore: the city's bright-red trolley serves downtown locations, ferries run across the bay, buses connect neighbourhoods. Or hop in a GoCar, GPS-guided storytelling three-wheelers.

Need to know: Christmas and New Year's Eve can be busy – book in advance.

Other months: Jan-Feb – coolest, quiet, whales; Mar-May,– warm, dry; Jun-Aug – hottest, busiest; Sep-Nov – warm, Santa Ana winds peak.

A black-maned lion surveys his Kalahari kingdom

CENTRAL KALAHARI
BOTSWANA

→ **Why now? For cheaper prices and greater game.**

In this immense wildlife reserve, covering 50,000 sq km (19,305 sq miles) and one of the largest in the world, rain does not stop play. Indeed, it positively encourages it. While December marks the start of the rainy season in Botswana, it's the best time to visit the semi-arid Central Kalahari. In the northernmost areas, around Northern Deception Valley in particular, the flush of wildflowers and grasses attracts great gatherings of grazers, which in turn attract predators – large numbers of hyena, leopard and the reserve's famed black-maned lions are all found here. This is also the best time for birding, as many species are wearing their breeding plumage and migrants are around. Roads may become trickier to navigate but the payoff is excellent wildlife viewing and, at times, soul-stirringly stormy skies. There are opportunities to engage with the San people too.

Trip plan: The Central Kalahari is 250km (155 miles) south of Maun. Most visitors accessing the park by road use Matswere Gate, 40km (25 miles) from Deception Valley. The easiest way to enter is by charter flight direct to a safari camp.

Need to know: The Central Kalahari lies in a no-risk malaria zone but malaria is present in other parts of Botswana, particularly the north. Malaria risk is highest during rainy season.

Other months: Nov & Jan-Mar – rainy season, wildlife congregates, cheaper; Apr-May – start of the dry season, wildlife still gathering; Jun-Oct – dry, busy, pricier.

© The Africa Image Library / Alamy Stock Photo

285

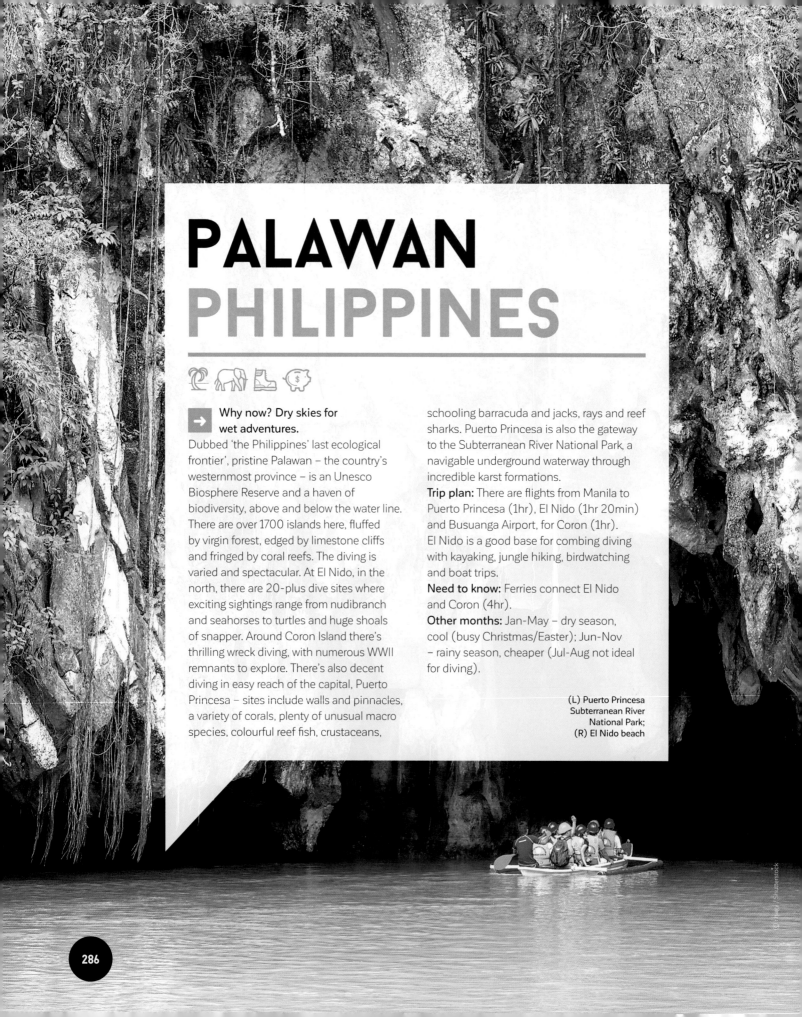

PALAWAN
PHILIPPINES

🌴 🐘 🥾 🐷

→ **Why now? Dry skies for wet adventures.**

Dubbed 'the Philippines' last ecological frontier', pristine Palawan – the country's westernmost province – is an Unesco Biosphere Reserve and a haven of biodiversity, above and below the water line. There are over 1700 islands here, fluffed by virgin forest, edged by limestone cliffs and fringed by coral reefs. The diving is varied and spectacular. At El Nido, in the north, there are 20-plus dive sites where exciting sightings range from nudibranch and seahorses to turtles and huge shoals of snapper. Around Coron Island there's thrilling wreck diving, with numerous WWII remnants to explore. There's also decent diving in easy reach of the capital, Puerto Princesa – sites include walls and pinnacles, a variety of corals, plenty of unusual macro species, colourful reef fish, crustaceans,

schooling barracuda and jacks, rays and reef sharks. Puerto Princesa is also the gateway to the Subterranean River National Park, a navigable underground waterway through incredible karst formations.

Trip plan: There are flights from Manila to Puerto Princesa (1hr), El Nido (1hr 20min) and Busuanga Airport, for Coron (1hr). El Nido is a good base for combing diving with kayaking, jungle hiking, birdwatching and boat trips.

Need to know: Ferries connect El Nido and Coron (4hr).

Other months: Jan-May – dry season, cool (busy Christmas/Easter); Jun-Nov – rainy season, cheaper (Jul-Aug not ideal for diving).

(L) Puerto Princesa Subterranean River National Park;
(R) El Nido beach

SOUTH CAROLINA
USA

Why now? To drive via empty beaches and busy skies.

Roadtripping along the Palmetto State's island-dotted coast is a super way to spend winter. Days pushing 15°C-plus (59°F) aren't unusual, but the summer crowds have disappeared – to the extent that, from November to the end of February, it's possible to horseback ride along touristy Myrtle Beach. And it doesn't matter that it's not sun-flopping weather because there's plenty to keep you interested. On Hilton Head Island, visit Mitchelville, the USA's first self-governed town of formerly enslaved people. Also on the island, take a tour to learn about Gullah culture, which upholds West and Central African languages and traditions. Explore historic Charleston (founded 1670), from its colourful French Quarter and Old Slave Mart Museum to its barbecue joints. Get your binoculars out in Huntington Beach State Park – winter is best for birding here; look for bald eagles and roseate spoonbills. And take a stroll along the boardwalk at Myrtle Beach for traditional seaside fun, out of season.

Trip plan: Fly in to Savannah/Hilton Head International Airport. Allow at least a week to drive along the coast. From Myrtle Beach, consider turning inland to Greenville and the cooler Blue Ridge Mountains.

Need to know: Look out for local oysters (in season September-April). Oyster boat trips are possible on the May River.

Other months: Jan-Feb – coolest, cheaper; Mar-May – warm, flowers blooming; Jun-Aug – hot, sticky, beaches busy; Sep-Nov – warm, hurricane risk.

SLOVENIA

Why now? Crowd-lite, multi-sport, fairytale snow fun.

While snug-sized Slovenia can't compete with Europe's winter-sport big boys, the country is still splendid when the snow starts to fall. For starters, there is good skiing, albeit on a smaller scale. Resorts such as lively Kranjska Gora, reliable Krvavec and family-friendly Vogel aren't huge but also aren't as busy as other Alpine hubs. But where the country really excels is in multi-activity winter breaks, combining downhilling and snowboarding with cross-country skiing, snowshoeing, snow-hiking, ice-climbing or even igloo-building and night tobogganing. The landscapes are thrilling too, with most resorts located in and around handsome Triglav National Park. Photographers will love the high peaks, frozen waterfalls, snowy forests, beautiful Lake Bohinj and magical Lake Bled, with its lake isle and castle shimmering in the frost.

Trip plan: Slovenia's compact size means its mountains are easy to access. Krvavec is only 8km (5 miles) from Ljubljana Airport; the drive from the airport to Vogel takes around 1hr 15min, to Kranjska Gora takes around 50min.

Need to know: Postojna Cave hosts a Living Nativity (25-30 December), with 16 Biblical scenes staged along a 5km (3-mile) subterranean route, freckled wth fairylights. Postojna is 50km (31 miles) from Ljubljana, accessible by train and bus.

Other months: Jan-Mar – winter, snow; Apr & Oct-Nov – shoulder months, mild; May-Sep – warmest, good for hiking.

OSA PENINSULA
COSTA RICA

Why now? To escape the increasing crowds.

Come December, Costa Rica is drying off nicely after the worst months of the rains and, consequently, tourists are beginning to descend: hotspots such as Arenal volcano and the beaches of Tortuguero will be filling up. But not so on the Osa Peninsula. Out of the way, on the country's southern Pacific coast, Osa is home to Costa Rica's largest national park – Corcovado – but sees only a tiny number of visitors. Perfect for a peak-season escape. Stay in an ecolodge and explore: this is one of the planet's most biodiverse enclaves, heaving with all manner of species, from howler monkeys and sloths to morpho butterflies, toucans, macaws and manatees; there are even chances to spot ocelots, harpy eagles and jaguar. Hike with expert naturalists, explore on horseback, abseil into canyons and kayak through bays and mangroves, looking for dolphins, turtles and whales (humpbacks might be seen from December to April). Offshore excursions to the biosphere reserve of Isla del Caño – for spectacular diving and snorkelling – are possible too.

Trip plan: Osa's main access town is Puerto Jimenez, accessible by flights (50min) or by road (6hr) from San José. To explore throughly, including hikes and diving, allow five days.

Need to know: It can rain even in dry season – be prepared for all weathers.

Other months: Jan-Apr – dry season, pricier, busy; May-Jun – increasing rain; Jul-Aug – wet, busy; Sep-Oct – wettest, some areas off-limits; Nov – drying.

© Karin Wassmer / Shutterstock

Eye-popping views
along the Lake
Waikaremoana Track

TE UREWERA NEW ZEALAND

→ **Why now? Find greater solitude
on a Great Walk.**

Start-of-summer December is a prime
time to tackle one of New Zealand's
10 official Great Walks. The most famous
ones, like the Milford Track, will be busy,
but the lesser-known Lake Waikaremoana
Track is rarely crowded, even now. It
is, though, quite special. This 46km
(28.5-mile) three/four day trail runs
through Te Urewera, a remote tract of
North Island rainforest that has been
passed back to the Ngāi Tūhoe (its

Indigenous owners) and granted the
same legal status as a person – a world
first. It's a one-way trail between Onepoto
and Hopuruahine, via its titular lake
(Waikaremoana means 'sea of rippling
waters'), rolling valleys, stands of podocarp
and kāmahi trees, magical Korokoro Falls,
Pukehou ridge and commanding Panekire
Bluff (from where you get the best views).
Anyone who hikes here is expected to be
a good *manuhiri* (visitor), respecting the
region's nature, spirituality and significance
to the Tūhoe people.

Trip plan: The nearest towns to Te
Urewera are Whakatane, Murupara and
Wairoa. Huts and campsites must be
pre-booked, as must transport to/from the
start/finish of the track – water taxi and
shuttle services are available.

Need to know: All native wildlife in Te
Urewera is protected and must not be
disturbed, destroyed or removed.

Other months: Nov & Jan-Feb – warmest,
busiest; Mar-May – warm/cool, quieter;
Jun-Oct – coldest, snow possible.

289

SOUTHERN FJORDS
CHILE/ARGENTINA

 Why now? To navigate to the end of the world.

At the very bottom of South America, it's as if the land just gives up to the ocean. This is where you'll find the Tierra del Fuego archipelago, a morass of islands edged by great glaciers and cut through by dramatic fjords and narrow channels; at its tip is Cape Horn, from where it's next stop Antarctica. The best way to explore this maze of waterways is by expedition cruise, which is only possible in the warmer months, when the ice has cleared and the weather is a little more clement (in December, expect highs of 10-15°C/50-59°F). Highlights include hiking through the rare sub-polar forest at Ainsworth Bay, taking a Zodiac ride to the Tuckers Islets to visit a colony of Magellanic penguins, and sailing through aptly-named Glacier Alley – in the milder months, you might glimpse ice chunks calving into the sea.

Trip plan: Cruises of three to seven nights run between Punta Arenas (Chile) and Ushuaia (Argentina). Both cities have airports. Ships, which carry a maximum of 200 passengers, are comfortable; all excursions and meals are included.

Need to know: Even in the summer, Patagonian temperatures can be cold and conditions can change quickly. Pack plenty of warm layers, including waterproofs and wellies.

Other months: Sep-Nov & Jan-Apr – cruise season (warmest/calmest Dec-Feb); May-Aug – cold, fjords unnavigable, no cruises.

© Boris Kasimov Photography / Getty Images

Ice meets
chilly waters
along Glacier Alley

Zakouma National Park, home to half the world's Kordofan giraffe population

© Guenter Guni / Getty Images

CHAD

→ Why now? To see resurgent wildlife, after the rains.

There's far away from it all, and then there's Chad. Sitting in the heart of Africa, it's a virtually untrodden land where southern savannah segues into parched Sahara, defiantly independent tribes live as they have for centuries, and landscapes – the Ennedi and Tibesti Mountains – look like outer space. It's had its troubles, but things are improving, not least in Zakouma National Park. Heavily poached in the early 21st century, Zakouma was taken over by non-profit African Parks in 2010. Wildlife numbers are increasing, notably elephant, buffalo, roan antelope and Kordofan giraffe (Zakouma is home to 50% of the global population) while rhino have been reintroduced and tourist camps are boosting local employment opportunities. The roads are re-graded after the rains (in late November) making December a fine time to visit, with landscapes lush, waterholes full and birdlife prolific.

Trip plan: Join a guided tour – this is one of the least-visited countries in the world and infrastructure is poor. Allow a week for a Zakouma safari, three weeks for a touring trip into the Ennedi Mountains.

Need to know: Chad is a predominantly Muslim country: dress conservatively and carry a headscarf if female. Check government travel advisories before you leave.

Other months: Nov & Jan-Apr – dry, best for touring, Zakouma open late November-late May; May & Oct – beginning/end of rains; Jun-Sep – rainy season, travel difficult, Gerewol Festival (Sep).

Hike the
Northumberland Coast
Path past dramatic
Bamburgh Castle

NORTHUMBERLAND
ENGLAND

→ **Why now? For cobweb-blowing coast walks.**

There's something about the Northumberland coast that makes it especially suited to winter. It's the low, delicate light, the enormous skies, the endless sands, the even emptier landscapes... Walking here, wrapped up against the howling wind or crisp December sunshine, just feels right. The region's whole shoreline is a designated Area of Outstanding Natural Beauty, and a long-distance trail – the Northumberland Coast Path – traces its length. En route are brooding castles (ruined Dunstanburgh, mighty Bamburgh), glorious beaches (dune-backed Druridge Bay; wide, sandy Alnmouth) and charming fishing villages like Seahouses and Craster, both good spots to warm up in a pub with fresh-caught fish and chips. December days are short but that's a good thing: Northumberland has legendary dark skies, perfect for stargazing – the Milky Way might be seen.

Trip plan: There are mainline stations at Alnmouth (for the south) and Berwick-upon-Tweed (for the north). Buses run between local communities though services are less frequent in winter – check in advance. The Coast Path is 100km (62 miles); allow four to six days.

Need to know: Northumberland's Farne Islands are home to a large colony of grey seals, which pup in autumn/winter and may be seen bobbing in the waves.

Other months: Jan-Mar – cold, dark skies, seal pups; Apr-May – spring flowers, attractions reopen; Jun-Aug – warmest; Sep-Nov – autumn colours, dark skies.

Keep eyes peeled for tigers in the Sundarbans wetlands

BANGLADESH

➡️ **Why now? For crowds without the crowds.**

You won't easily escape other people in Bangladesh – this lush, steamy, river-riddled nation is one of the most densely populated on the planet. But you will escape other tourists. Few make it here, so those who do find a country that's a little chaotic, perhaps, but eclectic and unforgettable. December is prime time: the rains have finally stopped, days are bright but not sweltering and nights are cool – ideal for landing in frenetic capital Dhaka (visit the National Museum and take a rickshaw ride around the old city) before exploring further afield. Take a boat trip through the Sundarbans wetlands, keeping an eye out for Bengal tigers and Ganges dolphins. Visit Unesco-listed Somapura Mahavihara, an impressive Buddhist complex dating from the 8th century. Enjoy a cuppa in the hills around Srimangal, which are cloaked in tea plantations. And make an effort to visit the jungly Chittagong Hill Tracks, where you can mingle with tribal peoples (including eleven distinct ethnic groups) whose lives have barely changed for centuries.

Trip plan: Allow at least two weeks and don't try to pack too much in – infrastructure is poor and travel slow. Mix road journeys with boat and train travel.

Need to know: A special permit is required to visit the Chittagong Hills; the Rangamati and Bandarban districts are the most picturesque.

Other months: Nov & Jan-Mar – dry season, cooler; Apr-May – humid, hot; Jun-Oct – monsoon, hot.

© neelsky / Shutterstock

FALKLAND ISLANDS

→ **Why now? To peek at the penguins.**
Far from anywhere, with wildlife out of this world (and red telephone booths and post boxes straight out of London) – is the singular Falkland Islands. Across this South Atlantic archipelago, which comprises East Falkland (home to capital Stanley), West Falkland and some 776 other isles, there are animals everywhere, from elephant seals galumphing on the beaches and albatross wheeling in the skies to whales blowing and breaching offshore. In December – when temperatures might just reach 10-15°C (50-59°F) – it's penguins that are the main draw, as chicks begin to hatch. Numerous species might be seen: Volunteer Point has the biggest colony of regal kings, Beaker Island hosts both Magellanic and gentoo, Pebble Island has rockhopper and macaroni too. Carcass Island is a great place for hikes and birding; take a boat trip from here to West Point, where 380m-high (1247ft) cliffs rise from the sea and 14,500 pairs of black-browed albatross hang out.

Trip plan: Access is via flights into Mount Pleasant Airport or by expedition cruise – some ships visit en route to Antarctica. It's easiest to get around by guided tour, though light aircraft flights and boat excursions can be arranged locally (book in advance).

Need to know: Both sun and wind can be strong – apply sunscreen and take a windproof jacket.

Other months: Dec-Feb – warmest, longer days, penguin chicks; Mar-Apr – wet, cold, good for whales; May-Sep – winter, coldest; Oct-Nov – spring, elephant seals arriving.

Elephant seals spar on a Falkland Islands beach

© Michael Heffernan / Lonely Planet

© Sean Pavone / Getty Images

Old San Juan dressed in
its festive best

PUERTO RICO

Why now? For a never-ending Noel.

→ Twelve days of Christmas? Pah! Sunny and spirited Puerto Rico stretches it to 60 days, starting with Thanksgiving (this is a US 'unincorporated territory' after all) and not finishing until mid-January. Visit in December and you'll likely come across shops stacked with festive trinkets, late-night *parrandas* (carol singing in the streets), church masses filled with *aguinaldos* (Christmas songs) and the hearty consumption of festive feasts: *lechón* (suckling pig), *arroz con gandules* (rice with pigeon peas), pork-and-potato

pasteles (steamed plantain tamales) and *coquet* (sweet spiced coconut drink). The Día de los Inocentes (28 December) is particular fun, akin to April Fool's Day, when people play tricks on each other – head to Hatillo for the best high-jinks. Season's greetings aside, the weather is wonderful right now for exploring this proudly Latino Caribbean idyll. Wander the bright alleys of Old San Juan (founded 1521) and lively second-city Ponce; venture into El Yunque for rainforest hikes; check out the surf at Rincón; and consider sailing over to the islands of Vieques and Culebra for quieter

sands and dazzling after-dark kayaking in Bioluminescent Bay.

Trip plan: Aeropuerto Internacional Luis Muñoz Marín in San Juan is served by regular flights from the US. The island is also connected to the Dominican Republic and Virgin Islands by ferry.

Need to know: Passport and visa requirements for entering Puerto Rico are the same as for entering the USA.

Other months: Jan-Apr – dry, busy, festive; May-Jun – quieter, hottest; Jul-Nov – wettest, hurricane season.

INDEX

PHOTO CREDITS

LONELY PLANET'S
WHERE TO GO WHEN

Published in October 2022 by
Lonely Planet Global Limited CRN 554153
www.lonelyplanet.com
ISBN 978 18386 9504 0
© Lonely Planet 2022
10 9 8 7 6 5
Printed in Malaysia

Written by Sarah Baxter & Paul Bloomfield

General Manager, Publishing Piers Pickard
Associate Publisher Robin Barton
Editors Hannah Cartmel, Anne Mason, Polly Thomas, Clifton Wilkinson
Cover Design Dan di Paolo
Layout Designer Jo Dovey
Image Researcher Ceri James
Print Production Nigel Longuet

Lonely Planet Global Limited
IRELAND
Digital Depot, Roe Lane (off Thomas St),
Dublin D08 TCV4

STAY IN TOUCH lonelyplanet.com/contact

Paper in this book is certified against the Forest Stewardship Council™ standards. FSC™ promotes environmentally responsible, socially beneficial and economically viable management of the world's forests.